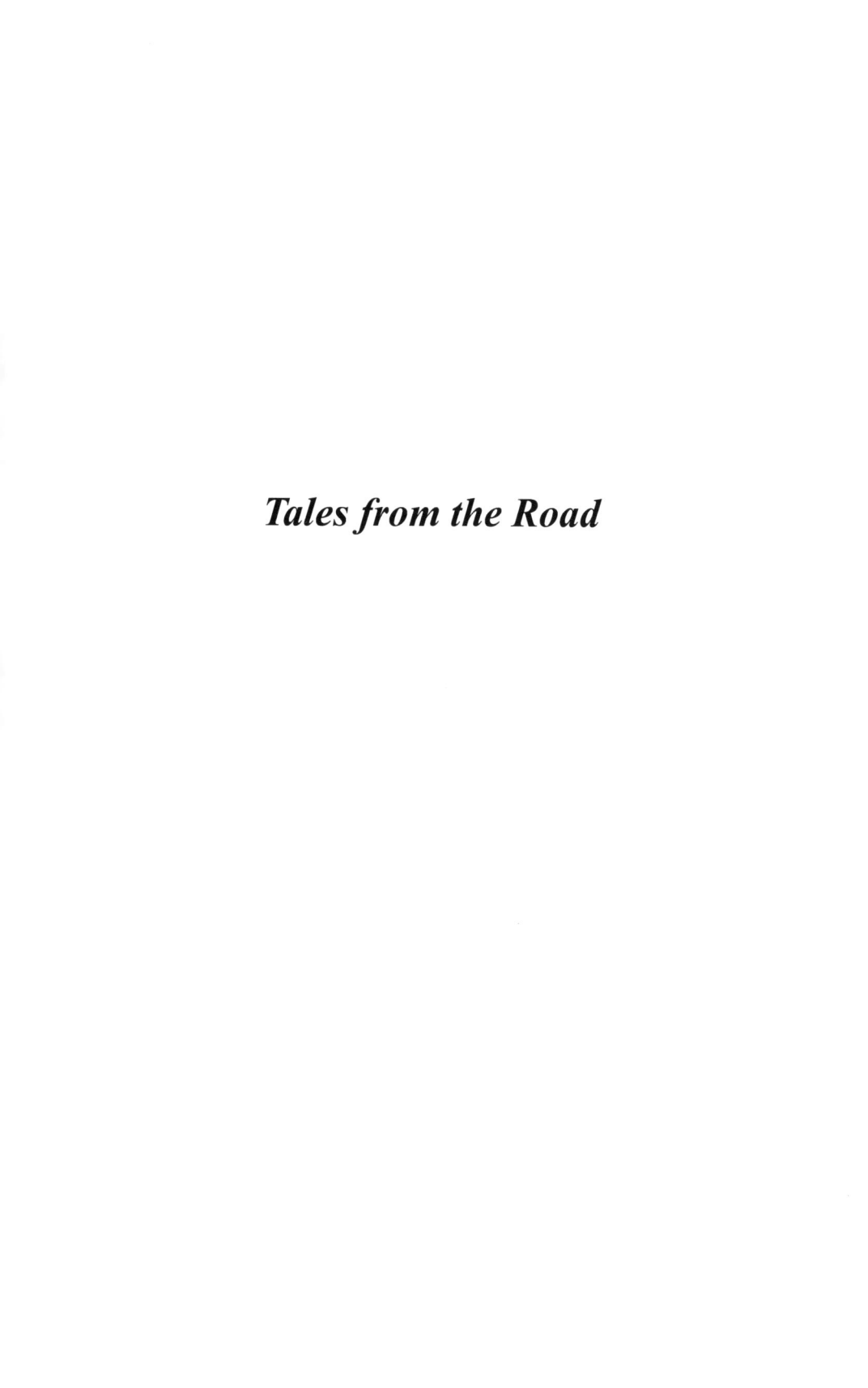

Tales from the Road

Tales from the Road

Lawrence Bransby

Copyright©Lawrence Bransby 2020

Facebook, Website

Lawrence Bransby has asserted his right to be identified as the Author of this work in accordance with the Copyright, Designs and Patents Act 1988.

All rights reserved.

No part of this publication may be reproduced or transmitted in any form or by any means, electronic or mechanical, including photocopy, recording, or any information storage and retrieval system, without permission in writing from the copyright owner.

Cover artwork by Danny Austin, with thanks.

ISBN: 9798696762951

To my dear Dad, who started it all

and

To my son, Gareth,

who led me into adventures I never would have had

without him there to lead me astray.

A journey only becomes an adventure

when something goes wrong -

so they say.

CONTENTS

Introduction
1. A Pass too far
2. That's how it all started
3. Night watch in the bush
4. First Desert Crossing
5. Ride like a twat
6. Riding with the Black Bears
7. Ten Points for the Old Lady
8. Outfits in the desert
9. It's like that with bikes too
10. Kazakhstan short cut
11. Tormenting a Dwarf
12. Desert crossing in Southern Morocco
13. The small dotted line
14. The tunnel
15. Desert ships of the Aral Sea
16. Why am I here
17. The raising of Lazarus
18. The defensive towers of Georgia
19. The Banya
20. This is Real
21. Road of Bones
22. True Bikers
23. Ford Fiesta desert crossing
24. Qu go Fish Ling-Ling?
25. Old biker still riding
26. Dempster Highway
27. Death Valley and Vegas
28. Two Lads and a Ural
29. Thin Red Line
30. Other books

Introduction

It's now been nearly five and a half decades of adventure travel, starting when I was twelve years old - most, but not all, by motorcycle; many, but not exclusively, shared with my son, Gareth.

Over the years, I have written and published a number of articles in adventure motorcycle magazines, each highlighting one small facet of a journey that was particularly meaningful to me. This volume collects all these articles together in one place for easy access and includes some others, written but unpublished, that, together, capture something of the joys and trials of long-distance adventure travel.

I have not organised the book in strict chronological order, rather randomly collated the articles so that, in progressing through the book, the reader will be forced to take a mental leap to some other part of the world, another bright snapshot flashed upon the mind's wall. The cohesive link, I suppose, is that each of these vignettes was personally experienced by me, alone or with a companion who shared the adventure.

My hope is that these stories, these Tales from the Road, will inspire others to make that dream of adventure, however small or tentative (which we all have somewhere hidden within our psyches), become a reality.

Lawrence Bransby

ONE

A pass too far

I suppose we should have realised that Matt's Pass in southern Kyrgyzstan wasn't all that the map implied when we tentatively made our way up its initial rocky switchbacks. We knew it was going to be difficult - a 32-kilometre, boulder-strewn track with difficult river crossings that one writer said was doable but, he added

hopefully, if you did manage to make it through, "your vehicle will be destroyed".

We didn't realise at the time that the comment was about ten years old and it wasn't long before we came to realise that no vehicle had travelled this pass for a very long time...

It had taken us three trips into Central Asia to ride the Bartang Pass, supposedly one of the more remote mountain passes in Kyrgyzstan. Even the usually bland Wikipedia gets just a little excited when referring to it: *"The Bartang is generally not passable except as an adventure".*

But (perhaps because the long years of expectation had raised our hopes beyond what the reality had to offer) we found the Bartang a little disappointing. We wanted more, to go "off-road and then off-road again" as a cyclist we met along the way commented when we told him of our plan.

So, after crossing the 132km Bartang Pass and, a few days later, riding to the Fedchenco Glacier, the largest in the world outside the Polar regions where we had a little fun with Gareth nearly getting washed away by a swollen river and, later, manoeuvring the bikes across the snout of a smaller glacier that had blocked the track (but that's another story) we decided to attempt Matt's Pass.

In retrospect, perhaps we should have listened to the policeman, who pulled up in his old Russian Uaz 4X4 next to where we had made camp, and who seemed to inform us that sleeping the night alongside the small but beautiful Lake Turumtaikul high up in the mountains above 4000m was not wise and that the road ahead was impassable. (We didn't know *what* road; he just pointed vaguely in the direction of Matt's Pass, shook his head sadly and made an X with his arms across his chest.) After he had driven away in a haze of blue smoke, Gareth just shrugged and said we'd give it a try.

I mean, if it was blocked we could always turn back.

The next day after a cold night in our tents and having to tow Gareth's DR350 to get it started, we breakfasted in a shepherd's shack on black tea and sour cream and then headed for the beginning of the pass. It didn't begin well.

A few kilometres before the turn-off, a river crossed the track. Gareth, who was ahead of me, rode straight into the water and, in an instant, he was down. The water was deep and he struggled to lift his bike against the current. Despite his efforts, the strong flow was dragging them down stream. I dropped my bike and rushed into the water to help but immediately my feet were swept out from under me and both of us, and the now fully submerged bike, were swept away into a deep pool where the water eddied darkly against the bank.

Working together, we eventually managed to drag the bike out. We stripped off our wet clothes and laid them out on the grass to dry while Gareth dismantled the carb and exhaust system to get the bike going again.

About 600m up river we found a rough wooden footbridge across the river and crossed safely. A few kilometres further on we came to the turn-off to Matt's Pass.

At first all seemed innocuous enough: the track was rough and littered with boulders that had dislodged from the slopes above but we could see where it made its way up the side of the mountain ahead in a number of tight switchbacks. Every so often a stream crossed the track and, on flatter sections, water had pooled to form bogs.

Halfway up, we paused for breath and Gareth said to me, "I don't think this pass has been used for a while," which I considered something of an understatement.

The switchbacks ended and the track began to follow a high, U-shaped valley that climbed gently upwards. We came across more fallen boulders and boggy sections and then some shallow river crossings that we negotiated without incident.

"How long is this pass?" I called to Gareth as we rode together.

He shouted back. I was sure he had said *Thirteen kilometres* and I thought to myself: This is going to be easy. We're nearly at the top and then it's downhill for a few kilometres and then we're through. I even felt a touch disappointed that it would be so easy. Like the Bartang Pass, I wondered whether we'd complete Matt's Pass and feel that we'd been cheated out of an adventure.

"Thirteen ks?" I shouted, looking for confirmation.

"Thirty-" he shouted back.

We peaked at about 4200m on a wide, rolling plain, flat and denuded of all vegetation. Patches of snow still remained on the ground despite the fact that it was mid summer. Then the tracks disappeared on the high Alpine plateau and we ranged about off-road until we picked them up again, faint and boulder-strewn.

If this was a pass, it clearly hadn't been used for a very long time.

The landscape changed and we entered a long rocky valley and, once again, began to climb. Then more river crossings, deeper now with wide, rocky entrances and exits.

As we struggled towards the top of the pass, I became aware of just how ill Gareth was. Days of diarrhoea had weakened him; at a brief pause to catch our breath he told me he was feeling dizzy and nauseous. We had reached a height of 4400m and I too began to feel light-headed and dizzy. After each river crossing or rocky stretch we were breathless and needed to rest and gather our strength.

At last the track began to descend but it had narrowed to just a few feet wide; even when going down hill, we found ourselves struggling over boulders to make progress. Then Gareth stopped. He got off his bike and crouched next to the engine, listening. Even inside my helmet I could hear an unpleasant, metallic clatter.

There was nothing we could do about it. We didn't have the tools to pull the engine apart so we continued on slowly, free-wheeling the bike down slopes without the engine whenever possible.

A short while later Gareth's bike jerked to a stop. I rode up next to him. "Engine's seized," he told me. "It's not going anywhere." There was an air of weary resignation in his voice.

They say a journey doesn't become an adventure until something goes wrong. I think ours had just become an adventure.

Our initial, and somewhat optimistic, plan was to push the damaged bike out working together but strength-sapping boulder plains and river crossings littered with hidden rocks soon convinced us otherwise. We had little choice but to abandon Gareth's bike and continue down the pass on mine. Going though our panniers, we dumped a lot of stuff. It looked forlorn scattered about on the edge of the track amongst the rocks, a cold wind moaning about us and reminding us of our isolation. What we decided to keep we loaded into my panniers and Gareth's rucksack. One of us would ride while the other walked; the track was too rocky to ride two-up.

He was clearly ill now and I began to worry. Fortunately, we were only about seven kilometres from a dirt road that would lead us out. We pressed on, the track so covered with boulders that progress was slow. We would leave the bike and walk ahead together, clearing a narrow track, lifting boulders out of the way and rolling them down the mountain into the river far below, then go back and get the bike, manhandling it over the rocks and through rivers that cut across the track.

Gareth was struggling. Just walking and carrying his pack was taking all his strength. At one point he sat down amongst the rocks, his head hanging, and he said to me, "I've got nothing left."

I was very conscious that if either of us were to become very ill, a heart attack or pulmonary oedema or suchlike, if either of us were to sicken to the point where we could no longer keep going, we would be in serious trouble. There was no way either of us could get the other out.

But we struggled on, Gareth digging deep and fighting his illness. Three times we lost control of the bike over large rocks and had to drag it back from where it hung over the edge of the narrow track, the river hundreds of metres below. Fortunately the little DR350s are light and together we were able to wrestle it back onto the track. And so we continued down the pass, lifting the larger rocks off the track twenty metres at a time and then going back for the bike and manoeuvring it through together.

It was late afternoon when we came round a steep bend in the track and I paused. Gareth came up to me, followed the track ahead with his eyes, then turned to me and said, "I think we've got a problem."

"Yes, we have," I said.

About a hundred metres in front of us the track simply disappeared - first into a bank of scree hundreds of feet high that had poured down the mountainside and, after that, where it should have emerged from the scree, there was nothing but large rocks and the river. After that, nothing. There was no pass any more. It was gone, disappeared.

We both knew that it was the end. It was getting late, the sun now low on the mountain ridge far above us and already the air was taking on that leaden coldness that one encounters at high altitudes. We had no choice but to abandon my bike as well and focus on protecting ourselves. We had to walk out.

But night would be on us soon and we needed to hurry. Again we sifted through our stuff, throwing out anything that would weigh us down; then, carrying what we could in dry bags, a bottle of water and a spare fuel container (despite his illness, Gareth was determined to return as soon as he was well enough and get my bike out, but we needed more fuel), we set off again, stumbling and sliding across the scree, clambering over massive boulders in the river bed.

It was about two kilometres later that we realised we had another problem. I had seen it a long way back and had hoped there would be a way round: the remnants of the track ended against a cliff face that dropped straight into the river, too turbulent and deep to cross. Alongside the cliff was a scree slope hundreds of feet high and impossible to climb.

"We're in trouble here," I said, more to myself than my son. With Gareth being very ill, we couldn't walk the 26 kilometres back out the way we'd come; we were very high in one of the most remote mountain ranges in the world and darkness was setting in. We had no food left.

In my reckoning, we had four options: attempt to cross the river; walk back out the way we had come; sleep the night in the mountains and try again the next day; attempt to climb around the cliff.

While we were pondering our options, Gareth said, "I'm going to have another look at the cliff - there might be a way through." He set off, clambering through a deep undercut at its base next to the river.

He was gone for a long time and I began to worry. But at last he returned and told me, "I think I've found a way. It's tight but I'm pretty sure we can do it."

For the third time we sorted through our stuff, discarding everything except money, our documents, camera, water and petrol containers; the rest we hid under a large boulder well away from the river and then, with Gareth leading, we followed a narrow track up and around the cliff, passing the fuel container to each other on the tight sections to free up our hands.

Once around the cliff face, we followed what was left of the pass in the gathering darkness and made our way down towards the dirt road where we hoped to get a lift to the small village of Langar, 32 kilometres away.

At last we reached the road and, in the dark, stumbled across some abandoned huts. We tried the doors and found one open. Gareth lay down on the floor of the hut while I waited on the side of the road, hoping to flag down a passing vehicle. None came. Eventually the darkness and cold drove me into the hut and I lay down next to my son. I could feel him shivering next to me throughout the long night.

The next day, cold and stiff, I dragged myself out of the hut and again waited on the roadside for a vehicle but nothing came past. There had been no sign of life on that road for the past sixteen hours and I began to worry that somewhere between civilization and us a landslide had blocked the road and we had been cut off. By mid morning, still nothing had come past so, despite Gareth's weakness, we decided we had no option but to walk out; if we kept going all day we should be able to reach Langar shortly after nightfall.

An hour later, though, as we plodded along the dusty track, a vehicle did eventually appear and stopped for us. We spent two nights recovering in Langar. On the third day a Kyrgh man took us back to the turn-off in his dilapidated Chinese 4X4 and, carrying fuel and water, we hiked back up the pass, scrambled around the cliff and reached my bike. Together we lifted and turned it and, once again clearing boulders from sections of track ahead, we managed to get my bike back to where we left Gareth's. Working quickly because a storm was threatening, we removed his fuel tank and poured what was left of his fuel into my bike then, while Gareth rode my bike back up the pass alone, I hiked back to the road and managed to get a lift with a local man to Langar.

Later that night, while I was lying on my sleeping platform worrying that my ill son had met with some disaster on his way back, perhaps had drowned the bike in some river and couldn't get it started again, had ridden off the side of a cliff somewhere in the mountains, there was a noise outside my room and a grinning Gareth filled the doorway. His trip up the pass and back around to Langar was, as he told me later, somewhat hair raising. It was such a relief to have him back.

And then, sadly leaving Gareth's faithful DR350 abandoned high up in the mountains, we rode the 600ks back to Osh 2-up on my little DR - a very painful trip which took us two long days.

* * * * *

This story wouldn't be complete without a more detailed account of how Gareth made it up the pass and back to Langar on his own.

One evening a few days later, I sat him down and recorded the following conversation on my phone:

"A good place to begin would be when you started riding off up the pass on your own..."

"After we'd swapped everything over?"

"Yeah, the fuel pipes and your toolbox and the spares. What were your thoughts of riding away and leaving your bike there?"

"I wasn't really thinking of my bike, I'd written it off already. The only thing that was bothering me was the weather that was closing in and the fact that I hadn't brought my jacket which I thought was quite an oversight but we were in a hurry to leave and we wanted to be as light as possible. But I should have taken my jacket because if it had started raining, I wanted to get going as soon as possible. I could see the rain coming."

"What were your thoughts about leaving me there?"

"I was worried about you going back via the cliff, I was hoping you would be able to cross the river and avoid it but I was also kind of preoccupied with the weather and I was still feeling pretty ill so I was just hoping that the trip was going to be all right over the top. I knew that once I'd got up I was going to be fine but I was concerned about how the pass was going to be but it turned out, it was tricky, it was actually tougher than I had remembered."

"Yes, that's what you said to me, that it was tougher than you thought it was going to be. In what way?"

"It was just rough, rough and rocky and then the two river crossings really caught me out. The one was quite short but was very, there were like three really deep gullies in it that we obviously bounced across coming down because going the other way it was an incline and there was a big step coming out the other side. That was a lot worse than I remembered."

"Was that the one where you stopped to..."

"Yeah. I stopped and made a bit of a ramp just to bump the front wheel up the step."

"Had you already entered the river?"

"No, I stopped before. It wasn't very long, that's the thing. It was quite a short crossing but it was nasty."

"Did you take the rocks from the river or did you carry them from the bank?"

"No, I didn't carry them far, I can't remember. It wasn't far; there were rocks all over there."

"And the second river?"

"The second one, that was tricky because I couldn't see, you remember, it was that really long one with the low, flattish rocks and I couldn't see where the road exited properly so I, when I left it I just ended up in this massive bog and I was scouting up and down to try and find out where the road went and the bike was sinking into the mud and I didn't want to get it stuck. But I stayed as close to the river as possible where it was firm and rode up and down a bit looking for where the track was."

"If it had been dark, you would have been in trouble, hey?"

"It would have been difficult in the dark, yeah."

"Because I remember on the way up, there were quite a few sections where the track just disappeared."

"Yeah, but I also had my GPS with me with the track that we had left, I had that in my pocket so I could see how far off I was."

"So it was just the two main river crossings and then you got to the top?"

"Yes, and then it was, yeah, the whole, that first ascent, it was just rough, rocky and rough. It started flattening out as I got closer to the top and that's when I could see this weather system coming in up in the mountains and it was spitting with rain and then that strange kind of polystyrene-type snow started falling."

"Were you worried you might get caught?"

"I was worried I might get wet but I managed to keep in front of it."

"Now on that section before you reached the top, were there any times when you stopped to clear the route by moving stones?"

"Only for that one river."

"And were you getting tired?"

"I was tired, and I know, I felt my arms and my shoulders were fatigued, and sore and tired. But I guess that's just from being ill *and having not eaten properly."*

"OK, so you got to the top. How did you feel when you knew you'd made it up?"

"I was pretty relieved. It had taken longer than I thought it would. But I was still pretty keen. Then my next thought was, right, when I go over that pass, what's going to be at the top? It was the same thing, the weather was, I didn't want to stop, I didn't want to camp, I didn't want to get there and then be forced to turn back and have to ride through rain."

"And the river crossing where you got washed away?"

"I got to it but I didn't bother. I didn't even look, really, I knew where I was so I went up to the little bridge, got across the bridge."

"Crossed that alright?"

"Yeah, it was fine."

"And then the next pass?"

"Yeah, it got quite small. It became like just a little track but a vehicle had been through fairly recently, I could see its tracks so I knew I'd either catch up with it or it would have gone all the way up and over. And it got, it was quite high, it was quite a high pass and there was snow right up on the top, big drifts of snow right up to where that river, that was quite a long river crossing, and it was flowing quite fast as well so I stopped and kind of peered at it but I couldn't see how deep it was so I turned around and I was, down from where the road crossed it, it was quite a bit wider there and I thought it would be shallower but it was still very rocky and rough and very boggy as well so I scouted around there for a bit to see if I could get across the, I wouldn't have been able, I think it would have been more difficult than actually crossing the river, so..."

"So you went back to it?"

"So I went back to the river and I walked the bike through the deepest part. It was almost like it had been dammed, you know, where the road went, there was quite a high section of rocks where

the water was going over it and I stood on there and just walked the bike through."

"And you were saying that the water was coming up quite -"

"Quite high, yes."

"Close to the plug?"

"Yes, it was high. It was a bit of a worry, I didn't want to drown it, it wouldn't have drowned the bike, just shorted the plug like it did before."

"And the bit you were walking on, was it firm?"

"No, quite slippery, lots of rocks."

"And once you were through there, you were -?"

"Yeah, it was quite a long pass down the other side and then, once it started getting lower, the valley opened up and I could see the black ribbon of tarmac on the main road but there was this other massive river right across it."

"You say another river crossing?"

"Yeah, that's when I stopped and looked at the GPS and saw that the road didn't actually connect, there was a gap and I was thinking: Oh, no, here comes another massive river crossing. I got right down to the river and the vehicle tracks, you could see that the car had turned off the road and it looked like it had driven straight across the river. I was just scouting around there and I couldn't see where it had crossed and the river was way too high so I just followed the road which was really indistinct and then about 2-300 metres up ahead I could see that there was a bridge..."

"Oh, you found a bridge!"

"Yeah, a bridge."

"And the car had gone over it?"

"I don't know. I couldn't see. Its tracks disappeared."

"And the river - was it flowing strongly?"

"Very strong, yeah."

"And how did you feel, was your heart in your boots?"

"I was fairly relieved when I saw the bridge..."

"Do you think you would have been able to get across?"

"I don't know. Possibly. It's hard to tell, you know. There might have been a section. The river was very wide, the valley was very wide so there might have been a section somewhere where it would have been shallow enough to ride across but I didn't stick around when I got to the bridge and the main road, that section of tar was really good, top gear, 80ks an hour, but then it deteriorated into fairly rough, that whole road was very variable that entire trip; sometimes it was good, sometimes it was hideous."

"And then you overshot by 20ks."

"Yeah, and then I ended up in Alichur. I assumed that that was where the turn-off was going to be because there was a town, so I stopped and looked at the GPS and I couldn't believe it, luckily that section of road was good. I turned round and rode back until I came to the actual turn-off. It was very small. In fact, if I didn't have my GPS I don't know whether I would have found it."

"And you were concerned that the army checkpoint at Kahrgush was going to be closed..."

"Yes, that road, the first section of that road was quite slow because there was a pass there and it was pretty rough but I just went for it, I was riding pretty quickly along there, got to the checkpoint and it was still open."

"And it was about 200ks?"

"Altogether, yeah. From the bottom of the pass, from where Matt's Pass joined the road at that little bridge, it was about 195ks, yeah."

"So, after the checkpoint it was all the way home. You must have been feeling quite relieved."

"Yeah, I was tired then. I was feeling really, I was focusing on the road, focusing on picking a line through the potholes and the sand and that. I was really feeling tired then. And when I got to where we'd spent the night, as I rode past, I slowed right down; I thought I was going to have to stop and look at the door but I could see where you'd scratched your name on the wall and I was about to go on and then I thought: Hold on, I'd better check and make sure you were not actually in there..."

"Yes, it was the first thing I did when I made it out, I scratched it, I made sure that I, I could have been lying there! Ah, man!"

"I stuck my head in the room and I was pretty relieved that you weren't there so, then it was, it was down to the home-stay."

"And I was there!"

"Yeah -"

"Yeah, that was great!"

* * * * *

And Gareth's bike, abandoned high up in the mountains? The article "The raising of Lazarus", later in this book, tells its story.

First published in Overland Magazine, Issue 19.

Excerpt taken from "A Pass too Far".

TWO
That's how it all started

I suppose you could blame my Dad for it, this wanderlust, this quest for adventure.

It was he who, when I was twelve, took me and my brother on a 370-mile walk from Durban to Lourenco Marques (now Maputo), in Mocambique. Averaging about 27 miles a day and sleeping on the side of the road in sleeping bags made for us by my mother, we completed the walk in two weeks. Although it was a long, hard journey, we wanted more so, two years later, the three of us rode those old, gear-less, black Phillips bicycles from Durban to Beira, a distance of 1,100 miles. Once again we slept wherever we could on the roadside, seeking shelter when it rained under trees, in a railway goods wagon and once in a jail cell at a rural police station.

Those two journeys kindled something within my brother and me, changed us forever, I believe. My wife and I attempted to sow similar seeds of adventure into the lives of our two children. It has always meant a great deal to me that many of the adventures in this book have been shared with my son, Gareth, a young man who has, over the years, led me into situations I would never have tackled on my own.

Perhaps growing up in the 50's and 60's in a small rural village in Natal, South Africa, ten miles up the coast from Durban also played its part. Surrounded by sugar cane fields and virgin coastal bush, it was ideal for little boys to explore and be innocently wicked in, with few adults around to order our lives or tell us what we couldn't do.

Even when small, our parents gave us the widest of boundaries in which to spread our wings and explore the world about us. We made *catties* by cutting off forked sticks and trimming them with our sheath knives, attaching strips of rubber cut from old car tubes to the prongs with string. We became quite adept at killing birds in the surrounding bush, I'm sorry to say, especially when we used marbles as shot. Later we progressed to bows and arrows. And then it was wooden carts with 2nd-hand pram wheels which my father made for us. These had no brakes, of course, and were steered with rope but we would whizz down steep hills, slide and roll off around corners and come home with bleeding knees and elbows - and no one, least of all our parents, seemed to mind. We were always bare foot; when out playing we didn't think of wearing shoes. And, mostly, shoes weren't necessary because the soles of our feet toughened over time with thick, leathery pads which protected them against most things - except those terrible devil-thorns which grew in the cane breaks and made us hop when we stood on them.

We treated the sugar cane fields as our own private playground. For hours we would watch the African men cutting the sugar cane with their sharp pangas, flicking off the chaff with deft strokes then lopping off the feathery green tops and piling the stems in neat rows to be picked up and loaded onto the little puffing steam train that bustled importantly along narrow contours kicking up clouds of dust (and we would run along behind the last cane-laden dolly and try to scramble on, much to the anger of the driver). Such fun! We would put pennies on the line and watch them bounce and flatten and then take them home and treasure them.

When we were a bit older we discovered the sea just on our doorstep and started surfing - first with belly boards which we saved up for and bought with our own money and, later, full-size surf boards which we would carry to the beach on our heads protected by a folded towel. These boards were heavy and about ten foot long (short boards hadn't been invented then) and I remember working a whole month at the local hardware store at R1.00 a day (that's 10p in today's money) to pay for it. And even though my brother and I were only about ten or eleven years old, our parents were quite happy to let us go surfing all by ourselves.

Our father sometimes took us camping on Salisbury Island in Durban harbour. We would sail to the island in our dingy, spend some time exploring the mangrove swamps and beach-combing; then we'd make a driftwood fire on the shore before retiring to sleep in the bottom of the boat which had been pulled up onto the sand above the high-water line. The next morning we would sail back.

And my Dad would take us walking through the coastal bush and all over the sugar-cane fields and it was on one of those walks one windy evening before I entered my teens that he suggested we might do a really long walk together, the three of us, an *adventurous* walk all the way up the coast north into the then Portuguese territory of Mocambique.

And that's how it all started...

THREE
Night watch in the bush

I settled down on my sleeping bag, the plastic Colgate shampoo bottle of ammonia clutched in my frightened hands. In their bags on

the other side of the fire, Neville and my father lay sleeping. I kept the fire going by feeding it wood from the large pile we had collected before it became too dark to see. The flames cast weird, moving shadows into the surrounding bush.

Remembering the lion tracks in the road alongside our camp the previous night, thoughts crawled about my brain: How far could a lion walk in a day? How far would the ammonia spray if a lion suddenly appeared and tried to attack me? Would I be able to get the screw cap off in time? Would the acrid ammonia fumes chase it away if I sprayed it in the eyes? What would it do if I missed?

Staring into the flames contracted my pupils, making it impossible for me to see into the surrounding trees and grass just outside the flickering pool of light cast by the fire, so there was no telling just what horrors lurked there in the darkness. Eerie night bird calls and strange rustles and whirrings came from the foliage about me - as if an animal was creeping towards me, stalking me...

As time passed I found it increasingly difficult to keep awake and on a number of occasions discovered that I'd dropped off briefly, awaking with a start. Then I'd quickly throw more wood onto the fire and peer into the encroaching darkness, wondering whether anything had crept up on me while I nodded off...

At the turn-off to Vilanculos, the pot-holed tar road ended and the soft sand began. I think we all knew that, at that moment, our adventure was about to begin. We set off, filled with excitement, on the road to Mambone. The track through the long grass and thorn bushes was very soft and we struggled, often having to get off our bikes and push.

Shortly after midday, we came across two African men on bicycles; they had bows and arrows slung over their shoulders and one had a dead Mpiti buck tied to his crossbar. It was as if we had been transported into an earlier time, into a sparsely populated world of hunter-gatherers. We stopped briefly. They looked at us and asked some questions we couldn't understand; we examined their home-made bows and arrows and the little dead buck about to be taken to their huts somewhere in the bush and eaten. It somehow made us realise just how remote the area through which we were riding had become.

The unmarked track forked and we made our way to the muddy banks of the slow-flowing Savi River. An old pont was moored against the river bank but we were the only people wanting to cross. We had not seen another vehicle for a while now. The operators, seeing, I am sure, some naive strangers to fleece, refused to take us across unless there were other vehicles to make the crossing worthwhile. Of course, they would take us on our own - for a fee. The amount they asked for was exorbitant so my father refused.

There was a dugout canoe pulled up on the riverbank and the pont operator said that, for a lesser fee, he would paddle us across in the dug-out. We agreed. He took two bikes across first and our hearts were in our throats as we watched our precious mounts, still loaded with sleeping bags, belongings, passports and money, gliding precariously across the swirling waters. But they made it across safely and he paddled back for Neville and me. We settled ourselves on the bottom of the dugout, balancing carefully because there were only a few inches freeboard when our paddler added his weight to the canoe, and we set off across the river, angling upstream against the flow. On the other side, we got out onto the bank and watched while he paddled across the river to pick up our father and the remaining bicycle.

Safely across, we set off again into the bush. After about six miles we came across a roadside store and, realising that this would probably be the last chance to stock up on supplies for the next 110 miles (which we hoped to cover in three days), we sat outside and ate all our spare food, drank as much as we could then stocked up with as many tins and packets of Maria biscuits as we could carry, topped up our water bottle and filled an extra bottle that we found behind the shop.

So, loaded with as much as we could fit on the bikes, we set off again following a soft sandy track with occasional rideable hard sections. But within half a mile my father's rear tyre went flat and we had to stop to patch it - our first and only puncture on the whole trip. We unloaded the bike, made the repair, pumped up the tyre but it immediately went flat again. After removing the tube again we discovered that there were *two* holes; we repaired the second puncture then pressed on.

The going was hard, especially with the extra weight on the back of the bikes. We had to do a lot of pushing and, after midday, we began to struggle in the afternoon heat. If one of us managed to get going, he did not stop or look back. It took total concentration to keep on the firmer wheel tracks and not stray onto the soft edges so looking back was not an option; and the sheer effort of getting going in the soft sand made one want to press ahead without pausing until the sand brought one to a grinding halt. Only then could one afford to look back and see how the others were coping. In this way we often became separated, each dealing alone with our personal devils.

It was late afternoon when we entered a band of tsetse fly country and they began to bite. Our (fortunately brief) taste of Hell had begun.

The tsetse fly had proved disastrous for livestock farmers for hundreds of years across Southern Africa. Any domestic cattle that entered a tsetse area were likely to die and it has taken many years and a huge effort to contain these lethal flies. Their bite is shocking, a stab of intense pain that cannot be ignored. They seem to be attracted to sweat and the ones that attacked us seemed to know just where the hard-to-reach places on our bodies were - like the middle of one's back or the back of the neck. Many times we were forced to drop the laden bikes into the sand, flailing our arms about trying to kill the biting flies. Once their stinging proboscis has entered one's skin, they do not fly away when flapped at like ordinary flies. They cling on, continuing to bite and sting until forcibly removed and crushed between forefinger and thumb. Slapping them, as one does to a mosquito, has no effect, no matter how hard they are hit; they seem to flatten their large, exoskeletal backs, take the blow, give themselves a little shake and continue to bite. You cannot ignore it. You *have* to get it off you, stop the pain and, of course, this requires removing a hand that is clutched to the handlebars when struggling through the sand or pushing the bike through a particularly soft section. Often the bike would fall over and have to be laboriously picked up again... and again... and again in the sweltering heat. Many hidden tears, I remember, were shed through this terrible section.

Fortunately, we came across the tsetses in the late afternoon and they settle as soon as the sun sets so we only had a brief taste of their cursed presence. The following day would be another story, though.

Remembering what we had been told by other travellers who had come through this section and realising that we were walking through ideal lion country, we decided it would be wise to light a fire for the night. So we pulled off the road into the long grass as soon as the sun had set and began collecting a good quantity of firewood from the surrounding bush. (I can remember keeping a nervous eye out for lions as I walked about looking for firewood.) My father wondered whether we should keep watches through the night but in the end decided not to. Perhaps this was because he had been feeling sick and we were all exhausted. Instead, we agreed that if any of us woke in the night we would pile more wood on the fire to keep it going. And this we did - although in the early hours we slept through and the fire was dead by morning.

Soon after we set off the next day, we were somewhat alarmed to come across lion footprints and fresh elephant droppings in the soft sand near where we had camped. They looked fresh and it appeared that they might very well have passed close by us in the night. We certainly heard nothing. Whether the lions were deterred by our fire or just didn't feel hungry we'll never know, but it was disconcerting. We realised that we would have to be more careful in future. How close we came to being eaten that night, sleeping under the stars out in the open and deep in the bush as we were, only God knows ...

It was early, as usual, when we set off - the most special time in the bush. In the early morning, before the sun is fully up, the harshness of the bushveld is softened, the dust less cloying, the long dry grass taking on a deep yellow glow before much of its colour is leached out by the brightness of the day. The air is still and calm, birds just waking and beginning to stir. We covered the coals of the fire with sand and pushed our bikes onto the track. Fortunately, for the first few cool miles, we made good time along a hard section of road. As the day warmed, we came across much game - a variety of buck, as well as wild pig, monkeys and baboons.

We were still very aware of lions and kept a wary eye out for them as we rode and pushed our way through the long grass and bush.

Then we struck more soft sand and, as the sun rose and heat seeped into the bush, we were rejoined by our friends, the tsetses, in full force. The torment that plagued us throughout that terrible day had begun. We struggled on, often separated so far from each other that, at times, it felt as if I was riding alone in a wilderness devoid of people. I was forced to contend with the soft sand, the unwieldy bike and the unending torment of the tsetse flies on my own. How often I fell during that day I do not know, but I remember crying out and even weeping in frustration as yet another tsetse fly jabbed its stinging proboscis into my back and I had to drop the bike to kill it; seeing Neville or my father disappearing around a bend in the track ahead while I battled to pick the loaded bike up yet again, push it through the soft, strength-sapping sand while trying to flap away the flies before they settled to bite again, looking for a section of harder track so I could start riding ...

My father wrote in his diary that night: *"As the day progressed, the roads became progressively worse, with sometimes only 10 yards of riding followed by a seemingly endless pushing through soft sand, with the heat always increasing and the tsetse flies viciously biting arms, legs, face, backs. We all agreed that this must be very close to Hell."*

Eventually, after covering what we estimated was about 55 very hard miles, we pushed the bikes off the track and made camp under a clump of trees. Because of the lion footprints of the previous night, we all agreed that we would build a large fire and keep it going all night. My father proposed we keep watch and divided the hours of darkness so that Neville and I would keep watch for three hours each while he took the four hours before dawn. We ranged about in the bush and collected a huge pile of wood (I expected to come across lions behind every tree) - enough, we hoped, to keep the fire alight until morning.

When it was dark I, being the youngest, took the first watch. I settled down on my sleeping bag, the plastic Colgate shampoo bottle of ammonia clutched in my frightened hands...

For a 14-year-old, that was a very scary time. My watch was from 7 to 10; Neville's from 10 - 1 and my father's from 1 until he woke us at 5. I admit to having used too much of our wood in my attempt to keep the fire burning brightly; I know this because by the end of

Neville's watch it was almost all used up; he had to walk out into bush in the dark to find more so my father could keep the fire going until dawn. I'm not sure I would have had the courage to do that.

I wonder what thoughts went through my father's mind during the four lonely hours of his vigil, with his sons sleeping opposite him in the darkness, his wife and daughter far away. I'm sure he spent much time in prayer, the silence and the vast canopy of stars overhead causing one to feel God's presence closely.

For me sitting in front of the fire, though, time passed slowly. I kept looking at my watch, willing the hand to move towards 10 o'clock. When I had to pee and couldn't hold it in any longer, I stood just outside the light of the fire, urging myself desperately so I could finish and get back to the safety and warmth of the flames.

Finally, the hands of my watch crept towards 10 and I was able to wake my brother. I climbed into my sleeping bag and, as so often happens, despite fighting against sleep for the past few hours, the moment I lay down I was wide awake and struggled to get to sleep for a long time, occasionally glancing up to see Neville's silhouetted figure sitting quietly against the flickerings of the fire.

When we woke next morning, Neville told me off for using up so much of the wood, forcing him to range about in the dark to collect more. He also told us he'd heard lion roaring - in the direction from which we had come.

The floods that had destroyed so many of the bridges in the area north of Lourenco Marques had turned the area we rode through the next day into a quagmire. The rainy season had passed but there were still places where the water had flooded the road and forced truck drivers to deviate into the bush, making their way around the flooded sections. The difficulty of getting any goods through this area was evident throughout the day. Riding (or pushing) along, we'd find that the track in front of us suddenly divided, both tracks heading different ways into the bush. Of course there were no road signs and at first we became quite concerned that we would miss our way, get lost in this wilderness that stretched all about us for hundreds of miles of flat, featureless grassland and bush. Sometimes the tracks would branch and then branch again, meandering through the trees to miss sections of land that were still waterlogged and muddy.

We often came upon evidence of the truck drivers' struggle: loads dumped in the bush on the sides of deep mud - obviously in an attempt to lighten the trucks. I assume they would return and collect their goods at some stage when the countryside had dried sufficiently for them to make it through. The ruts the trucks had made were sometimes as deep as our handlebars and we struggled to make our way through or around them. Sometimes you could see where deep ruts broke off the main track onto the bush in an attempt to circumvent a particularly bad section of mud and then they would plough on, churning up the ground until they reached the main track again; some just ended where a truck had bogged down; all about was evidence of digging, cut branches which had been thrust under the wheels in an attempt to get the trucks free.

Fortunately by then we seemed to have passed through the tsetse fly belt and that made life so much more pleasant. We battled on until, with the sun up but before it became hot, we came across a group of three trucks well and truly bogged to their chassis in a massive mud hole. It was clear the Portuguese drivers and their African crews had been there a long time. They were unshaven and had that pinched look about them that people get when they've been sleeping rough for a while. It was clear the trucks were going nowhere soon; some of their loads had been removed and lay scattered about and there was evidence of their attempts to extricate the trucks by digging beneath the wheels.

We stopped to enquire the distance to the Buzi River and these rough, grizzled men greeted us warmly and invited us to share some food with them. Before we could protest, they produced a loaf of bread, opened a tin of meat and, while we tucked in, they boiled a kettle on a fire and made tea. After that, one of the drivers produced a bottle of red wine, poured some into a mug and offered it to my father. When he protested, suggesting that they keep it for themselves, the man shrugged and said with a smile, "When it's finished... it's finished!" They told us they had been there nearly a week and were waiting for someone to come out and rescue them, help them dig the trucks out. And, while we shared the little they had, deep in the Mocambiquan bush, we briefly established that special bond that people down on their luck experience when they happen upon each other in the anonymity of wide-open spaces and share what little they have with each other with that unique generosity one so often finds in adversity.

Rested and touched by their openness, we reluctantly pressed on. The "road" - if you could call it that - became nothing but a succession of diverging and converging tracks, very rutted, but at least it was no longer soft sand. But progress was still slow and the riding more technical, choosing which rut to follow, which diverging fork to take. Eventually the track improved, though, and we began to speed up.

At noon we finally reached the Buzi River pont. This time, there was a truck waiting to cross so we didn't have to trust ourselves to dugout canoes again. Some locals had gathered to cross as well, including a woman who, to escape having to pay the full fare for her son (who must have been at least ten years old) had strapped him to her back like a baby and covered his head with a cloth, but his long legs stuck out in front of her as a testimony to her deception and, despite her protestations, she had to pay!

The truck was carefully driven onto the pont and we followed, taking our place amongst the other foot passengers. The river, however, was so shallow that, despite straining with all their might against the cable, the pont crew could not move us away from the bank; we were stuck fast on the muddy bottom. Obviously having done this before, the truck driver started up his engine and by rolling back as far as the pont would allow, then driving forwards and jamming on the brakes, he nudged us forward about a foot. Doing this repeatedly, we slowly bumped and nudged our way across the river.

We had 40 miles to go to reach the main tarred Umtali-Beira road and by means of some hard riding, reached this just before nightfall. My father, keeping a promise he had made repeatedly as we struggled with the soft sand, heat and tsetse flies, laid down his bike, got down on his hands and knees and kissed that road. Never before had a tar road been such a welcome sight!

Excerpt taken from: "By Bicycle to Beira - Reminiscences of a 14-year old"

FOUR
First desert crossing

Loaded up with extra fuel, water and food for two days, we headed out of Merzouga like schoolboys off on an adventure. At last, after four days riding through persistent and depressing rain across Spain and over the Atlas Mountains, we were about to dip our toes into the desert. The weather had turned hot and dry and already we were overheating in our riding gear.

Gareth checked on his GPS and found the track; the bikes felt sluggish and heavy with the added weight, rolling slightly and slow to respond. Within minutes we had lost our way in the maze of small tracks that meandered from the town into the desert; ahead of us the track crested a rise, the sand turned a reddish orange and Gareth, who was in front of me, ploughed to a stop half way up, his wheels deeply buried in the sand. I stopped on the hard ground before the rise and went to help him. There was no way he could get the bike to the top of the low hill and he couldn't budge it backwards. A Spanish man travelling through Morocco in a car had also attempted this hill and got stuck; he came over to help us. Together, the three of us pulled the heavy KTM backwards out of the sand and onto hard ground again.

So, our first brush with sand and we had very quickly come to grief. The heavily laden bikes were very difficult to move once buried and, in places, definitely needed more than one person to extricate.

Had we bitten off more than we could chew here? Already stuck and we hadn't even left the outskirts of the town.

Getting badly stuck the first time we tried to ride our heavily laden bikes through soft sand had been a sobering lesson for us both and added to our uncertainty about the wisdom of what we were attempting.

After dragging Gareth's bike out of the sand, we found the correct track and set off on one of the most difficult and memorable rides I have ever done.

At first the track was easy. Dust- and heat-haze obscured the last buildings of Merzouga behind us; the beautiful, chocolate-box dunes of the Erg Chebbi disappeared below the horizon and were replaced by a desolate landscape of sand and rock. And, suddenly, a sense of release, of freedom came over me. This is what we had come so far to experience. At last we were nudging our way into the desert, devoid of people, camper vans, advertising hoardings, local men dressed in gaily-coloured *djellaba* calling, "Hello, my friend!"

We passed large sections of desert where rows of palm trees had been planted and crude barriers erected in a vain attempt to halt the migration of the dunes. As I rode past these puny constructions, a picture of King Canute came to mind. Nothing is going to stop dunes migrating once the fierce Harmattan begins to blow, lifting the sand grain by grain until the air turns to milk and visibility is reduced to a few yards.

The ground was firm beneath our wheels, slightly stony with occasional corrugations. In the distance on both sides of us, low ranges of hills, rocky and black, seemed to channel us along through a broken land. The *piste*, a stony dirt track, twisted and undulated around and over small hills, dipped to cross wide, flat river beds; the land was starkly desolate but still the occasional tamarisk tree gave perspective to a dry sameness which stretched to the horizon. We rode standing up most of the time, feeling the bikes responsive under our feet, the extra weight no longer really noticed. There were no sand drifts, no dunes and we were making good progress. In fact, all about there was *nothing* except for the desert and the thorn trees and us, making our slow way along tracks that, as the afternoon progressed, became increasingly smaller and more indistinct across the barren landscape. Every so often the *piste* would split and branch, usually where the terrain was rough or very rocky and vehicles had decided to find their own way. Gareth kept an eye on his GPS (mine had given up through this stretch) and, where tracks of equal size diverged, would point left or right to keep us heading in approximately the right direction.

What we hadn't realised, and were to learn as we explored deeper into the remoter sections of the desert over the next two weeks, is that there is never a single track, even though on the map it might be shown as such. For those who know the land, who are able to recognise a mountain range or pronounced landmark in the distance, it is usually not a problem. But for novices, crossing an unknown and uninhabited stretch of *reg* for the first time, it was somewhat disconcerting. We would certainly have turned back without the GPS which, although it too, on maximum zoom, showed a confusing maze of tracks radiating across the desert landscape, at least we knew we were heading in vaguely the right direction. We would have been completely lost without it.

At last we came across a Moroccan man on a small Chinese-made Docker motorbike; we stopped to speak to him and, although it was difficult for us to understand each other, he seemed to be warning us about a river crossing some twenty miles ahead. There was nothing we could do about it so we pressed on, no longer quite sure that we were doing the right thing or heading in the right direction.

As the afternoon progressed we began to come across dunes again; on either side of us were long lines of low mountains, buttes where the hard rock cap had not been worn away, rounded where it had. They were particularly beautiful in that the sand was a deep red-brown colour whereas the rock was black, creating scree slopes of black overlaying the brown. As the miles fell away, the sand changed colour: grey, yellow, red, brown - and always the overlay of black rocks providing contrast. Later the track descended onto a flat, firm salt pan extending to the horizon in front and on either side of us and we sped up, loving the smoothness of it, the rush of cool air against our faces.

Then we began to encounter soft sand.

At first it was just short, isolated sections that we could cross with a burst of speed. But progressively the deep sand became the norm rather than the exception and we began to struggle. The *piste* had descended into a wide dry riverbed, the tracks almost continuously soft and deep. We bogged down regularly and it was sapping our strength.

Lose speed, have to change into first gear and the front wheel ploughs into the sand instead of riding on top of it, the rear wheel spins madly, digging you in until you come to a stop. Usually the bike would be so deeply dug in that you could climb off and leave it: it would keep standing on its own. Sometimes we would need to come to each other's assistance, help push to get a bike going again; sometimes we would have to push the bike whilst stumbling alongside, feathering the clutch to keep the revs up and then either trying to jump back on (very difficult with a load on the back of the bike) or push onto firmer sand when one could start again.

We were quickly becoming exhausted, overheating and consuming our limited supply of water at an alarming rate. At one point we became separated and I shudder to think of what could have happened. The problem is this: once you get unstuck and begin moving, you dare not stop until you reach firmer ground. Controlling the bike and negotiating a way through the soft sand takes all your concentration so it is impossible to be aware of where the other rider is at the same time. At one point both Gareth and I got stuck in deep drifts. He was somewhere ahead of me, I couldn't see him but could hear the revving of his engine. I was exhausted and collapsed next to my bike, deciding I would wait for him to walk back and help me. The problem was that Gareth, also bogged down in the sand, thought I was *ahead* of him. He managed to get his bike moving again and pressed on, hoping to overtake me. I was well behind now, waiting.

Eventually I recovered sufficiently and decided I would try, one more time, to extricate the bike on my own. I don't know how I got it going again out of the soft sand but I did and, a while later, came across Gareth, who had stopped when he heard me behind him. There is no mobile reception that far into the desert, there were tracks going all over the place and we could have lost one another completely. A scary thought.

We wondered what to do. Both of us were exhausted. We had no idea how far this stretch of *fetch-fetch* went, for all we knew it could have been as bad, or even worse, for the next fifty miles. Should we turn back while we still could, while we had some water left? And we still had the river to cross. We didn't know how deep it was or even whether it existed but we remembered the barely understood warning given us by the local man on his motorbike and the unprecedented flooding we had ridden through when crossing the Atlas two days before. I was concerned I might drop my bike when crossing the river and drown it.

Realising how close to the end of my strength I was, Gareth volunteered to ride ahead and see whether he could find the river. To make it easier, he unloaded his bike and, with a great deal of shoving and an impressive rooster-tail of sand spraying up behind, he set off along the tracks. I collapsed in the shade of a stunted shrub and vaguely hoped he would be able to find me again.

A while later, I heard a revving engine and stood to look out for him. As soon as he came into view I could see that he was struggling. The bike was digging in, slewing from side to side between the tracks, and he was having to paddle hard with his legs from time to time to keep it going; at one point the front wheel dug in and he fell but quickly picked up the unladen bike and accelerated hard to reach me. He was so exhausted he could no longer hold the bike up and it fell over. He lay on his back in the sand, not speaking. I gave him water. After a while he sat up and told me he was shattered, his muscles quivering with exhaustion.

Again, I wondered whether we should turn back. I didn't know how much more I could take and our meagre water supplies were diminishing fast. But Gareth assured me that the river was about a mile away and that it looked fordable. The bad news was that between us and the river was soft sand all the way.

We rested a long time, drank more water and discussed our options. We agreed that we'd press on to the river, cross it and see what the desert surface was like on the other side. Neither of us wanted to turn back.

Then we looked carefully at the track, trying to work out the best way to tackle it without exhausting ourselves or damaging the bikes. Over the past few hours we had started to recognise what the firmer sand looked like and where to find it; we were just beginning to learn to "read" the sand, like a kayaker learns to read the currents in a river and adapts his stroke, body position, angle of approach, to take advantage of it. We had learned quite quickly that to press on in the deep sand of the tracks was going to exhaust us and we would end up overheating the engines or burning out our clutches if we persisted. Off *piste* the land was broken, ridged and chaotic, covered with small dunes, some the classic Barchan shape, others just random humps or accumulations of sand. We were learning how to cross these, to use the curving edge of a dune to get around an obstacle, power over the smaller accumulations in a straight line, the wheels seeming to rise and float over them.

But in this section of *fetch fetch* we realised that the accumulated sand around the base of small, stunted shrubs, raised above the rest of the land, was quite firm. The plan was: firstly, leave the tracks; then, carefully, plan a route from one firm rise to another, using the short downhill run to pick up sufficient speed to get over the soft stuff and up onto the next. Pause, scout the land and plan the next rush. After a while, we learned to pick out a route while riding, making our way from firm ridge, across the soft stuff, onto the next section of firm sand, pick up speed, power across a soft section, rest on firm sand, check where the other rider is, move on. We learned to use any rocks, sticks or vegetation to give the wheels extra traction when we started to bog down.

We weren't getting stuck so often any more and in this way, we reached the river. It was wide but seemed fairly shallow. Gareth removed his boots and socks and waded across: "Quite firm," he called to me from the other side, "but soft in places. If you wiggle your feet about, they sink."

There were no rocks so we decided to cross at speed, making sure we did not sink in. To be safe, we decided to unload, carry our kit across and make the crossing unladen. I stood in the water to help if Gareth became stuck and he started his bike, changed quickly into second gear, ramped over the bank and hit the water with a great flurry of spray. He crossed without a problem, accelerated across the firm sand and made it up the soft bank with relative ease.

Then it was my turn and, with Gareth standing on the opposite bank, I selected first gear and accelerated. To my consternation, the back wheel just dug in and I struggled to pick up speed and get the bike into second. But at last the rear wheel rose to the surface, I accelerated and was across without incident, hitting the soft sand of the far bank and skidding to the top. Encouraged, after a short rest we loaded up the bikes and set off again.

It was getting late now; we were very tired so decided to look for a place to camp. But we still had to cross a belt of soft sand a few miles wide, this time interspersed with low dunes. We picked our way through, gaining experience all the time on how to cope with the sand, learning how to read the desert surface, recognise the very soft parts and avoid them if possible and, if not, how to power across them without sinking in or falling over.

Finally, ahead of me, I saw the ground change: the colour turned black and I knew we had almost reached a section of flat desert called *reg*, firm sand covered with a layer of round black pebbles no bigger than your fist and great for riding over. I picked my way through the last of the soft sand, around the last dunes and felt the smooth, firm surface beneath my wheels. Relieved, I stopped and waited for Gareth.

The sun was now low on the horizon; every muscle ached, but soon we would be setting up camp, preparing a meal, drinking tea and reflecting on the day in the comfort of our tents. But Gareth was still battling through the sand. I sat on my bike, watching him. He only had about thirty metres to go and I was sure he would be alongside me in seconds. Just one more dune to cross...

As I watched, he accelerated up the face of the dune and the bike stopped as if he had hit a brick wall. The front wheel had disappeared as if into water and he almost went over the handlebars. I waited for him to extricate himself but he couldn't move. In the end I got off my bike and walked to where he was stuck. The big KTM was deeply bogged down to the engine and there was no way it was going to move forward up the slope of the dune face. We tried to pull it back but it was as if fixed in concrete. And yet, it was a perfectly normal looking dune face. And so we learned, as many desert travellers have learned before us, that there are deceptively soft patches in the sand which act almost like swamp-water into which a foot or vehicle just sinks. The two of us, working together, could not budge the bike an inch. In the end we had to lie it on its side and drag it around before Gareth could pick it up again and ride it onto the firm ground via a different route.

The day was almost over. A cool wind was blowing, lifting the sand and blowing it in little stinging cascades across the ground. Shadows lengthened across the desolate landscape all around us.

We rode on, the ground becoming increasingly rocky; by now we had lost the main track but knew we were approximately where we should be so were not worried. We would find the track again the next day. On the lower slope of a smooth-sided mountain, capped with the distinctive black rock found in the area, we saw a lone acacia tree and made for it. There was soft sand nearby so we decided to stop for the night. We unpacked, stripped off our shirts and revelled in the cool evening air. Soon our tents were up and water boiling for tea. And as the sun began to set, the two of us climbed to the top of the mountain that overshadowed our camp and sat in quiet contemplation, watching colour leach from the land, the sky turning deep orange and then red before the darkness set in.

And I was filled with a sense of peace and satisfaction at what we had achieved. We hadn't turned back. We had persevered. We had made it through. We had learned.

Tomorrow would be easier.

Excerpt taken from: "There are no Fat People in Morocco".

FIVE

Ride like a twat

Today, physically, I came very close to the end of my tether. Partly I suppose it was because for the previous 30 hours fluid has been draining out of me every hour in the worst case of diarrhoea I have ever had. In retrospect it probably would have been wiser to delay and get my strength back, but we finally reached Marsibit (260ks from Isiolo) in eight and a half hours, riding in the blazing sun over one of the worst roads I have ever driven on, full of rocks and corrugations and bull dust for the entire day; a bike-breaker of a road, a spirit-sapping road. But we made it (only half way, though - another 250ks of the same to the Ethiopian border).

We will rest up tomorrow, and tackle that section on Tuesday; we, physically, and the bikes, mechanically, need a rest.

(Gareth was 17 when we did our first long journey together, trans-Africa. We were riding two old XT500s which we had bought second-hand for the trip.)

At 8.30 we reported at the police barrier to join the convoy, but it had already left half an hour before. "But you can catch it up," the policeman told us, seemingly unconcerned by the threat of Shifta bandits, the reason for the protected convoy in the first place; and then he tried unsuccessfully to get some money off me.

At first, as always, the road wasn't too bad, but that is usually because one is fresh and the world rosy. Physically I was feeling OK and even had tinges of the old joy of riding coming back. This was what we had come for: Africa in all its harsh rawness. The dirt road stretched ahead across a flat land with, every now and then, a massive mountain, pale blue and rocky, thrusting itself out of the ground. It was a starkly beautiful landscape, devoid of people or habitation. And then we saw camels, a large herd, crossing the road ahead. At intervals we came across Samburu tribesmen walking in the dust along the side of the road; they wore dark-red, toga-like garb leaving one shoulder bare and carried spears. Some had painted their faces in intricate patterns of yellow ochre, their fine features set off with beads and silver jewellery, head-bands and feathers. One could almost call them beautiful, but in a proud, masculine way. A dignified people; when I asked whether I could photograph them, they refused; one young girl, about 15, wanted to attack me with a fist-sized rock when I proposed a photograph along the side of a deserted stretch of road where she was walking with her goats!

On this shockingly bad section of road, our troubles started when Gareth fell badly, injuring his leg. I had lost a Jerry can which hooked on a high ridge of loose stones and went rolling across the road spewing petrol. (These longitudinal ridges are built up by convoys of trucks and, if one hits them at an angle, it takes all one's strength and skill to keep the bike from going over. In the direct sunlight before and after midday, when perspective flattens and shadows disappear, they are almost impossible to make out, blending as they do with the dusty whiteness of the road.) Behind me, Gareth braked hard, his front wheel dug into the loose gravel and over he went. He was up quickly but there was blood on his knee where his jeans had been ripped. We got the bike up - it takes both of us to lift a downed bike; one water bottle was badly crushed and my Jerry can holed. Gareth stripped off boots and jeans. The flesh had been deeply torn away on his left knee and the palm of one hand. He accepted my ministrations with his usual stoicism.

At about 11.30 we came across a big bike, front wheel missing, propped up on rocks. As we stopped, a large man emerged from the shade of a thorn bush where he'd been sheltering from the heat, tools and kit spread about in the sand.

"You got a spare tube?" he called out hopefully.

We nodded and dragged out the tube we kept inside our spare tyre.

His name was Carl, an Australian biker on a round-world trip. He had been riding with five other bikers, American, German and Danish, in a loosely cohesive group and was at the back, travelling at about 80kph, when his front tyre went flat. Somehow he managed to keep the bike up and brought it to a stop. He found rocks to elevate the front wheel and had spent the last two hours trying to repair the tube. The others hadn't come back. He said a few words about his companions in choice Australian dialect, mostly beginning with 'F'. On his petrol tank was a formal-looking sticker which said:

WARNING

Remember to put fuel in the tank.
Try to wear a helmet.
Ride like a twat.

Australian humour.

He'd used up all his patches, taken the tyre off and replaced it about nine times he told us (with accompaniment of choice language, I'm sure) and even tried to stuff his spare 18-inch rear tube into the 21-inch front rim without success. In the end he had given up and was hoping to flag down a truck and persuade the driver to take him back to Nairobi.

We quickly fitted our spare tube, replaced the wheel and rode on together. (I was sad to lose our spare with the rest of North Africa still ahead of us, but the unwritten rule of the Good Samaritan in these remote places must always take precedence.)

Perhaps it was my exhaustion taking its toll on my concentration, the appalling road and the weight on my bike, but during the day I fell three times, twice hard, ripping my knee open deeply and grazing my arm. We bandaged me up and the blood and the shock made me physically ill. *(On this trans-African trip, other than boots, helmet and gloves, neither Gareth nor I wore any protective gear. At home we didn't have any and, at that time, the cost of purchasing armoured riding jacket and trousers was more than we could afford.)*

The road seemed never ending, the corrugations shaking our bikes to bits. At one point we discovered that a bolt in Gareth's brake assembly had rattled off but we managed to find another to replace it - not quite the right size but it would do; then one of Carl's brake pads rattled loose and was lost, the aluminium calipers and remaining pad badly ground away. Lying in the dust and heat under his bike, we managed to fit a spare.

And as 3 o'clock moved slowly to 4 and then to 5, I found myself weakening. I had difficulty kick-starting the XT; the falls and the heat and the strain of trying to keep the bike up had taken a tremendous toll on my physical reserves. What was so touching to me was the way Gareth noticed and, without fuss, helped me, quickly offering to kick-start my bike when he saw me struggling. I accepted gladly. Two or three attempts and, if the bike hadn't fired up, I was almost too exhausted to lift my leg, especially with the heavy boot attached, let alone give the tremendous kick required to start the big thumper. I found that I was having difficulty holding my head up and every muscle in my body was crying out for rest.

Then Carl's bike broke in half, the frame snapping on both sides. It was that kind of road.

We waited with him, knowing that, for him at least, it was the end. Fortunately, it wasn't long before a truck trundled along and the driver agreed to cart the bike somewhere more civilized. So we left Carl and rode on into the late afternoon.

We finally reached Marsibit after five as the sun was setting, and checked in to the local hotel. There we met the other riders, two Germans on a KTM and a Tenere, an American on a BMW, and a young Dane riding a rather tired XR500. (They were a little sheepish about their desertion of Carl, but insisted they thought he was in front and had ridden ahead. They claimed that Carl had only two speeds regardless of the road conditions: full speed or stop, and I can believe them!)

In my airless room, for a long time I lay on the bed, exhausted and unable even to wash. But, despite our crashes and injuries, we had made it. Half of the notorious Isiolo to Moyale road completed.

We had been told that from Marsibit to Moyale on the Ethiopian border the track was worse than the first half and only 10ks shorter. We planned to rest for a day, tending to our wounds, having the Jerry can welded and giving the bikes a once-over. We would then tackle the next stage slowly and carefully, caring for both ourselves and the bikes; we couldn't afford any further injuries and the bikes needed looking after if we were to nurse them across the rest of the continent. Not having a spare front tube was also a worry. The other bikers were also leaving for Moyale after a day's break and we hoped that we might ride together, support each other when things got bad. Their plan was to reach Europe via Saudi Arabia, Jordan, Israel, boat to Greece, boat to Italy and home. They were shunning Egypt, they told us, because of its reputation for hassling overlanders and the difficulty of obtaining visas. Despite my cunning self-validation of our carnets in Nairobi, my gut feeling was to do the same.

A day later we woke to the mournful wail of the muezzin calling the faithful to prayer. It was still dark outside. I had not slept well, knew it was time to get up, but lay for another 15 minutes enjoying my bed. Woke Gareth (as always - he sleeps with the pillow over his head and simply cannot wake on his own) and, while we packed, we ate a breakfast of hard boiled eggs bought the evening before. Our ripped knees - ugly wounds, Gareth's flesh ground away deeply and mine ripped open and needing stitches - we bound tightly with all the bandages we had, trying to give protection in case of another fall.

In the before-dawn stillness, the five other riders were also getting ready. As we prepared our bikes together in the dark courtyard under the sleepy gaze of the night watchman, there was that feeling of excitement one gets when a child, rising in the dark to prepare for a long holiday journey. By then Gareth and I were seasoned travellers (and had the wounds to prove it), and felt able to take our place in the loose camaraderie of the group. The others decided to wait for first light and to have coffee first, but Gareth and I set off on our own, anxious to get away and make the most of the cool of morning, knowing too that we would probably be riding slower.

As we rode through the dark deserted streets, dusty and littered with plastic, I felt the old twinge of joy I so often feel when starting off the day, the unique pleasure of riding a motor bike along little-used roads through a wild and foreign country, the cool air blowing against my face, the excitement of the unknown ahead. My body had recovered well and my stomach was fine. It was good to be well again.

And then a massive Fiat truck and trailer pushed me off the road, overtaking me in the dark and, long before he was past, cutting back in. My dim yellow headlight showed nothing but the clouds of dust thrown up by thundering wheels just inches away from my shoulder, the road was rutted and covered with large stones and thick ridges of sand and suddenly I realised that unless I took evading action the trailer was going to hit me. Swerve into the blackness on the left and onto the soft shoulder, the bike slewing to one side and lying down.

Fortunately I was going slowly because my leg was caught under the bike. Choking dust swirled about me as I dragged my leg free and watched the small red lights of the truck as it lumbered away into the night. So much for slow and careful. Five minutes of riding and already I was down.

Gareth was ahead and hadn't noticed my near escape. I lifted the XT and set off after him. The police barrier loomed up in the darkness. Already about five trucks and trailers were lined up for the convoy. We parked and made our way to the police shack.

"When does the convoy leave?" I asked.

"Maybe 7.30 - 8," the soldier said, waving a nonchalant hand which implied Africa Time.

Bitterly disappointed, Gareth and I sat down in the dark to wait. Around us, truck drivers were drinking sweet black tea served by a woman with a child strapped to her back. I wished she would offer me a cup. Already the sky to the east was lightening, but a cool wind had begun to blow clouds across the sky from the east - perfect for riding.

After ten minutes of frustrated waiting, we approached the soldier again. He told us that the Shifta usually attack about 6ks down the road and he pointed to a hill in the distance. "There, where the road goes around that hill - but they won't attack motor bikes," he assured us with a casual certainty.

"Could we go on ahead on our own?" I asked, looking at Gareth who nodded.

"Yes," he said looking up the road as if checking for Shifta. "When you get past that hill you should be alright."

We would accept a "should". Quickly we fired up the bikes, the soldier lifted the barrier and we set off carefully along the dark road, hoping we wouldn't come across a line of rocks blocking our way.

We passed the six-kilometre hill as the sun rose. The semi-desert landscape was beautiful as only it can be in the late evening or early morning. We paused to look into a large volcanic crater below and to the left of the road, an eerie sight in the pale dawn light, and then on again, making good time on a smooth dirt road. The land flattened and the semi-desert turned into pure desert, rocky and desolate, not a blade of grass and only a few stunted and dusty acacia trees to break the monotony. We had entered the Chalbi Desert, the road was remarkably good and, as I rode, I thought, as I had done before in Malawi and Tanzania: This is raw Africa - far from the tourist routes, deep into the desert, a slightly frightening but incredibly beautiful place.

After an hour or so the other bikers caught us and we rode on together through heat of the day. Contrary to expectation, the second half of the Isiolo to Moyale track was better than the first, increasingly sandy and firm instead of stony and corrugated and we made good time.

As we neared the Ethiopian border, the change from southern sub-Saharan Africa to the more Arab Sahel became increasingly apparent: camels appeared more frequently, staring contemptuously out of the bushes; English almost disappeared; the Muslim religion became prominent with Islamic verses in flowing Amharic script on the walls of small roadside shops; the features of the people became more Arab than Negroid, both the men and women slight, spare of flesh, delicately boned. The women wore brightly-coloured loose clothing, almost like the Indian sari, covering the head but leaving the face clear, their skin light brown and beautiful, moving like bright jewels against the arid and dusty landscape. One is reminded of Biblical scenes: women drawing water at wells, a Madonna-like serenity of movement and facial expression. Men walked about hand-in-hand in unaffected, asexual familiarity, often with a teeth-cleaning stick in their mouths like a cigar, or chewing bright green Khat leaves, a mildly intoxicating drug.

At last, by late afternoon, we crossed into Ethiopia, leaving the desert and the notorious Isiolo-Marsibit road behind us.

Excerpt taken from "Trans-Africa by Motorcycle, A Father's Diary".

SIX

Riding with the Black Bears

It all begins, as these things so often do, with a chance encounter on the side of the road. Cold, tired and a little wet from the morning's showers, Gareth and I sit at a rain-speckled plastic table with the hot roar of Moscow-bound trucks passing just behind us. In a small, wooden booth, a plump Russian woman with no lower teeth and a flower-print dress serves us sweet black coffee and feeds pieces of thinly-chopped wood into the samovar that smokes and bubbles on the counter.

A young Russian biker sees us as as he passes, pulls up and approaches us. His name is Sasha. He's a member of the Black Bears Motorcycle Club, he tells us, on his way to the White Sea coast north of Archangel. It's the club's annual get-together and would we care to join them?

What followed was a memorable four days.

We spend the first night camped in a field full of inebriated Russian bikers about 18 miles east of Vologoda. The next finds us in the apartment of Alexi, a local club member, which is where this article begins...

It's one o'clock in the morning. Eight Russian bikers and two girlfriends, Gareth and I fill every available space in Alexi's small apartment. His 17-year-old daughter sulks in the bedroom playing a TV game, resentful of this sudden invasion of her space. Three-litre plastic bottles of beer have appeared, as well as cognac - the drinking has begun. As if out of nowhere, Russian sausage, soft cheese, sliced tomatoes and bread are put on the table and roughly chopped with a wicked-looking sheath knife with a bone handle.

A girl sitting pressed against me on the couch - early 20s, dark hair with a lock dyed red which hangs over her forehead - leans over me and with beery, sausage-laden breath murmurs huskily in my ear, "You're going to have a Russian experience." The warmth of her body against me and the intimate, beery way she speaks makes me wonder whether this Russian experience might involve things of a fleshly nature and whether they will blow my head off with a shotgun if I refuse.

The other girl sits quietly, almost haughtily (she doesn't speak to us at all, I think because she has no English) and I realise she was the one I saw emerging naked from the outside sauna the previous night, her pert breasts braving the cold.

Then a type of ravioli, a Russian favourite, is brought to the table and someone drenches it with sour cream. People lean forward and help themselves; a fork is pressed into my hand and voices encourage me to eat. I do and it is delicious.

In the corner of the room, the TV continues to play some badly acted local soap, as it has done since we got here, part of the mutter of background noise. The talk, mostly in Russian, is about the ride that day, the accident. One bearded biker has a thick layer of sour cream spread on his sunburned nose - an effective remedy for wind and sunburn, they tell us. More beer is poured and then the bottle of cognac is cracked open. It is late and after a while, I quietly excuse myself and head for the bedroom. Two bikers lie in sleeping bags on the floor. Alexi's daughter still sits stoically at the computer, playing games, ignoring us. They have all insisted that Gareth and I sleep in the double bed...

Then, before I could get to sleep, a phone-call: one of the bikes had broken down 25 miles outside Kotlas and Alexi left us to take his dilapidated van to rescue it and the riders. Later, another phone call: one of the biker's luggage had shifted because of the bad road surface, come into contact with his exhaust pipe and caught fire. His mate, riding behind, saw the fire and accelerated to catch him and wave him down but in the ensuing confusion, they both crashed. Some damage to the bikes and some broken ribs but they decide to carry on (although they would back-track 120 miles to the main road so they wouldn't have to ride the long sections of dirt).

The next day, another early start and a long, hard twelve hours' riding - 400 miles - but such a joy. Even the long sections of dirt were enjoyable in a way - testing but seldom dangerous for Gareth and me on our big trailies. Sasha struggled somewhat on his road bike and on a number of occasions I thought he was about to crash, legs flailing, bike slewing this way and that when he hit a particularly large ridge of sand but, fortunately, he never went down. Probably about 60 miles of the 400-odd we did today were on dirt; it rained a little during the morning which at least helped settle the dust.

As we made our way north, the trees became shorter and less thickly self-seeded, their growth stunted by the long, cold winters and weak summer sunlight; the Sevdvina River, alongside of which the road made its way north, was wide and shallow, the water level very low at that time of the year but still beautiful and slow-flowing. As we neared Archangel, we linked up with other motorcyclists along the way, many of whom we recognised from our camp in the field two nights before and who greeted us warmly.

We passed Archangel, stopping to drink a toast of vodka from a motorcycle indicator lens ("Isn't there supposed to be a 0% blood-alcohol level for drivers in Russia?" I asked. Sasha pointed to the biker pouring out the vodka: "He's high up in the police," he laughed. "It's not a problem."); then on further north until we took a soft sandy track that led us onto the beach, the heavily laden bikes slithering and roaring and throwing up high rooster tails as we struggled through the sand to our camp, shaded by a grove of low pine trees, the White Sea just 40 yards in front of us. Across a small bay, the smoke from Severodvinsk was visible in the distance. (We only realised later that we were camping in an area restricted to foreigners and were liable to arrest and a hefty fine - Severodvinsk is where the Russians build their nuclear submarines and, obviously, a rather sensitive place.)

It was 10pm before we had the tents up, the sun still well above the horizon where it seemed to hover while the earth turned slowly beneath it for hours of twilight at this high latitude - 64.5 degrees North, just south of the Arctic Circle at 66.6 - and, even though it was mid-Summer, the temperature dropped very quickly at night or when the wind blew. A driftwood fire had been lit, rock music was playing, powered by a small generator, potatoes cooking in the massive cast-iron samovar which had been transported to the beach (with a more than ample stock of booze) in the back of a van.

News had come through that another two bikes had crashed on the way: Daniel and his wife Anastasia were evidently barged by a "redneck" in a car; a few of the bikers decided to rough him up but, in the push and shove, trying to manoeuvre the offending car off the road by barging it with their bikes so they could get at him, two of the bikes crashed and Anastasia fractured her leg.

It had been a long, hard day and, with the noise of Russian voices all about, rock music beating into the night and the fire flickering in the darkness, I retired for the night filled with a sense of satisfaction that *this* was what we had come to Russia for. And it was so good that my son was sharing it with me.

The following day was a well-needed rest day spent socialising with our new friends. We were tired and it was good to take a break. The distances we had had to cover through Russia were vast and required long and hard riding; in retrospect, we probably needed another two weeks to do the route justice: time to explore more, to savour the countryside at a slower speed, meet more people, pause more often.

Gareth was still determined to find a route from Archangel to Murmansk following the White Sea coast. A brief look at the map suggests that this is logical - the alternative is a 1,200 mile route which dips far to the south then west and finally north again to Murmansk. But all the small roads seem to end in the wilderness or double back to the main road after heading purposefully in the right direction for a while. We had both seen a "road" that went the whole way but, on closer inspection, it turned out to be a railway track.

Whilst pouring over the map after breakfast, we were joined by about eight Russian bikers, all of whom had opinions about the viability of the route. But the consensus was clear: it was impossible. One told us that a year or so ago, five bikers from Moscow attempted it but only two made it through and one died on the way. I don't know whether that is apocryphal, though. They told us that the topography between Archangel and Murmansk alternates between islands of dense forest surrounded by lakes and swamp. One commented wryly that, when looking at small roads on any map of Russia, one must treat them as little more than pictures on a page: they *look* good but in reality many of them do not exist at all - just in the minds of the authorities who would *like* there to be a road there so they draw it on the map, something we discovered for ourselves later in the trip.

The rest of the day was spent mixing with the bikers who went out of their way to talk to us, examine our bikes, ask about our journey, about England and, more important, what we thought of Russia. The fact that we are father and son travelling together was greatly respected by everyone. As the drink started to flow and their inhibitions towards us lessened, grizzled bikers would approach us and shake our hands warmly, sometimes without a word being spoken but their eyes made us welcome; sometimes their comments were translated by those around us whose command of English was a little better. One large biker, maudlin from drink at midday, hugged me to his breast and tearfully admitted that he'd forgotten an English word. This seemed to have upset him greatly. At other times we would communicate with snatches of words and gestures but the gist of the communication was apparent - like when one large, tattooed biker approached us, pointed wordlessly to each of us in turn, indicating father and son, pressed his hand against his heart and then hugged us tightly to his massive chest. When he let us go, there were tears in his eyes.

We met Walter whose nickname we were told is "Killer". Later when he had moved away from the group around us, Malvina (she who lolled against me on the couch at Alexis' flat and spoke of us having a "Russian experience") told us almost *sotto voce* that he, Walter, is the Black Bears' "killer". We didn't understand and asked her what she meant. Again, seeming to look furtively about to make sure no one was listening, she said quietly that sometimes the bikers come into contact with criminal gangs and need his "assistance". For what, she didn't say and we didn't want to ask. The almost conspiratorial way she told us spoke volumes, though.

And we met Konstantine, whose brother had been murdered in the UK a few years ago. He wanted to say something to us and asked one of the bikers who spoke English to translate: "When I first learned that you were from England," he said to us, "I felt aggressive towards you." The translator explained to us about Konstantine's bother and how he had been killed while on a trip to the UK. Then he continued, "But now that I know you, I feel differently." He hugged us, pressing us against a tattoo right across his barrel chest saying: "The Great". He pointed to it and said tearfully, "For my brother."

Later in the afternoon, Gareth and I took our unladen bikes for a fast and invigorating ride along the low-tide beach until a heavy burst of rain drove us back. One very inebriated Russian biker, who had managed to get his Africa Twin onto the beach, managed to ride it drunkenly for 100 yards before he crashed it. He was not particularly happy about his cracked plastic and bent crash bars, looking at them through drink-blurred eyes as if wondering why they were shaped like that. He needed help getting his heavy bike over the low, very soft dunes back to camp when he buried it down to the engine in the sand.

Back at our tents, Gareth commented on the tremendous sense of camaraderie and fellowship we could sense amongst club members, almost as if they band together, wearing their club insignia and distinctive leather cut-off jackets as a kind of defence against a system which has broken down - the state on the one hand, criminals and perceived enemies on the other - and the feeling of brotherhood gives them not only protection in numbers but a sense of belonging in a country they feel has lost its way and is ignoring the ordinary man in the street. But behind the acceptance of us into their midst - because without doubt, they welcomed us into their fraternity and made us one of them in a way that was most moving - both Gareth and I had a sense, a feeling, just below the surface, that *anything* could happen; just a wrong word or gesture away, was the brooding potential for violence or something - just what we could not say - especially with people the worse for drink as many of them were. (But never towards ourselves; we never felt anything but complete acceptance, a brotherhood of bikers.) Strangely enough, later that night that *something* that we had felt simmering just below the surface materialised, although we obviously knew nothing of it then.

What happened was that, later that night, two men were badly beaten up by a group of the bikers. Gareth saw it, I was otherwise occupied. Evidently two locals had come into the camp intent on selling drugs. The Russian bikers took exception to this and beat them up rather badly. Afterwards, while they were staggering away, they came across the 11-year-old son of one of the bikers and, in revenge, hit him over the head with a large stick, knocking the boy to the ground.

Later, around the camp fire, Malvina, in her breathy, tactile way, assured us, "It's OK - they are still alive."

Sasha, standing next to the fire with us, said with a grin, "But they don't have their own faces any more."

A little while later, Walter sat next to Gareth and me and showed us his bloody hands. He spread his fingers and considered them with apparent satisfaction then said, "Blood - not mine!"

At midnight, exhausted, my senses and emotions overloaded from the experiences of the past few days, I crawled into my tent to sleep.

The next day we would begin the long ride to Murmansk, not knowing that we would quite innocently stumble into another area forbidden to foreigners and be arrested.

Published in Overland Magazine, Issue 5, under the title: "Drinking with Bears" and

in Adventure Bike Rider, Issue 16, under the title: "Black Bears and Motorbikes".

Excerpt taken from "Venture into Russia, Three Motorcycle Journeys".

SEVEN
Ten points for the old lady

Both animals and humans in Ethiopia make riding more than a little trying. Herders of animals make little or no effort to get them off the road to allow a vehicle to pass; pedestrians not only don't move aside, but step into the road without looking then leap back like startled hares as if shocked that there might be a vehicle trundling along behind them. Children are worse. Every child in Ethiopia seems to find it obligatory to scream, shout, throw a stone, pretend to throw a stone, roll a ball under the wheels, poke a stick into your spokes, act as if he is about to commit suicide by leaping under the wheels of your bike or (the preferred option) attempting to push his smaller friend into the road just as you pass by. Perhaps they have lessons in school: Maim a Motorcyclist with a Single Stone; Three Ways to Push your Little Brother into a Motorbike without Getting Caught.

Both animals and humans, unless given a very wide berth, tend to panic and run in any direction (except off the road) and, as both Gareth and I discovered, sometimes under the wheels of our bikes.

I write this by the light of a 40-watt bulb hanging from the ceiling of a blue-painted, wattle-and-daub room. In places the mud has fallen from the walls revealing the sticks beneath. We are on the second floor so I hope the house holds up until tomorrow. I have washed in a bucket of icy water and feel reasonably clean despite sharing the "bathroom" with an unmentionable hole in the floor which passes as a toilet. Gareth is not feeling well but, as usual, he doesn't complain.

Setting off from Lalibela this morning, we were thoroughly searched on the outskirts of the village by a group of sullen-faced policemen who were looking for the large, solid-gold cross that had been stolen from one of the churches the day before. Finding nothing, they waved us off. Having re-packed all our belongings, we managed to find a little-used dirt road which took us for 80ks through the Simien Mountains.

These mountains in northern Ethiopia are particularly remote and we rode alone along a narrow track with only the occasional goat for company. Once we passed a lone tribesman standing on a far-off ridge watching us, his old bolt-action rifle held loosely across his shoulders.

It was when making our way down a steep pass that we came across a group of women herding a flock of goats and cattle blocking our way. The women didn't attempt to urge the animals off the road so we had to manoeuvre our way through; the goats, being more intelligent, nimbly avoided us; the wide-horned cows, slow and stubborn, had to be nudged a little. Suddenly an old woman, who had obligingly moved out of my way, seemed to change her mind and darted across the track immediately in front of me. There was little I could do. Despite locking my wheels, I hit her in the legs and knocked her down. Fortunately, because of the cows, I was going slowly. She sprang to her feet and turned on me, her face suffused with anger. I leaped off my bike, ran to her apologising as sincerely as I could despite knowing that she would understand nothing of what I said. Fearful that I had injured her (she was an old woman and very slight of build) I checked for bleeding. Fortunately nothing seemed to be broken and I could see no blood so, continuing to apologise, I tried to give her a hug (but what I really wanted to say was, *Why run in front of my bike, you silly old faggot?*)

By this time all the women had crowded angrily about me, shouting and gesticulating, letting me know in universally understood terms that they thought me lower than a camel's turd and, if they were able, they would lay hold of me and do me a serious injury.

Knowing there was nothing more I could do and wanting to put as much distance between us as I could before their husbands/boyfriends/second cousins arrived carrying sticks and bolt-action rifles, I re-mounted and attempted to start the bike. Of course, the old bitch simply refused to start, letting me down when I needed her most. Seeing my intentions, the old crone grabbed hold of the handle bars to prevent me from making a hasty retreat. A tug-of-war ensued, me all the while trying to select neutral and then kick-start the heavily-laden old XT without dropping it on the road.

Suddenly I realised what the old woman was doing: she had my sleeping bag, attached to the front luggage rack by bungee cords, half out and was tugging at it madly, obviously attempting to claim it as compensation for my attack on her person. I snatched at her hands shouting, "No you don't!" but her fingers were all bones and tendons and had hooked themselves into the bungees and she wasn't going to let go; that sleeping bag was hers by some universally accepted Ethiopian tribal rite, probably a sort of eye-for-an-eye thing, and she was going to extract payment.

Gareth, during all this, was sitting on his bike watching with a grin on his face, offering no assistance whatsoever. (Why on earth did I bring him if it wasn't to leap to the aid of his poor ageing father in his hour of need?) Fortunately we were heading downhill so I gave up trying to kick the big 500 single to life (those who have tried to kick-start a reluctant XT500 will have some idea what I was going through. Add to that a crowd of screaming, grabbing women and an old crone who had her claws into my sleeping bag, attempting to drag it out and have me and the bike over, and you will see that I was in trouble.) I leaped off the bike, ripped the grasping fingers free and, in a rather undignified fashion, pushed the bike down the hill, leaped on and dropped the clutch. Fortunately she fired immediately and we accelerated away. When I glanced back, all the women were picking up rocks and throwing them at us.

In retrospect, we were *very* lucky: first, that I hadn't injured her badly and, second, that there were no angry men close by carrying spears and ancient bolt-action rifles. What we would have done had I broken her leg or injured her seriously doesn't bear thinking about. We were deep in the mountains and very far from any form of civilization. A very lucky escape.

After the excitement, we climbed steadily into the mountains until we entered cloud and rode through semi-twilight with visibility down to about twenty metres. The rains here had been heavy, the road slick and glutinous with clinging mud which threatened to have me down several times. Then, finally, we emerged from the clouds and followed the track down a beautiful pass with range upon range of the Simien Mountains disappearing into the purple distance on all sides, wide cultivated valleys between and a sense of endless space.

The next day, heading south through more populated valleys, Gareth managed to ride into three animals, something that has to be a record: a cow, a donkey and a goat, the latter sprawling ass over tit in the road before scrambling to its feet none the worse for wear (I hope) other than an assault on its dignity. Fortunately, in all these encounters, Gareth managed not to spill. Needless to say, we didn't stop to discuss compensation (like sleeping bags) with the owners.

Gareth's nine points for his three animals doesn't beat the ten points I got for the old lady, so I win.

Excerpt taken from: "Trans-Africa by Motorcycle, A Father's Diary".

EIGHT

Outfits in the desert

Gareth and I had completed the first two *pistes* from Merzouga to Zagora and Mhamid to Foum-Zguid in Morocco; both we and the bikes had taken a bit of a battering and were in need of some serious R&R. I was looking forward to a day or two of stress-free riding, a gathering of reserves before we attempted the next *piste,* a two-day desert crossing close to the Mauritanian and Algerian borders.

That was the plan.

But on trips like these, plans have a tendency to be shouldered aside by circumstance - like meeting a bunch of Russian bikers the previous year off on a jolly to Severodvinsk and being invited to join them.

So it was that, shortly after leaving Foum-Zguid on the long run south, we passed a tatty garage outside of which were parked some strange-looking contraptions that could have come straight from the set of Mad Max.

Of course, we had to turn back and investigate.

And there, parked on the side of a dusty road in central Morocco, was a sight that would make the heart of any lover of outfits and adventure travel beat a little more erratically: dusty and travel-worn, four custom-built outfits, pared to the bone, rested, as if gathering strength for whatever next Africa was about to throw at them. These were hand-built, sidecarcross bikes with designs that spoke of strength and resilience, specially constructed for long-distance, off-road travel; there was a utilitarian robustness about them that drew one's eye. We checked them out, less discretely now, noting the design of each: a cunningly mounted heavy-duty air cleaner here, a switch-operated electric motor to engage the sidecar wheel for extra traction through mud or soft sand tucked away there; tool boxes and spares carefully stowed; heavy-duty grab-rail for the standing sidecar passenger (sometimes known as the "monkey", for obvious reasons) to cling to while leaning to counter the massive centrifugal forces generated in the turns. It was clear that these bikes had been modified and refined on the test track of extreme journeys; nothing for show, nothing extraneous; each bit bolted, welded and strapped into place for a reason.

We were intrigued and wanted to meet the riders. It wasn't long before one of them, a wiry-looking Frenchman with red-rimmed eyes and hair matted with dust strolled over. His hands were calloused and leathery; lumps of knotted muscle corded his forearms; his grip could have crushed bones.

Introductions were made. They all looked dusty and trail-worn. With them was another Frenchman riding a KTM300 trail bike.

Our French was non-existent; their English poor but we understood that they were a loosely cohesive group of outfit riders who liked extreme challenges; they embarked upon one major trip each year, alternating between Africa and some of the more extreme parts of Europe (where, for some strange reason, they revelled in travelling in sub-zero conditions just for the hell of it). This year it was Africa and they had hired a guide, with two 4X4 back-up vehicles, who was leading them into some of the more remote parts of Morocco. They were, in fact, on the point of heading into the Jebel Sarhro Mountains, following *pistes* that are not found on conventional maps. The plan was to *bivouac* - their word - in the mountains that night and did we have food, tents etc? If so, would we like to join them?

Gareth and I looked at each other and grinned. We did and we would. Suddenly, I didn't feel tired any more. All thoughts of R&R were pitched out the window. If tagging along with them would be anything like the time we spent with the Russian Black Bears, we were in.

We quickly filled our tanks and spare fuel containers at a nearby garage and looked for food and water to last us the next two days in the mountains.

Purchases completed, bikes fully fuelled, we joined the Frenchmen drinking coffee and were introduced to their guide and fixer, Bruno, an ascetic-looking paraplegic, thin and darkly-tanned, his nose aquiline, shoulder-length grey hair tucked into a worn baseball cap. Despite his apparent handicap, he was very involved in rallying; a member of an international rally co-ordinating committee, he gave advice on routes in Morocco including sections of the Pari-Dakar. He employed a driver for the lead 4X4; his pared-down wheelchair, as utilitarian as the outfits he was leading, was stowed in the back of the ageing Range Rover.

Coffee finished, we fired up our bikes and set off with our new companions, heading south. About twenty miles out of Tissnt, we turned off onto a rough dirt road that followed the bed of a wide river valley into the mountains towards Taliouine in the north. At midday the leading 4X4 pulled off across a stretch of soft sand and stopped next to a small clump of palms, kept alive by water seeping through the rock to pool in a natural depression. In the still air the desert was oppressively hot. Lunch was provided for the French outfit riders while we sat in the sand, apart, not yet integrated into this group who had so kindly invited us to join them.

Then it was on again, heading deeper into the mountains. The valley narrowed as we climbed, the road degenerating into a track that followed the *oed*, repeatedly dropping down steep-sided banks to cross the dry river bed, boulder-strewn from numerous flash floods that characterise the flow of rivers in this desert terrain.

So much for our period of R&R. The day before it had been sand; today it was rocks.

With one 4X4 in front and one at the back, the Frenchman on the KTM300 ranging about whenever we crossed a wide, rocky, river bed looking for the track again on the other side, we rode up and up through desolate mountain valleys, usually following dry river beds along tracks cut out of the sides of the mountains. Occasionally we lost the track and would have to ride over wild, rocky terrain to find it again. My heavily laden KLE500 wasn't suited for this terrain and my bash plate took a hammering as I bounced and slithered over rocks the size of footballs that littered the river beds.

In the late afternoon we stopped next to the sandy bed of a small *oed* and set up camp. Almost immediately the French riders started pulling their outfits apart, doing maintenance and repairs. Trunks of tools and spares were carried in the two 4X4 support vehicles. If I had to do an arduous trip across forbidding terrain, far from garages or help, these are the kind of bikers I'd be happy to travel with. While the spaghetti was being cooked in a massive aluminium pot, one rider, Vincent, got down to work and replaced his bike's worn rear tyre with a new knobbly, then replaced his chain and the sidecar's shock absorber, working until well after the sun had set.

Slowly we began to integrate with these hardy, rough but most likeable Frenchmen. We sat down just outside their circle to prepare our meal, not wanting to presume to join them without an invitation, but one of them held up a bottle of red wine and we were drawn into their close-knit circle. As the evening progressed, we clustered around a gas lantern, sitting on jerry cans and tin trunks and spare wheels, they talking animatedly amongst themselves about the day's adventures (I assume) while we sat, part of the group, absorbed into their camaraderie. One of the French riders, we learned, was a seven-time Paris-Dakar entrant. No wonder they seemed to know what they were doing.

Much later, under a crisp desert sky, bright with stars, a bottle of Sake was produced and passed round until it was finished; then out came a plastic bottle of whiskey. This too was passed round. We played *Spin the Bottle* in the desert sand to decide who would have the last mouthful. The sense of bonding was quite palpable.

The next morning, before the sun was fully up, some of the Frenchmen were already working on their bikes, preparing them for the day. After breakfast we set off on another day riding through the mountains.

About midday, we came across a small village almost hidden in a deep cleft, the houses built from the same rocks into which they were nestled so that, from a distance, they blended in and seemed to become part of the cliff face itself. In the valley floor grew hundreds of palms, their dusty olive-green fronds shrouding the road in places so that we seemed to be riding through a rustling, shaded tunnel between the mountains. We rested there for a while, walking into the dense thicket of palms and seeing the intricate network of small canals leading water to their fields, bright green with new wheat, all with raised earthen borders to contain the water. Women in brightly coloured *djellaba* worked the fields - purple and lilac, red, orange, yellow - so bright they looked like iridescent beetles against the background of dun earth and dark rocks, gentle-faced women who eyed us shyly as we passed, slim-bodied and sleek of skin like whippets.

Then the track began to climb up the side of the valley, a narrow ledge of road cut from the rock that zig-zagged its way up to above fifteen hundred metres onto a high, wind-swept plateau. It was intensely beautiful and, when we looked down on the village from near the top, seeing the splash of green from the palms, the small rectangular stone houses, I had to pause quietly and absorb it, *will* my mind to take and hold it like a mental snapshot.

Making our way down into another valley, we realised that we had lost the KTM rider who often roared off ahead on his own, exploring. We paused in the sand of a dry riverbed and waited.

And waited...

Some of the outfit riders headed back the way we had come, looking for side tracks he might have taken by mistake; others rode on ahead to look for him, checking in the dust for his tracks.

After a while they returned: nothing.

The driver/mechanics settled down to do some maintenance: petrol was leaking from the tank of one 4X4 and oil dripped from the transfer box of the other. They lay under the truck, removed the prop-shaft and repacked the oil seal.

There was still no sign of the KTM rider. The mechanic had sorted the prop-shaft so we rode on until we reached the next village where again we paused and waited for over an hour.

During this time, as always happens, we were surrounded by little boys who clustered around the bikes touching things; they climbed onto the sidecars and were allowed to rev the engines, much to their delight. A small group of girls, veils covering their heads like young Madonnas, held back, smiling shyly but turning away warily if we approached them.

Still we waited. The KTM rider hadn't turned up nor could any of the French riders find him. Vincent was entertaining a crowd of giggling boys, teaching them to sing:

"*Alouette, gentille alouette,*
Alouette, je te plumerai"

followed by a spirited rendition of "*I like to move it move it!*", much to their delight. Then he filled his mouth with water and chased them screaming around the dusty village square.

A silent group of adults gathered on one side and watched, smiling. They did not approach us.

Later some of the Frenchmen set off again to look for the lost rider and, this time, they found him. He had taken a wrong fork a while back and then broken down. (They managed to cram his bike into the back of a passing van and repaired it the next morning.)

Finally off again, we left the 4X4s behind and all rode fast across a vast high plateaux, forty to fifty miles an hour along a rocky, undulating track, snow-capped mountains in the distance, until we reached the main road again.

That evening during our meal, Vincent asked us whether we would like to ride with them for another day. They were heading north, he said, following a similar *piste* higher into the mountains up to four thousand metres. One of the other Frenchmen, usually silent and reserved, said to us in faltering English, "It has been a pleasure to have you with us."

A very special moment.

Sadly, when we woke the next morning it was raining hard and Bruno decided it would be too dangerous to head into the mountains because the rivers would be high. It was not to be.

That is my one real regret of the trip, that we missed out on spending one more day in the remote High Atlas mountains with this very special bunch of Frenchmen, that we hadn't had a chance to ride one of their outfits. They had given us lasting memories and it had been a privilege to ride with and get to know them.

So we parted company in the rain: they making their way to Marrakech; we heading south to attempt one of the very long *pistes* near the Algerian/Mauritanian borders before making our way home.

First published in Adventure Bike Rider, Issue 29, July 2015 under the title: "Riding with Mad Max".

Excerpt taken from "There are no Fat People in Morocco".

NINE

It's like that with bikes too

When I see the lived-in lines etched into the face of someone like - let's say Judy Dench - her left front tooth slightly out of kilter, her skin holding within itself the patina of umpteen gazillion physical and emotional bumps and scrapes that this wonderful thing called life flings at us, I am impressed. I like her wrinkles and her liver spots; I like the tired folds at the corners of her eyes. And I like her even more because she has the guts to say: *This is who I am.*

Some people, however, seem to fear the ageing process. They fight their inevitable demise with every last breath in their tight-nipped, tucked and Botoxed bodies; they flash fake smiles with their fake white teeth, bland and characterless.

Listen, teeth *need* to be a little crooked; faces *ought* to be etched, stained and marked by time and the living of life and loving and not loving. It's the bumps and scratches, the daily, slow wearing out of things as they age, that give character; it's a revealing of that which lies beneath the surface, captured in time.

Bikes are like that.

How often have you seen people walk past the bland sameness of gleaming plastic, smooth and unsullied, never pausing for a second look; a polished engine that's never smelt the dust (perhaps with cute blue LEDs making the bike look alluring at night, like a tart on a street corner), riders standing about in matching gear, clean and expensive... and then watch as they pause to stare at the rat-bike or the travel-stained adventure twin, tired and worn, bits held together with wire ripped from a fence somewhere where the roads are dusty or muddy and the locals have calloused hands and trousers that hang loosely from bony hips?

The rat-bike is a conscious reaction against the sameness, the bland uniformity, the characterlessness of many bikes you see on the road today. The rat-bike builder says: I'm so bored with polished bodywork I'm going to paint my bike by hand... badly. Black - so it won't look pretty.

As a statement.

I'm going to muck about with my bike until it's got some personality; I'm going to make it mine. Not the Touratec adaptations that are as impersonal as the bikes they adorn. The owner of a rat-bike wants something that is different, unique, hand-crafted; wants to stamp his personality on it, create in his bike the laughter lines and liver spots and the broken and re-welded bones that cause a man to walk with a limp.

And, like the rat-bike, it's the adventure-stained big trailie leaning a little too low on its side stand as if taking a quiet breather before heading off again into the setting sun that causes the passer-by to pause and stand and stare, often with a wander-lust in his eye as if he wants to tag along, please. The watcher flicks his eyes over the bike, noticing the patina of hard travel: holes drilled in the front mudguard to allow just that little bit more air to reach an overheating engine; spare cables zip-tied to the originals ready for a quick change-over when the last strand of wire snaps; weeping oil seals from the hammering the engine took to make it over a high pass in the Hindu Kush, snow-covered and rocky; dust held still in hard-to-reach crevices from a fall in the deep hot sand of some God-forsaken desert; character-lines of scratches and dents from life on the road, from falls and slides and that close-call with a truck in India; rubber cut from a car inner tube holding something down or up or closed or open; weld-splatter around a cracked frame, roughly patched by a dark-skinned, crouching man welding in the dust on the roadside without goggles, who lines up the parts and then closes his eyes quickly before the bright flash of arc burns holes in his retinas; here a rim just a little bent from the rock that was seen too late; wire and zip-ties zipping cracked edges of plastic together, holes drilled with an awl borrowed from a gaunt man who repairs shoes in the shade of his verandah; angle iron and flat bar bent and welded and bolted by a bush mechanic in a cobwebby workshop which held the bike together just long enough; a jerry can bolted onto the frame, testimony to the fact that it has travelled somewhere remote and fuel-less; a bash plate beaten out of shape like the face of a boxer who has lost too many fights; rusting crash bars, having taken one too many for the engine; "we were here" stickers peeling at the edges bearing mute testimony to places long relegated to the fading clutter of memory.

These are the Judy Dench bikes of adventure travel; bikes that don't have to be pretty because their true character is held deep down beneath the skin; unpolished bikes that cause us to linger a little and stare and wonder at the stories that could be told.

It's the man with tired eyes from too much staring into the sun or the distance or his own soul, with laughter lines and crooked teeth, a smudged tattoo, perhaps, on arms taut with muscle; an old scar from a motorcycle accident or a fight or both, with jeans worn with the wearing, comfortable as if they'd made friends with his body over the years, it's this man that I'd like to share a beer with or sit with in companionable silence watching the sun expire, rather than the plastic man with a manicured smile and carefully clipped nails, gold chain and designer watch, hair trimmed just so, face slick with fake tan.

It's like that with bikes too.

First published in Overland Magazine, Issue 16, under the title: "National Treasures".

TEN
Kazakhstan short cut

There's a sandy track that makes its way across the semi-desert of the Steppe between Shykar and Aral in central Kazakhstan. It meanders a little, separating and coming together making a filigree of patterns across the plain. The dry grass across which it travels is dull yellow and dry until, in the evening when the sun is low, it flares golden and seems to burn with light. The tracks have been worn into the sand below the level of the surrounding plain and the parallel hollows are sometimes firm and sometimes soft so that your tyres glide and hum, bite and drift as you ride.

Twice this track has eluded us but it still calls out, across thousands of miles of unforgiving Steppe, to be ridden. Not *conquered*. You don't "conquer" the Steppe. It's too big; too old. It endures; you don't. It might let you cross a few times, but don't take it for granted.

It'll freeze you in winter and burn you in summer. Its roads break bikes.

A year ago Gareth decided it might be interesting to attempt this dirt track crossing from Aral to Shykar instead of following the normal tar route across Kazakhstan a few thousand kilometres to the Russian border. Just for fun. It was within our fuel range and we'd carry food and water and camp along the way.

We set off, not knowing what to expect. Like in Russia, a road marked on a map might be somewhat different to what you experience on the ground. The tracks seemed to follow the rail line and that was a comfort because in the vast emptiness of the Steppe, the occasional long, slow trains that trundle past with an uncompromising air of purpose offer some companionship, as do the power lines that rise and dip across the plain until they reach their vanishing point on the horizon and then disappear.

But somewhere or other we took a wrong turn and ended up in deep sand on the wrong side of the rails. The track we were following slowly thinned and then disappeared. In front of us was a high dune, blocking the way. Even when we climbed it on foot and looked out across the seemingly endless Steppe, we could see nothing but the rail line and some equally small, sandy tracks crawling across the dry, grassy surface. The temperature was over 40 degrees, we were tired and there was no way we were going to be able to battle our way through sand that soft for the next 150kms. Disappointed, we turned and made our way back to Aral and the tar road to Russia.

But back in the UK, looking at the satellite image of the area, we could see that there *was* a track. We found where we had taken the wrong turn, then followed the tracks we should have been on as they angled their way across the Steppe to Shykar. So, we decided, on our next trip into Central Asia we could attempt it again. Obviously this wouldn't be the main purpose of the trip: we'd just take a short cut across a giant loop in the road on the way from Georgia to Kyrgyzstan.

That had been the plan, anyway...

As soon as we enter Kazakhstan, the road turns feral. Deep potholes and ridges have been squashed up like plasticine by overloaded trucks travelling across a road with inadequate foundation. We play *Miss the Pothole* for the next hour, riding past mud brick houses, sleek-skinned horses, the occasional camel, the road straight to the horizon, quivering in the heat.

Then we reach the oil fields. Kazakhstan floats on a lake of oil. Vast untapped reserves - between nine and eighteen billion barrels, so they say: the Pre-Caspian Basin, the Mangistau-Usturt Basin, the Central Kazakhstan Basin, the Western Siberian Basin to mention a few of the huge ones. No wonder Russia was somewhat peeved when the USSR broke up and the various oil-rich 'Stans got their independence. As we ride, the horizon is littered with small oil pump jacks, slowly nodding their pelican heads and sucking up the black stuff. We pull over to get a closer look, keeping a wary eye open for men in uniforms and dark glasses. A man in a pickup drives up but he is friendly. We take photographs.

Later we eat *bilash* with a truck driver with silver teeth. A slight, thin-armed man, he is wrestling his large truck all the way to Armenia. He - and all other truck drivers in this place - have our respect. Many a time we have come across a driver, alone, lying in the dust under his truck in the heat, wrestling with a wheel wrench or sitting amidst a pool of oil with the entrails of an engine or gearbox around his feet. Modern day cowboys, riding their iron steeds alone across the Steppe.

After Atyrau the road reforms itself and we barrel along blissfully for a hundred ks through a region of flat land - well, *flatter* - covered with small salt lakes and larger salt pans, some partially filled with water. When the sun occasionally breaks through the cloud, they shine with a crystalline whiteness. In fact, this land bordering the north-west shore of the Caspian Sea is ten to twenty metres below sea level for over 1000ks and 150ks inland. Its extreme flatness gives little scope for river systems to develop properly and drain the land, so shallow lakes form in every dip and undulation, evaporating and depositing salt.

Then, after the small town of Dossor, the road degenerates again and we attempt to dodge the worst of the broken, ridged, pot-holed bits as best we can, choosing always the sections least likely to destroy our suspension any more than they have already been.

Evening and we stop for the night. The sweet lady who shows us our room (she has no English) assures us that not only does the hotel serve no food but there are no cafes or restaurants in the town. She can offer tea, she suggests helpfully. Later she brings us a loaf of bread, a salami, two one-litre cans of beer and a newspaper to use as a tablecloth. The beer is 12% proof so we tell her we only need one, thank you. We settle ourselves in the spacious upstairs lounge but she asks us whether we won't, please, eat in our room. She is so gracious - and she's obviously walked to the local store and purchased these things for us specially - that we comply without remonstrance. The lounge is for show, like a pre-war front room, reserved for the visits of special guests, and two rather grubby travellers spoil the effect.

In our room I break out the emergency rations of peanuts and raisins and dried apricots and my son and I sit cross-legged on one of the beds, quaff our beer and consume a most pleasant meal.

This is Kazakhstan. Here, if you want, you can buy vodka for £1.00 a litre bottle.

Soon after leaving Maqat the next day, the road gives us ample warning that it's about to turn very bad. Multiple pot-holes have eventually caused the entire road to break up and soon we are riding on dirt, the surface of which is made up of the road foundation, broken-up bits of tar and the occasional razor-sharp plateaus of the original tar road just waiting to burst a tyre. Obviously many truck drivers have been badly bitten by this road and have headed off into the Steppe on either side to make their own way. We spend the next four hours ranging about seeking out the bits of track on either side that will least destroy the bikes. Every now and then, though, we come across a set of smooth tracks and we fly along, listening to the tyres sing on the firm, smooth sand. Then this, in turn, begins to break up; take another fork and then another, Gareth and I sometimes separated by hundreds of yards, each following different tracks.

Every now and then we come across heavy Kamaz trucks, most of them carrying fuel, lumbering along and throwing up a storm of thick, red dust. Overtaking is difficult and dangerous. Sometimes we can find a parallel track and get past before it joins again; occasionally we have to head off road and hope for the best.

At some time during the morning we stumble upon a small, square, breeze-block-built building and are served fried eggs, dry bread and coffee by a pleasant lady; then on again, the bikes, as Gareth commented on one of our pauses, taking quite a beating. Poor things.

The *vastness* of this place. The emptiness, the infinity of it is difficult to grasp. Riding across this small corner of the Kazakh Steppe heightens one's sense of insignificance. The dry, undulating grasslands fall away from horizon to horizon like a video on a loop, forward, back, side to side; an ocean of semi-desert grass. Above, a vast dome of sky. At times one needs the perspective given by electricity pylons that mark out the pulse of this land, the gentle rise and dip of their wires, watch as they disappear into the vanishing point on the horizon. One clings to the reality of steel and wire, something tangible to allow one's brain to grasp the enormity of nothingness that surrounds you, to give it some sense of scale, of reality. I suppose this is something felt by deep-sea sailors when confronted by days, weeks of nothing but sea.

We drive ourselves and the bikes on; it's a race against the punishment of the land and our diminishing allotment of time.

At the small town of Bayganin we fill up our tanks and spare fuel containers - enough for a range of 500ks. The plan is to head directly east across the plain following tracks Gareth has found on Google Maps. They wobble about a little, come and go, separate and reunite - but there seems to be a way across. It's another unknown. We are also not sure whether we will be allowed through the oil fields that can be seen on the satellite photographs or whether we will be arrested for straying into a forbidden area - again. Like the Russians, for some reason Kazakhs are rather tetchy about foreigners poking their noses into places they ought not to be.

At first the road seems deliberately constructed, raised a little above the level of the plain on a low causeway. We make our way to a small village. A collapsed bridge over a muddy stream has been replaced by three metal pipes. We cross without incident and run the gauntlet of camels, scrawny dogs and children. The road now becomes a well-used track across the plain which leads to a shed and some horses who run away at our coming. No one is about. After the shed it's clear that we have entered terrain seldom used.

We follow two tyre tracks through the dry, overgrown grass. They diverge and split and become less distinct. I can't see us making it all the way through on these.

The tracks we have been following begin to curve away from the GPS waypoints. Eventually we have to leave them and head across country to see if we can pick up tracks heading in the right direction. Blundering about through waist-high grass, we cross a number of deep, dry gullies that must be water-filled in the wet season. The ground is rough. Eventually we come across a line of telephone poles and, logically, following the poles, we find the track. It's a good one, smooth and lightly covered with sand so we make steady progress. The riding is fun. Eventually the telephone poles angle away and leave us and we ride across the pure Steppe, uncluttered by man-made things, a waving sea of yellow, slightly undulating ground.

After 65ks of this we stop on a ridge and set up our tents. It's been a great day. With evening comes stillness. The whole world is beautiful. The yellow grass seems aflame against the setting sun. In the distance gas flares lighten the sky. We are close to the oil field.

We collect firewood and, later, we sit around the fire and eat. There are no clouds: it's going to be cold.

The next day is our worst. A *bad* day. After thirteen hours of riding I am very tired. We both got pretty badly beaten up; the bikes took a beating too.

We are up early - partly because of the cold but also because we want to get through the oil field before anyone is aware of us. Although we have nothing for breakfast, we agree that it's best if we don't stop; just a quick, unobtrusive ride through and, if any police are about, hopefully we'll be gone before they register our presence.

In the cold, Gareth's bike won't start so we push it down the ridge and it fires up. In no time we are skirting the town. No one pays us any attention. It is large and sprawling with massive electricity pylons feeding power in, and above-ground pipes taking the oil out. Despite its size, there is no trace of it on our map. We can't find a name for it either. An anonymous oil town somewhere in the anonymity of the Kazakh Steppe.

Once through, the road is good tar, specially built for the oil field and its infrastructure. I ride along, enjoying its smoothness, the cool morning air in my face, thinking our road troubles are over.

Sadly, it doesn't last. We come to a junction; to the left, the good tar continues to the horizon; we turn right onto a beaten-up track that also stretches to the horizon. I glance sadly at the tar and make the turn.

Soon the road has deteriorated to such an extent that I decide to try my luck on a side track. It is very soft and before I can get my speed up, the soft centre ridge has caught my front wheel, slewed me about and in a flurry of dust I am off, the bike somersaulting and breaking my mirrors. I whack my head but fortunately the ground is soft. Nothing damaged but my dignity. Gareth sees my flailing arms, legs, bike and dust in his mirrors and turns back.

"Oh, my dear father!" he is supposed to cry. "Are you alright? I was so concerned! Here, take my arm - let me help you up..."

He doesn't. Instead he laughs like a drain and looks about in the sand for broken bits of my bike. Fortunately the old DR350s are built to last.

Back on the hellish road we continue to beat ourselves and the bikes almost to death. My oil-less suspension bottoms out again and again and I wonder how long it can possibly last.

We pause to take photographs of a pot-hole as deep as my knees. Occasional sections of good tar lure us back onto the road, tempt us to increase our speed until - *Wham!* we hit another cluster of pot-holes so numerous that there is no safe way through. Then it's back to looking for a smoother track running alongside the road or, more often, riding along a narrow strip of dirt between the road and the steep drop onto the plain. But these, too, have been badly beaten up with steep dips and occasional washed-out gullies. We have to be careful but the pressure of distance pushes us on, far faster than we ought to be riding. 20kph would probably be about right for this road; we are riding at twice that.

Having had nothing to eat or drink since we set off, at last we come across a place that seems able to sell us some food. We are hungry and, remembering the fried eggs of a few days before, Gareth points to some eggs in a basket and makes beating motions. The lady doesn't understand but we persist. Eventually she shrugs and presents us with some eggs on a plate. They are hard-boiled and cold. As we eat them a large, heavy-set man, florid with close-cropped hair, walks up to our table, glass in hand, and silently toasts our coffee with vodka.

We struggle on. At some time in the afternoon Gareth is ahead of me and slightly to my left. The road is very bad. He sees a gap in the road edge leading onto a parallel track, brakes and turns. Unable to stop, I T-bone him at about 30ks an hour. Fortunately I don't hit his leg but my front wheel is wrenched sideways and, as I go down, my handlebar smashes him in the back. He doesn't fall but is doubled over on his bike, obviously in trouble. I pick up my bike. My forks are twisted but otherwise all seems OK.

After a long time Gareth is able to get going again. He is in a lot of pain. An hour or so later we reach the small town of Shykar. We need fuel. I am exhausted but relieved because, in my stupidity, I think we have reached Aral. I say to Gareth that we should just find a hotel where we can rest and lick our wounds. I can already feel the warm shower water easing my aching body, the cold taste of beer sliding down my throat.

And it is then that he tells me we have only reached Shykar. There's over 300ks to go, 130ks of those over a bad track.

Part of Gareth's original plan was to attempt the track that eluded us the previous year, a track that followed the rail line and ended in sand so deep that we had to turn back. But Aral to Shykar was one of those "because it's there" tracks Gareth wanted to attempt. Part of the reason for taking the short-cut across the Steppe to the oil town and the hellish road we had just ridden was to get to Shykar and have a go at this soft-sand track from the other side.

While we rest and consider what to do, I discover that, in the accident, I have bent my front brake disk and it's binding and smoking hot. Fortunately, as these things so often happen, a Kazakh man is working on his car just five metres from where we are resting and, next to the car, we can see a large monkey wrench. We ask if we can borrow it. With some painful leverage, Gareth straightens the disk.

Then he says to me, "I think I've broken something - feel here -" He lifts his shirt. I feel his ribs and press; the bones rub together with an unpleasant grating sound.

Suddenly Gareth wants to faint. It's the grinding together of the broken edges of his ribs that does it. Pale in the face, he strips off his gear and sits in the shade of a tree. While he recovers, two confident little girls, immaculately dressed (as all little Kazakh children seem to be), approach me. They want to take selfies with us. Much to their delight I agree. Later they come back and give us flowers.

It is a long time before Gareth recovers sufficiently to begin making enquiries about the Shykar-Aral track. The man working on his car waves his hands in negation - No! He points to the other road, the one that takes the long way round. To make sure, we approach a man in a truck. He agrees. The road is too bad. Don't go there.

Reluctantly Gareth gives in. We can't risk it. Not with his broken ribs. The thought of wrestling a bike through heavy sand, having to pick it up in a fall is too daunting. He is in too much pain and, to be honest, after the day we've had, I'm worn out. I feel like I've been ten rounds with the road and lost.

We discuss it and agree: we have to take the long way round. It's late afternoon. Only another 330ks to go...

After a long rest and with the sun low in the sky, we set off again. The first fifteen ks are wonderful. I begin to relax. Head down, let the mind wander, tick off the miles, we'll be in Aral in no time.

Then the road begins to deteriorate, a slow but progressive falling apart. It becomes one hundred and thirty ks of being beaten up all over again, just as bad as the hellish road from the morning. There is nothing to do but suck it up and endure. Again I wonder just how long before my rear spring snaps. I begin to despair of this torment ever ending.

We finally reach the main road at 5.30. Only 200ks to go. We buy petrol from a man who sells it in ten-litre plastic bottles he keeps in a shed, and set off again. The road, thank goodness, is smooth.

So we race the setting sun across a flat, yellow land, our shadows lengthening. The sun flares white off the grass tips, dims and becomes a dull, red ball. It is beautiful and lifts my spirit. The harshness slowly leaves the land - and then it is dark.

We struggle to see through visors covered in dust. When the good road ends and we are diverted onto a rough dirt track, thick with bull-dust, Gareth tries to stand on the pegs but the pain is too great and he stalls. He struggles his way through, back onto the tar. Finally, after being in the saddle with various short breaks for over thirteen hours, we stagger in the dark into Aral and find a hotel.

Bad day.

In a way, I'm sad because riding like this you can't really enjoy the land through which you are travelling, appreciate the subtle changes to its expansive sameness. You are so focused on staying on the road, missing rocks and pot holes, controlling the bike as it slides and bounces around on the loose, stony road surface, focused on not killing yourself by sliding off the edge or hitting something that will have you off, keeping yourself and the bike going just one more kilometre until the end of the day. It becomes an endurance test instead of a ride; tiredness of mind and body take away the joy of travel.

Of course, we were riding too fast for the condition of the road - not out of the sheer pleasure of speed or the excitement of controlling a bike along a challenging track but just to get there, to end the pain. But we had made it reasonably intact. Gareth was suffering but able to cope. He doesn't complain.

Anyway, it was only one rib - he's got lots more.

And the Aral-Shykar road? Maybe another day.

First published in Overland Magazine Issue 17, April 2016, under the title: "Short Cut Across the Kazakh Steppe".

Excerpt taken from "A Pass Too Far, Travels in Central Asia".

ELEVEN
Tormenting a dwarf

Siberia. The road climbs and follows the edge of a wide, slow-flowing river that meanders across a treeless flood plain; far below me a rail line follows the river and, while I watch, a long train pulled by two diesel-electric locomotives makes its silent way. The increased height gives perspective to the endless boreal forest beginning outside the confines of the flood plain and continuing dark green to the horizon far, far away.

And then the plains are gone and the taiga comes close, pine and birch, hemming in the road. In places, large swathes of forest have been burned and the blackened trunks of trees cling to the hillsides like the shattered, branchless trunks left behind after the Somme.

The day is done; I look for a place to stay for the night. A small town beckons. My GPS assures me there is a hostel here. I do not believe her but decide to investigate, even if she's lying, as she often does in Russia, leading me through deserted streets towards promised accommodation that does not exist, and I ride through its narrow streets, ever hopeful. Finally I stumble upon a hostel patronised by a gang of road workers. They have finished work for the day and loll about, shirtless, their massive 6WD Kamatz truck parked in the road outside.

The lady of the establishment shows me a pleasant room that I share with another man; the road workers occupy a large, open bunkhouse with attached kitchen.

After checking over my bike, I make my way past the bunkhouse and am greeted by Victor, skin burned dark from exposure to the sun, heavy-duty camouflage jacket and no shirt, his chest pinched and thin. His friend Maxim joins us. We sit on wooden benches and they smoke. Men and smoking are Siamese twins in Russia. Maxim tells me he has a family who live in a small village about 800kms away. I get out my map and he shows me. It's a hard life but they have to take whatever work they can get, even if it's far from home. Victor digs out his phone and shows me a picture of a prairie dog he has shot. "Big mouse," he says and they laugh.

Maxim produces a two-litre plastic bottle of beer and we toast each other while he and Victor blow smoke over me.

Later my room mate, Alexi, leads me to the local *magazin* and I buy food for my supper as well as some beers for my new friends. On the way back, a distressed cow bellows as she trots along the pavement; gusts of wind stir the dust in little eddies, cold and then warm, and I can see that it's going to rain. Snow-showers of pussy-willow fluff are whipped into the air and dark clouds mass in the west. On the street two drunken men square up to each other, shouting, but a woman manages to separate them, scolding them both roundly like children. They stagger off down the street in opposite directions, shouting insults over their shoulders as drunks do, becoming more confident in their aggression as distance lends them courage.

I make it back to the hostel just before the rain and it beats down on the small wooden shelter roof, the large drops leaving marks like pennies in the dust. Lightning crackles behind the clouds and the smells of ozone and newly-wet, warm earth rise about us. The Russian workers all crowd into the shelter and light up, the damp air hazing and blue with acrid cigarette fumes. As each squeezes himself onto a bench, he introduces himself: Zinka, Pauille, Zandra, Alexi, Alexandra. Their hair tends towards the shaven, tattoos loose and smudged under the skin; the atmosphere is thick with testosterone, working men's smell, their bodies sun-browned and rough, smokin', drinkin' men who, in the absence of women, scratch their crotches and hawk and spit and who welcome me into their presence like a brother.

And, later, of course, as is to be expected in Russia, they invite me to share their meal. We sit on stools and benches, pressed together in the large kitchen with its gas stove and sink, its fridge and plastic tablecloth; some, who have nowhere to sit, stand shirtless with plates in hand, lean across to help themselves from a large pot of *borscht* made with potatoes and hunks of bony meat, sliced tomato and cucumber with sour cream, dry bread and my offerings from the *magazin*. They encourage me to eat, smiling and urging me not to hold back, offering me black tea to drink after the meal and then we retire to the shelter again to smoke and talk. Later, as we swig strong beer from a two-litre plastic bottle, they pass around a phone and laugh as they watch a video of men tormenting a dwarf, as you do.

Much later and my throat and eyes are raw from smoke; the men are still drinking and their tongues have thickened and slowed. A different plastic bottle is now being passed around. When it reaches me, having been warned never to drink Russian spirits from an unlabelled bottle, I ask, "Wodka?" and they laugh and say,

"Nyet - Peeva!" - beer. I take a swig. It is dark and strong.

Alexi points to a small man with a pleasant, open face, explores the unfamiliar words a moment with his tongue and then says loudly and slowly, "I like wodka!" The small man smiles bashfully then points to his jugular, holds out his hands as if riding a motorbike, makes revving noises then mimes falling over. They all laugh. The plastic bottle is passed around again. I decline. One of the men attempts to tell me he has a motorbike and has ridden to... and he mentions a country in Russian.

"Ukraine?" I venture because that's what it sounds like.

As one, the men whoop in derision. Maxim puts up his fists like an old-fashioned pugilist. Clearly there are no kind feelings towards Ukraine here. Eventually we work out that he means Poland.

I notice from their watches that I've entered another time zone. The plastic bottle is empty. Maxim attempts, I think, to encourage me to go to the *magazin* and buy more alcohol but Alexander, an older man with heavy features, swept-back hair and a thick Stalin moustache waves him away. The men begin to slope back to the bunkhouse but Alexander stays with me, different from the others, older. When we are alone, he shows me a photograph of himself wearing dress uniform, his chest covered with medals. "Twenty years," he tells me.

"Afghanistan?" I ask him.

He nods and then adds, "Chechnia." His face is sombre. Then, in turn, he pulls up his shirt sleeve and trouser leg to reveal two large, ragged scars, each six to nine inches long.

I lift my arms, miming a rifle. He nods then waves his hand dismissively, as if it is of no consequence.

"Chechnia..." I say, shaking my head.

"*Da*, Chechnia," Alexander echoes, his heavy features etched in sadness.

TWELVE
Desert crossing in Southern Morocco

*F*or a while now, the tracks we had been following across a stony, desert plain in the south of Morocco near the Algerian and Mauritanian borders had been getting disturbingly more indistinct until what was left seemed to be little more than the deep scoriations of a ripper attached to a heavy-duty grader roughly demarcating the route of some future or abandoned road.

It wasn't the route we thought we'd be following; that was somewhere to the left across the desert, supposedly part of a long-past Pari-Dakar route marked with cairns.

We had enough fuel to turn back to the safety of people and houses and, more important, petrol; and, if we didn't encounter problems or get lost, we probably had just enough to make it to the Al Mahbas - Zag road which, if we kept going long enough due east, we were bound to hit.

According to the map there was supposed to be a town or village somewhere nearby but the last village - also marked on the map - had strangely disappeared.

What to do...?

This was our third desert *piste* since entering Morocco and we were slowly gaining confidence in ourselves, the bikes and our ability to ride across sand; but the fear of the unknown, of getting lost in the enormity of the Sahara is something entirely different.

Crossing our first *piste,* from Merzouga to Zagora in east Morocco, we had learned the hard way how to cope with riding laden bikes across soft sand and small dunes. By the end of it we were certainly no experts but we were coping.

The second, more ambitious, *piste* took us from Mhamid to Foum-Zguid through the dune fields along the edge of a wide flood plain. Recent heavy rains - which had drenched us throughout our crossing of the Atlas Mountains - had brought the Oued Draa down in flood and made the normal *piste*, which follows the easier route of the flood plain, impassable.

Seeing our indecision, a local man with a 4X4 and a flair for business approached us. He assured us that he and a Bedouin guide could lead us through the wide expanse of dunes around the flooded region to another old Pari-Dakar track clearly marked (yeah, right!) by cairns every 500m. With persuasive logic, he added that hiring him and his guide now would cost us less than if they had to rescue us and our bogged bikes from the mud of a flooded Oued Draa later...

Needless to say, it didn't turn out like that - but that's another story.

Now, much further south, we were attempting our third and most ambitious *piste* - a remote section of desert recommended by the legendary desert biker Chris Scott. But the track we had been following was becoming disturbingly indistinct until, eventually, we paused, unsure of what to do: turn back; head off into the desert and try to pick up the track Gareth had marked on his GPS or keep on following the ever-diminishing grader tracks and hope they wouldn't just peter out into the sand.

At first, when we set off that morning from Al Aiun, carrying food, fuel and water for two days, there was a tar road with signs, just two, spaced twenty miles apart: a warning triangle with a picture of a camel underneath. Why?

As the morning progressed, the landscape became more desolate. There were almost no cars on the road. No people, no houses, no animals (I lie, there was one donkey, I remember it distinctly) - just a flat land broken briefly by a few stunted trees and rocks; then the plants disappeared; then most of the rocks.

I must admit that, as we neared the turn-off to the east that would take us four hundred miles into the desert, I felt both excited and apprehensive. After the first two hundred miles, the plan was to find a *piste* that Gareth had marked with way-points every twenty miles or so on his GPS, an old route he'd found on the Internet.

The tar road ended and became dirt; the dirt degenerated into a track and then there were just the two grader tracks with the marks of ripped soil between. Worryingly, as the tracks became less distinct, they angled away from our intended route. And the problem was, we just didn't know what was ahead of us, whether there were vast sections of soft sand to negotiate, steep-sided wadis or rivers to cross.

In the end, we chose the *known* over the scary thought of heading off across the sand hoping to find a line of irregularly-spaced cairns that might or might not be there any more. The track ploughed by the bulldozer was something tangible; we could see it meandering faintly into the distance until it became lost in the blur of heat-haze.

So we just pressed on, the GPS waypoints moving further and further away from us. We still had about 180 miles of desert to cross.

Eventually we stopped, a little fearful now. We poured over the map. Gareth checked his GPS. Neither of us wanted to make the decision.

According to the map, there was a village - Jdiriya - twenty miles ahead of us as the crow flies (but it turned out to be forty miles across the ground). Perhaps we could get fuel and directions there. In the end, we decided to head for Jdiriya and make our decision whether to press on or turn back once we got there.

The track, very rough and stony now, followed a long range of rocky hills to our left for miles before finally turning into them. We entered through a steep-sided valley then made our way up onto a broad plateau. Finally, in the distance ahead of us we could make out a few buildings and an antenna held in place with cables. We made for the closest building, outside of which were three men standing in front of a broken and stripped Land Cruiser, ex-army it would seem, from the machine-gun mount bolted onto its rusted back. We stopped in front of them and after exchanging greetings we asked where we could get fuel.

"Pas d' essence,"- a shrug as if to say, "What did you expect?"

Jdiriya turned out to be an army outpost and not a village. No fuel, no shops. We topped up our tanks with the extra fuel we were carrying, were given a few bottles of water, and set off again. The soldiers had drawn a crude map for us in the sand: here, the track where we had entered and, here, a turn-off to the left just outside the camp. We hadn't seen any turn-off when we came in and were concerned that we might miss it but they insisted (using sign language, of course): "Straight on... then sharp left," pointing over the hills to the west.

Hoping we would not get lost, we set off. Yes, a vague track did branch to the left but it was as if a single car had turned off the road onto the rocky plain so the driver could relieve himself, not a *piste* to follow for the next hundred and forty or so miles across the desert. But Gareth assured me we were heading in the right direction according to his GPS so we pressed on.

And it was about then that we began to gain confidence. As we had learned in our first attempts at crossing a desert *piste,* there never is just *one* track, there are always many and, so long as you keep travelling in vaguely the right direction, you should reach your destination in the end, especially if you are heading for a long road at right angles and not a point. So, with the sun now low on the horizon, we rode on over gently undulating terrain, looking for somewhere to camp for the night.

Sometimes the track was easy to follow but then, at intervals, it would disappear altogether. But we no longer felt that tightening of the chest: I'm lost! We knew that somewhere ahead other tracks would appear. And they always did.

Finally, as the sun began to set, we came across a dry river bed with some old, gnarled tamarisk trees to give focus to an otherwise featureless desert plain, the sand in the river bed almost pure white, fine-grained and soft. We stripped off to bare torsos because of the heat, set up our tents and collected firewood. Then we indulged in the civilizing luxury of tea.

One hundred and thirty miles to go before we met the Al Mahbas - Zag road. We would just make it on our petrol with a little to spare.

The sun set over the desert, softening the atmosphere as it always does. We were very far from anywhere. The air cooled. We lit a fire and a gentle darkness slowly covered the land. Stars began to emerge from an indigo sky and a low moon appeared on the horizon turning the pale sand of the river bed strangely bright against the darkness. The desert all about us became hushed and still.

Stripped away was all the clutter that complicates life and distracts one from the important things: just Gareth and me, father and son, together in the desert. It was like a Boys' Own adventure coming to life. It was something Enid Blighton could have written. All around us was a deep sense of isolation; inside, a feeling of contentment. The bikes were going well; the desert surface we had been travelling across was forgiving but sufficiently challenging and varied to make it interesting. It was the isolation that was the challenge, the realisation that, if we were to break down, we would be in trouble that lent a certain *frisson* to life.

The next day we set off early while it was still cool, the sky overcast and grey. And for the rest of the day we rode across the desert in an almost straight line; we saw nothing man-made, nothing living except for a falcon that flew over us in the late morning and seemed to pause quizzically and watch us passing below before flying on and disappearing. Even the tracks we followed showed no tyre marks at all, suggesting that the last vehicle had passed this way a long time ago, certainly not since the last rains, and who could tell when those had been? The indentations were there for us to follow, although they forked and converged, at times other tracks suddenly appeared out of the desert at right angles, crossed ours and disappeared into the distance going who knows where? And, although the direction of our travel seldom varied, the colour and texture of the desert did: sometimes it was a pale cream as we crossed a dry riverbed, then a deeper orange, then black stones with yellow sand beneath. When the tacks crossed the bed of an ancient lake, the bikes would hiss along like we were riding on silk, then it would change again as we rode at walking pace over stony ground, picking our way between the rocks that clanged against my bash plate, making me wince.

Then, after riding for two hours or so, Gareth pulled up with a puncture. We unloaded the bikes, piled extra weight onto the rear to lift the front wheel off the ground, removed it and found the culprit: a large thorn had penetrated the tyre and tube. We fitted his spare. Looking at the stripped bike standing disabled on the vast desert plain, the wind gusting over us and blowing sand into everything, made us feel rather vulnerable. Riding across this expanse of desert *reg* was exhilarating when everything was going well, but even this slight hitch suddenly made us aware of just how exposed and vulnerable we were. With the engines stilled, it was only the gusting wind and intermittent hissing of blown sand grains that peopled this vast emptiness with sound and emphasised our loneliness and isolation; the disabled bike without its front wheel, our bits and pieces strewn about the desert surface, gave the impression of a major accident. And there was no one about to offer assistance. We were entirely on our own.

New tube inserted, we re-fitted the wheel, packed up and set off again. But shortly after midday the same tyre went flat again. Another thorn had penetrated the tyre. Again we stripped off our luggage, removed the tube and patched it.

As the afternoon waned, we paused to fill our tanks with the last of our petrol. The wind howled over the desert surface lifting grains of sand and turning the atmosphere a pale, milky white. Gareth kept looking at his GPS and counting down the miles to the village - town? - of Al Mahbas (not shown on the map; just a waypoint Gareth had copied from a book), worrying that it wouldn't be there, that we would be stranded in this windy desolation, the tracks continuing on towards the horizon and our fuel running low.

Then, in the distance, we saw a pair of radio masts and knew we had made it. And suddenly the Al Mahbas-Zag tar road was in front of us. We mounted the soft bank onto its firm surface, relieved and yet deeply sad, pausing to look at the track we had been following for a day and a half continuing on into the wind-swept desolation of the desert until it disappeared into the heat haze on the horizon.

We didn't want the adventure to end; both of us wanted to continue on, following the tracks until they led us somewhere deep into the emptiness of the desert.

First published in Overland Magazine, Issue 11, under the title: "Taking the Piste".

Excerpt taken from "There are no Fat People in Morocco".

THIRTEEN
The small dotted line

*A*fter previous trips together to Russia and Morocco, Gareth and I were looking for something completely different.

Central Asia, perhaps?

This was the plan: Fly the bikes into Almaty in Kazakhstan, head into the Pamir Mountains and the Pamir Highway, the Silk Road, then press further south through Kyrgyzstan and Tajikistan.

There were two tracks we were particularly interested in: the first was a dirt road that hugged the Afghan and Chinese borders along the Wakhan Corridor, a thin finger of Afghan territory designed to keep the Russians and British apart during the 19th century; the second was the remote Bartang Pass, described by Lonely Planet as: "the stark and elemental Bartang Valley, one of the wildest and most beautiful in the western Pamirs... at times the fragile road is only perilously inches between the raging river below and sheer cliffs above."

Then, after three weeks playing in the mountains we would ride back to the UK across Kazakhstan, southern Russia and Ukraine.

We'd given ourselves five weeks to complete the trip but, when travelling in Central Asia, it's best not to make too many detailed plans...

Let's be blunt here: Kyrgyzstan is not a *normal* country.

If I hadn't suggested we stop to gnaw on a gristly sheep's leg for lunch we would have got over the Taldyk Pass before the landslide blocked the road. But I did.

So we ate our dubious lumps of meat, then pressed on up the pass heading for the beginning of the Pamir Highway and the Afghan border only to find that, just minutes before we got there, half the mountain had collapsed onto the road, blocking our path.

Can't complain too much, I suppose - we could have been under it. What to do? Our way effectively blocked for the next ten days while they brought in graders to clear the road, we were faced with a six-day detour through the mountains, or attempt a small goat track that Gareth discovered marked on the map as a minute dotted line climbing over the 3615m Alau Mountain Range. It was a few hundred kilometres away but better that than travelling half way across Kyrgyzstan and Tajikistan to get around the rock fall.

The next day we attempted the pass, knowing, deep down, that there was little chance of our making it - not with loaded bikes and snow covering the upper reaches of the mountains.

At Kyzyl-Kyya we filled up our tanks and one spare fuel container from a bucket scooped out of a 44-gallon drum locked away in a dusty shed. Gareth looked up from his GPS and informed me, "Twenty kilometres and the map runs out..."

No more data. We would be on our own, half way up a scary range of mountains, with just a dodgy map and the track.

The sun beat down on us from a sky in which cumulus clouds were just beginning to form. At least it wasn't going to rain - yet, I thought. At times, when I could chance taking my eyes off the road, I looked up at the mountains ahead that barred our way and I could count five consecutive ranges, like massive waves in a turbulent sea, each higher and more hazed with blue than the next, the final mountain covered with snow and completely dominating the horizon. My heart sank but I didn't voice my concerns.

At the first army checkpoint behind a high, gated fence, our papers were scrutinized by a young soldier with a firearm slung over his shoulder. The "office" was a converted metal container. An army 4X4 was parked out back; the track ahead still had signs of tyre marks and the soldiers didn't laugh in our faces when we showed them on the map where we intended to go so, momentarily, my hopes rose. If a 4X4 had made it to this point, maybe others had made it right over the top and, if they could do it, surely we could too?

Papers checked and the gate opened to let us through, we pressed on along a stony track that quickly narrowed and became steeper. We had to push our way through large herds of horses and sheep making their ponderous way up the pass, a rock wall on one side and a steep drop-off into the river on the other. The Kyrgyz drovers, usually two or three on horseback accompanied by a few large, ragged dogs and a donkey carrying their belongings, largely tolerated our presence with an ageless phlegmatism. About half an hour later a metal pole across the track signalled the second army checkpoint. In a single-roomed building were soldiers and a bed. One was asleep and roused himself drowsily to speak to us. He checked our papers, asked us where we were going and then insisted, *"Daroga nyet!"*, crossing his forearms in front of his chest and shaking his head.

Not willing to give up until we were forced to, we persevered, showing the soldier the track we originally intended to take and indicating, with the same crossed-arms gesture, that the Sary-Tash road was blocked. Eventually we managed to persuade him and he raised the barrier to allow us through. We continued on up a track that grew still narrower and more covered with rocks that had tumbled from the steep mountain slopes all about us.

Then we came upon the third and final army checkpoint. And here the tracks ended. No vehicle had travelled further than this that we could see.

We made our way across a rickety bridge, rotten wooden slats through which the river could be seen tumbling its way down the mountainside, towards a square building, table and benches outside under a large tree, shirtless soldiers playing soccer in the heat. The officer in charge welcomed us to his barren outpost and listened politely as we explained what we proposed to do, showing him the track on our map. But he shook his head. Using gestures and the little Russian we could understand, one of the soldiers explained that just eight kilometres from the checkpoint the track was blocked and we would only be able to proceed from there on foot or on horseback.

Again we prevailed upon them to allow us through so we could see for ourselves and we pushed on along an even steeper, narrower track, jostling once again with herds of sheep and horses plodding their way up the pass. It was very hot and the bikes were overheating. So were we. We struggled on through breathtaking scenery, always the mountain barrier high and implacable in front of us, until, almost exactly eight kilometres from the military checkpoint, just as the soldier had predicted, our attempt ended.

The track ahead was completely covered with a thick, sloping layer of scree. I accelerated into the loose stones but bogged down almost immediately. A metre to my left dislodged rocks dropped off into the river fifty foot below. I tried once more to get moving but the moment my rear wheel began to turn, it slipped sideways closer to the drop. While I waited, more scree slid down from the mountain above me, pooling like water around my wheels and feet, starting to cover them.

Fortunately I wasn't riding alone and soon Gareth had made his way up to me and we manhandled my bike across together.

Gareth then tried to power his way across on his big KTM but he hit a rock that pushed him towards the edge and the steep drop-off to the river below; he tapped off, righted the bike and accelerated again but immediately bogged down in the loose tumble of stones. It was impossible for just the two of us to get the heavily-loaded KTM going again across the deep scree. Every movement of the rear wheel caused the bike to slip closer to the cliff edge and the turbulent river far below. We unloaded it, dragged it on its side to safety and, again both pushing and accelerating, made it across.

We could see that the track continued on its way up the mountain but we both realised it was the end. Clearly this was a track used by drovers taking their animals across the pass and not intended for vehicles. We hadn't even climbed a third of the three thousand or so metres that lay ahead of us and already we were struggling.

And so, thirty kilometres from the top as the crow flies, our attempt came to an abrupt end. Reluctantly we turned the bikes and made our way back down the pass.

The soldiers at the third checkpoint smiled wryly when they saw us returning. They offered us tea and gave us a loaf of flatbread and we spent a pleasant half hour with them in their Spartan, isolated outpost high in this desolate but beautiful place.

So, there was nothing to do but set off on the long, six-day detour west and then south to Dushanbe to get around the rock fall. This was a long, hard slog. The road, a section of the Silk Road, is badly beaten up by the many heavily-laden trucks that crawl through this mountainous region and, at times, we wondered just how the bikes could stand up to the beating they were receiving. The heat in the lowlands was oppressive, over 40C, yet when the road climbed over mountain passes, snow was thick on the ground. Distances here are deceptively vast and we were riding between 8 and 12 hours a day just to make sufficient progress. Our soft panniers began to disintegrate and my exhaust mountings broke off but we managed to strap it up with pieces of fence wire.

Finally we reached Dushanbe and turned south-east towards Khorog, the setting-off point for our dip south to the Wakhan Corridor. And this isolated corner of the world, tucked inside the tectonic push and shove of mountains and high Alpine plateau where Afghanistan, Kyrgyzstan and China rub shoulders in an uneasy and suspicious relationship, was the highlight of the trip: isolated and remote, almost devoid of people - just a few Tajik shepherds and their families living in adobe shacks high up in the mountains, poor people scraping an existence in this harsh terrain but whose hospitality towards us was touching in the extreme; clear streams running alongside the track, snow-capped mountains a constant presence - the Pamir Mountains to the north and the Hindu Kush to the south, Afghanistan just a stone's throw away, Bactrian camels making their solitary way just across the river.

At Khargush, the Pamir Highway turns north. The road was blocked by an army checkpoint but we managed to persuade the officer in charge to allow us to continue east towards Lake Zorkul and the Chinese border. The "road" degenerated into a jeep track, sometimes no more than two wheel ruts across the high Alpine plateau, occasionally disappearing so we had to range about to find it again. We camped alongside Lake Zorkul as a light snow began to fall.

By now, Gareth's KTM was battling with the altitude - some sensor not functioning - and he was using double the expected amount of fuel and struggling to keep the engine going at low revs. A lot of clutch slipping, especially when crossing the many small rivers (and when getting stuck up to the hubs in mud). Finally we came to a small village where we hoped to get fuel but there was none. We didn't have enough to reach the next town - unless we got the bikes over a rather deep-looking river. Fortunately, it was spanned by a narrow, tatty-looking cable-stayed footbridge that a local man assured us would take the weight of the bikes so we stripped off all our luggage and gingerly made the crossing.

Still not knowing whether the landslide had been cleared, we continued on our way, re-joining the Pamir Highway at Murghab and heading north, back towards Kyrgyzstan. We were running out of time. Fortunately, when we got there, a narrow, one-lane gap had been bulldozed through.

Then it was the long ride home: 1,700 miles across the flat desert-like steppe of Kazakhstan and into Russia; 1000 miles across south west Russia, into Ukraine (north where there wasn't any fighting) then across Poland, Germany and on to Rotterdam where we took the ferry to Hull and home.

First published in Adventure Bike Rider Issue 27, April 2015.

Excerpt taken from "The Wakhan Corridor - A Motorcycle Journey into Central Asia".

FOURTEEN

The tunnel

We continued steadily along a fairly good road for most of the morning although the fierce heat was a constant and unwelcome presence. Then, at last, we began climbing the first of two mountain ranges above three thousand metres that we needed to cross before reaching Dushanbe. Near the top of the first pass, we came upon the opening of a tunnel and were waved to a stop by a policeman.

As he walked towards us, I thought *Now what?* After pleasantries had been exchanged, he informed us sadly that we were not permitted to proceed through the tunnel. This in sign language, of course - hands gripping handlebars, right hand revving then arms held across his chest in a clearly negating **X**.

We asked why. I saw our attempt on the Palmir Highway receding once again: Kazakhstan 3: Brits 0.

He pointed to some writing engraved in a plaque at the entrance to the tunnel: *Motorcycles and bicycles prohibited from entering this tunnel* he translated in sign language. Gareth asked if there was a road around the tunnel, pointing at the surrounding mountains and describing a wide loop with his arm.

No, there was no way round. He looked conciliatory and, using his hands, expressively indicated a motorcycle crash, then put his forefinger to his temple and pulled an imaginary trigger. Loose translation: "If I let you two jokers through this tunnel after I have been expressly forbidden to do so (and, look, it's even engraved on stone for all to see) and you are idiotic enough to have a crash, then I'm a dead man. I may as well just blow my own brains out because, if I don't, someone else surely will."

As you can see, I have developed a sophisticated understanding of sign language.

Anyway, we stood around, looking at inconsequential things for a while. It's best not to rush these things. After riding for days trying to get round the rock fall, you don't just say, "OK" and go home when someone tells you that you're not allowed to go through a tunnel, even if he's wearing a uniform. And we weren't even going to think of offering a bribe.

We waited.

He waited.

I got the water out and we had a drink; it was like sucking at the spout of a recently boiled kettle.

When enough time had elapsed for his dignity and authority to remain unblemished, he approached us and, in a low voice, (in case those who might put a gun to his head might be listening) muttered, "Just go quickly and no one will notice - you don't tell, I won't tell -" well, that's what his facial expression, conspiratorial tone and hand gestures implied.

We didn't need a second invitation; in seconds we had started our bikes and were heading for the entrance. It was a good tunnel, long and dark but perfectly serviceable, and both of us wondered why they had imposed a restriction.

But it was the *second* tunnel that was scary, though. And we realised - afterwards - that it was *this* tunnel we were being protected from, not the first. And only after we had ridden through it did we understand why.

Later, Gareth told me he remembered seeing on the map, somewhere around here, a warning in italics and with exclamation marks (well, I'm not so sure about the exclamation marks - but if there weren't any, there should have been) saying: "*Dangerous Tunnel!!!!!!!!!!!!*"

Well, *that* was an understatement!

We came around a corner near the top of the second mountain range and were confronted by a cluster of broken-down trucks, bits of gearbox strewn in the dust, a few trucks haphazardly parked near the entrance to the tunnel; but from the black hole in the side of the mountain was pouring a thick pall of blue-black smoke. Gareth and I pulled over and switched off, both of us thinking the same thing: *a truck has caught fire inside.*

I am ashamed to admit - but this is an honest account and all my manifold weaknesses will be brutally exposed - that my first thought was not for the driver and his passengers being turned into toast inside that black hole and all the other drivers caught in there asphyxiating whilst frantically trying to reverse out; no, my first thought was: *Bummer, our way is blocked yet again...*

I didn't actually try to calculate how many days it would take for the tunnel to cool down and all the dead bodies and twisted, burned-out wrecks to be removed (which we did when trying to work out roughly how long it would take to bull-doze the rocks out of the cutting so we could get through after the rock fall), probably because at that moment two of the waiting trucks started up with a belch of diesel fumes and began to move towards the smoking tunnel entrance. Both Gareth and I glanced quickly at each other and leapt on our bikes, firing them up and pulling in just behind the second truck: If they could get through, so could we.

The trucks crawled towards the entrance, both of us tucked in behind, so slow that we had to walk the bikes along to stop them falling over. We followed them inside, smoke billowing about us, the noise loud and oppressive. Then Gareth poked his head round the side of the truck immediately in front and pulled away; I followed, seeing just enough to hope that I wouldn't meet something coming the other way with its lights off. We made it past both trucks, our lights like two pale fingers probing the darkness in front of us.

As with any tunnel that is totally dark, it doesn't take long before you begin losing your sense of direction; with no points of reference, the mind begins to play tricks, you can no longer tell which is up or down; you have no idea where you are headed and your sense of balance leaves you. The easiest solution for me was to focus on the dim red point of light receding into the darkness in front of me that was Gareth's tail light and head for it.

I became aware, with not a little concern, that I was breathing almost nothing but exhaust fumes. The smoke wasn't smoke at all; it was diesel fumes. My throat felt raw, my lungs seared; my eyes began to burn. To add to the Stygian feeling of the place, the murky, swirling, stench of underground darkness, all about us was a noise so loud it threatened to overwhelm my senses. I tried to identify it, to place it, but couldn't. It was the kind of noise that makes your ears bleed; a noise that, in normal countries, you would be prosecuted for allowing your employees to work in; the kind of noise you might hear moments before a Kamatz truck rides over your head. And, in the darkness and smoke and chaos of the tunnel, it seemed, after a while, to be coming from the centre of my chest.

At first, the road surface was pot-holed tar. But this soon degenerated: most of the tar disappeared and the road - could it be called a *road?* - became broken and ridged. Everything was wet and all the potholes had filled with water. As the floor of the tunnel was also wet, the holes weren't visible - you just had to hit them and hope for the best.

We came upon more trucks trundling their slow way through and, taking a deep breath and praying that we wouldn't hit something or meet something coming the other way or be thrown under their wheels which thundered and bumped and splashed just a few inches from us, we overtook them.

Suddenly, without any warning (because I couldn't see it) I fell into a deep, water-filled hole. The potholes had degenerated into craters that could cover half the "road"; and you didn't know what half because the entire floor of the tunnel - I keep on wanting to type "cave" because that's what it seemed like - was wet and running with water which glinted dimly in the headlights until suddenly *Whomp!* you'd go down again. Some of these lakes were hub-deep with sharp edges and, again, we had no option but to hit them and plough on, bashing and sloshing our way through.

Suddenly, the noise level increased (if that was possible); it felt like being on a runway with a 747 about to land on your head. I braced myself, not knowing what was about to hit me. Then out of the darkness appeared a huge industrial fan, the blades about ten feet high, with no protective grill. I was sure it was going to suck me in as I passed, spit me out again as a fine spray of blood and minced flesh. (Gareth said afterwards that he was worried a truck would kick a stone into the blades which would be shot out at us like a cannon ball. These fans were *sooo* big and *soooo* bad that a rock hitting a blade and being whipped out would punch a hole right through your helmet and head and bury itself in the engine block of a following truck.) And there was no warning; no lights; no refelective paint - nothing. Just out of the swirling, smoke-filled darkness and terrible noise appeared this monstrous, madly-spinning *thing* and we only realised what it was once we were alongside it.

And, of course, all this time trucks were coming the other way, sloshing and bashing through the water-filled holes, some without lights or any reflective devices whatsoever. They just appeared in front of you, out of the gloom.

Suddenly, right in front of us, was a broken-down truck. Again, no lights, no warning, so nice man waving a flag. It was the first of three abandoned trucks we came across in the tunnel. (I don't know whether anyone ever checked whether there were dead people inside them. Probably not.)

Another thundering industrial fan to scrape past; more hub-deep, black holes to wade through.

Please, Lord, don't let me drop my bike in here! That was my main worry (and my oft-repeated prayer). If I dropped the bike - and that was a definite possibility - no one would see me; Gareth would ride on, oblivious, until he came out the other side and realised I was no longer behind him. The trucks wouldn't see me before they had driven over me. Considering the condition of the "road", they probably wouldn't even have felt it. What's the *Bump! Bump!* of a motorbike or a body when you're driving underground through thick smoke across a murky bomb site in the dark?

A few more broken-down trucks and then, out of the gloom appeared an entire mechanical drill rig, just to one side but allowing enough space for one truck at a time to squeeze past, *working in the tunnel!* While trucks (and us) were bashing their way past in the darkness, this drill rig was digging out the ceiling! And there were workers in there, walking around like ghosts.

I wondered how many had died inside there. I know I was getting worried that one of us might pass out. It took us at least fifteen minutes to get through the tunnel and we must have been inhaling, continually for this whole time, the amount of exhaust fumes your average suicide pumps into his car with a hose pipe. I genuinely started to check my symptoms while I was riding and look closely at Gareth in front of me, wondering when one of us would fall over and die from asphyxiation. But we didn't.

Suddenly, through the gloom ahead, appeared a lighter patch which grew until, far ahead we could just make out the mouth of the tunnel.

We were through.

Excerpt taken from: "The Wakhan Corridor" A Motorcycle Journey into Central Asia".

FIFTEEN
Desert ships of the Aral Sea

There is something about the image of sea-going ships beached in the middle of a desert that piques the imagination. One's mind struggles to assimilate the sheer incongruity of it. Ships imply water; deserts the absence thereof. And yet here, on the vast bed of the Aral Sea, now the Aralkum Desert in Kazakhstan, ocean-going

ships lie beached. Instead of water, desert sand laps against their rusted sides. The image draws one back.

In 2014, Gareth and I managed to find the rusting remains of one ship after wandering about in the heat following small desert tracks and showing a roughly-drawn sketch of a fishing boat on the sand to bemused Kazakh sheep and camel herders. We eventually stumbled upon what was left of a ship, its outer plates stripped away and little but the superstructure left to brave the elements. Having explored it, we turned back; it was just too hot, the road too bad and, to be honest, the remnants of that one ship so disappointing that we just wanted to leave.

But when we got home and looked at the satellite images more closely, we could clearly see more beached ships, some of them just a little further on from the one we had discovered. We decided to return to look for them.

When entering Kazakhstan, there is a feeling of having lost a century somewhere. The roads are deeply ridged and potholed by overloaded trucks making their way across the flat, grassy steppe. We ride past small, isolated communities of mud-brick houses, large herds of cattle and sheep, hay being stored for the winter. Occasionally a small town appears and passes: nondescript, ugly, dusty, soulless and treeless. Oil towns, I assume. There's nothing else here. We press on. There is no reason to stop.

In the distance whirlwinds of dust make columns in the still air.

Gareth's front fork seals have gone. Oil blows onto the engine, his boots, riding gear. When we pause briefly for fuel or coffee, men saunter up to the bikes, eyeing them obliquely. Then, glancing up at us, they ask, *"Eskuda?"* (where are you from?) and we tell them.

They shake their heads. Sometimes they shake our hands.

And always the camels, gazing at the horizon with supercilious disdain. When close to the road, their rank odour, like a pack of wet hounds in a kennel, lingers long after we pass.

Aral is a fascinating example of Russian hubris, of the manipulation of a land and its people that went too far, that led to what has been referred to as one of the world's worst environmental disasters. The first studies of the Aral Sea were conducted by a Russian expedition in the 1840s. It was far bigger than they could have imagined: 426 ks long and 284 ks wide, an inland sea 68,000 sq kms in area with a maximum depth of 68 metres. Water from the Tian Shan Mountains as well as a vast drainage basin that included Uzbekistan and parts of Tajikistan, Turkmenistan, Kyrgyzstan and Kazakhstan flowed into the lake, keeping it full and viable. It was alive and richly stocked with fish.

The Russians saw its potential and wanted to control it. So, in 1847 the town of Aralsk was founded as a naval base, near the mouth of the Syr Darya River. Two naval vessels were designed to patrol the area. Because the sea was not connected to other bodies of water, the vessels - two-masted schooners named *Nikolai* and *Mikhail* - had to be disassembled in Orenburg on the Ural River, carried in pieces on the backs of camels overland to Aralsk, and then reassembled there. *Nikolai* was a warship; *Mikhail* a merchant vessel meant to serve the establishment of a fisheries industry. In 1848, these two vessels surveyed the northern part of the sea while a larger warship, the *Constantine*, was being assembled. The Russians were there to stay. Commanded by Lt. Alexey Butakov, the *Constantine* completed the survey of the entire Aral Sea over the next two years.

Soon a thriving fishing industry had been established, employing over 40,000 people and producing one-sixth of the Soviet Union's entire fish catch.

The Soviet government then concluded that the region would be ideal for growing cotton - if only they could irrigate it. It was decided that the two rivers that fed the Aral Sea, the Amu Darya in the south and the Syr Darya in the east, would be diverted to irrigate the desert. The construction of irrigation canals began on a large scale in the 1960s. Many of the canals, however, were poorly built - porus and massively wasteful, with most of the water being lost through evaporation and leakage even before they reached the cotton fields. The Qaraqum Canal, the largest in Central Asia, lost up to 75% of its water in this way.

Despite these setbacks, the plan succeeded, for a time, and in 1988, Uzbekistan was the world's largest exporter of cotton. The problem was that the canals consumed 90% of the water that flowed from the Tian Shan Mountains into the Aral Sea.

Inevitably, it began to shrink. Each year its level was lower, its shores retreating into the desert. By 2007 it had declined to 10% of its original size, splitting into four small lakes which, in their turn, soon dried up. The region's once-prosperous fishing industry had been essentially destroyed, bringing unemployment and economic hardship to the entire region.

Waves of sand now lap the ships' rusting sides and grass and salt-resistant shrubs have colonised the sea bed. Camels and sheep graze where fish used to swim in their millions. The Aral Sea, once the world's fourth largest inland body of water, has become the Aralkum Desert, a sand and saline wasteland. The former fishing towns along the original shores became ship graveyards, their harbours and jetties empty and dry, miles from the shore.

We set off from Aral early so we could have time to explore. The 80k causeway to the small village before one reaches the first of the stranded ships was as bad as we remembered it. We shuddered our way along, gritting our teeth and sucking it up. There was no alternative, not even the option of smoother tracks on either side. Once a faint path revealed itself and we headed off the causeway onto the flat sea bed but the tracks were soft and short-lived. Made by animals, probably. So, it was back on to the corrugated road.

Camels, alone or in small groups, grazed close to the road and at one small village horses were corralled. These are in beautiful shape despite the poor quality of the grass. With horses this hardy, able to thrive so well under such harsh conditions, it is understandable why the Kazakhs and, even further back, the Mongols, depended so much on them.

Somewhere along the way Gareth paused and pointed to the left of the road. A strange mesa of soft, heavily-eroded clay rose out of the flat sea bed. There were tracks leading up the side that faced us. A mutual nod and we were off. The slope was steep and fairly soft but not a real challenge. At the top a small flattish crest gave us somewhere to park the bikes, right on the edge where the land fell away steeply to the sea floor hundreds of feet below. Its height gave us a bird's-eye view across the dry sea bed stretching to the horizon, flat, parched and covered with a thin layer of scrubby bushes.

Then back to the road and on to the small village whose people cling to life in this wilderness with their flocks of sheep and their camels. The sky had become heavily overcast and a strong wind was blowing. We rode through the village and immediately the tracks narrowed and turned to sand. It was cool compared to the previous year when we suffered badly from the heat, especially when struggling through sand. The tracks undulated across the flat plain, deeply worn below the surface of the land. I passed the long stretch of tracks where, the previous year, the soft sand had got the better of me and had me down. Now, with the smaller, un-laden bikes and knowing what to expect, we stood up on the pegs and hit the soft sections at speed. Treat it with contempt; hit it hard and fast.

And then the familiar shape of a ship's superstructure appeared out of the sand ahead, a stark reminder of a time long gone. It rusted quietly in the wind. We stopped in the shade of the hulk and stripped off our gear. I looked up and tried to picture deep blue water lapping the ship's hull forty metres above my head, the smell of fish, the shouts of fishermen winching in their nets.

The mental image was absurd, surrounded as we were by little other than wind-blown sand.

This time we clambered up the hot, twisted plating, sieved with rust holes, and into what was left of the hull. We climbed scabby steel ladders onto the bridge and looked out from the darkness inside onto a sea of sand, not water. The low, scrubby plants were a mottled green and maroon, the sand beneath fine and white. On the rusted steel plates, the Banksi-like white line paintings were still there: a disconsolate fisherman, smoking a pipe and sitting on a fuel barrel, who lost his livelihood when the sea dried up; another fisherman wearing a cap swigs from a bottle of beer, drowning his sorrows; a depressed-looking man sits on a wooden crate, his head resting on his hand, obscuring his face; a man urinates against a wall, looking over his shoulder, a quizzical expression on his face as if unsure as to why we are still watching him.

We explored the ship, trying to imagine how it must have been back then, before the Soviet leadership decided to play god with an entire land and its people. Eager to probe, we fired up the bikes and followed the tracks a little further. It wasn't long before we came across two more ships, the superstructures of both still painted blue, glassless port holes bearing testimony to their origin. Again, most of the outer plating had over the years been cut away. But when we climbed inside one of them, up onto the bridge and looked down from above, the shape of the hull was clear, still buried in the sand, curved bow plates protruding.

Where last year we had turned back and retraced our steps along that soul-destroying eighty kms of corrugated road, this year we had noticed on satellite photographs a number of tracks leading on and around a section of the sea bed and planned to make our way back to Aral following these.

I must admit to looking about the desert surface as we rode: surely there are the remains of other wrecks still here, something that had floated metres above our heads when this whole area as far as the horizon was blue with sea, a wreck, perhaps, that has been missed by others who passed this way. Fanciful hopes.

The surface became corrugated and I headed off onto an area that looked and felt like an ancient salt pan; soon Gareth followed and for a while we did silly things on the smooth, yielding surface.

We rode on, the tracks separating and coming together in a filigree of patterns, the sand fine-grained and white, the low bushes touched with muted colours of red and maroon and olive green. Following a different path, Gareth lost sight of me, stopped and turned back. He thought I was behind him somewhere. I saw him heading back and flew after him, keeping him in sight. It would be all too easy to lose each other in that place. He would have been OK - he had the track marked on his GPS; I didn't. Eventually, after some exhilarating riding I caught up with him.

"How did you get in front of me?" he asked then noticed that my fuel pipe had been snagged by a bush in my mad scramble to catch him and was spewing fuel over my engine.

A bit further and I was sure I could see water. We rode across the scrubby vegetation to investigate. It *was* water and Gareth, ahead of me, sank into the mud. He managed to get out without bogging down and I remembered the Russian biker on a GS who had gone down in mud the previous year. It took six of us to drag his bike out.

The water is a good sign. In an attempt to save and replenish at least a part of the original sea and realising that trying to turn the clock back was an impossible dream, a section of the North Aral Sea has been dammed. The project was completed in 2005 and this smaller section of the sea began to fill. Salinity has dropped and the fish are returning. It was this water that we stood in front of - a partial return of the sea.

Further on still we came across a strange concrete structure, cracked and leaning. We rode across to investigate. Only when we were close did we realise that it was the remains of a concrete dock for large ships, an abandoned jetty, collapsing now that the water has retreated. Looking closely, we could still see the wooden and metal bollards where the ships used to tie up. A surreal picture, this crumbling jetty in the middle of a desert sea.

What looked like a channel, wide and deep, had been dug from the jetty out into the white sand. And it was then that I remembered reading about the desperate attempts of the fishermen trying to keep their ships afloat and maintain access to the retreating waters. They started digging a trench, longer and deeper each day until, eventually, even the most hopeful realised that it was too late: the water was drying up, shrinking faster than they could dig. Their livelihood was evaporating with the Aral Sea, now shallow and mostly unnavigable, into the hot endless skies of the Kazahk Steppe and the dust bowl left behind. In the end they gave up. The hundreds of ships that used to ply these waters became stranded, lying scattered on dry, wind-swept land. Many have been there for twenty years.

These trenches can be seen on satellite photos of the Aral sea even today.

Finally we made it back to Aral through increasingly soft sand tracks. We bought oil and other essential fluids and gave the bikes a good service in preparation for the next stage of the trip, across Kazakhstan and into the mountains of Kyrgyzstan.

We were satisfied with the ships we had seen, but there are more out there, waiting to be explored. The best are, I understand, in Uzbekistan but more difficult to access.

Perhaps another day...

First published in Overland Magazine, Issue 14, under the title: "Ships in the Desert".

Excerpt taken from "A Pass too Far".

SIXTEEN

Why am I here?

I was tired, hot and sweaty; all I wanted to do was drink copious amounts of water, have a shower, consume a cold beer and collapse onto my bed. But the heavy-duty zip-ties holding up my broken exhaust had again sheared and the silencer had been bashing against the brake calliper every time the rear suspension compressed. I needed to secure the exhaust before it did any more damage or broke off altogether so, sitting in the hot dust outside the home stay while small children chirruped across the street, I unbolted my pannier rack to gain access and strapped the exhaust back into place using a piece of wire I had picked up on the side of the road the previous day (just in case), a piece of washing line I "borrowed" from the property next door and, just to be certain the exhaust would not break free again no matter what the condition of the roads, my cable lock.

It was past nine before I was finished and darkness was setting in (although it did nothing to ameliorate the heat).

Before turning in that night, I wrote this in my journal:

There comes a time in any traveller's life when he pauses for reflection and asks himself: Why?

It's getting dark, the temperature is hot enough to roast a chicken, you are up to your elbows in oil and there's sand in your hair; your bum itches, insolent flies drink moisture from the corners of your eyes, your stomach is tightening and coiling in that ominous way that signals the imminent evacuation of all your intestines from your rectum; your bike is falling apart bit by bit and you're not sure whether it's going to get you home before the last piece falls off; your nose is blockled with cement and whenever you blow it, it bleeds. Your body stinks. Your eyes are gritty. The last drop of water you've got is warm and you dare not attempt the brown stuff that stutters from the tap in your unspeakable bathroom in case it kills you.

Filled with self-pity, you plaintively ask yourself: Why am I here? What am I doing in this place? I could be at home, right now, sitting in my comfortable chair with a cat on my lap and a cold beer in my hand, watching MotoGP on the telly or Charlie and Ewan doing their thing instead of me (with a back-up truck, of course, and film crew just out of sight so we all think they're doing it alone and their fancy aluminium panniers are full of tools, spares, food and water and other essential stuff that's not tuckled away safely in the support truck).

But then, as darkness begins to fall and the children have gone to sleep and the piece of wire you pulled from the fence and the clothes line you cut from the yard next door have been tightened and your exhaust is so well secured that you know it will never fall off even if hit by an avalanche; you're rather pleased with yourself and your back-yard mechanics, your "boer maak 'n plan", and you've had a cold shower in your hot room and got most of the grease off your arms and all the sand out of your hair and the flies have gone to sleep for the night and you've changed your clothes. Later you find some quaint, smoky bistro down a side alley that sells cold beers and, quite coincidentally, at the same place are a couple of intrepid cyclists with stories to tell and a twenty-something young woman who's hitching from Katmandu to Marrakesch or Ulan Batour or Timbuktu or Tashkent - some exotic-sounding destination - and she smells like a woman should and looks great and you know she sees your grey hair and grizzled beard and wrinkles as signs, not of age, but of untold wisdom and experience - and suddenly, as you drink deep of your beer and the aches ooze from your muscles - you know why you're here...

Excerpt taken from: "The Wakhan Corridor - A Motorcycle Journey into Central Asia".

SEVENTEEN
The raising of Lazarus

*L*azarus was stinking when he emerged from the tomb. His sister, Martha, remonstrated with Jesus, "Come on, he's been dead for four days - there will be a smell."

This is the story of a plucky little DR350 that my son, Gareth, re-christened "Lazarus". Like the rotting, cloth-wrapped body of Martha's brother, this bike was resurrected from the rocky grave of Matt's Pass in Tajikistan in a manner that rather smacks of the miraculous.

There were two DR350s, both twenty-five years old; Gareth and I purchased them for £1500 each from a dealer and rode them home. We planned to use them for a few trips into Central Asia, opting for lightness and durability to cope with the Bartang Pass and other things that riding in the Pamir Mountains tends to throw at one. Very little preparation was needed: new wheel bearings, pannier racks designed and welded, new chains and sprockets, long-range tanks. Sorted.

In 2015 we rode them from the UK to Osh in Kyrgyzstan via Turkey, Georgia, Russia and Kazakhstan where, on a particularly bad piece of dirt, I T-boned Gareth and broke a couple of his ribs - but he's got lots so we carried on, making it over the Kegeti Pass just days before a snowstorm closed it for the rest of the year. In Osh, we left the bikes under a corrugated-iron lean-to in the walled yard of MuzToo, a company that runs tours around Central Asia and has handy workshop facilities for riders in the Pamirs with mechanical problems. Judging by the number of wrecked bikes in their yard, that would be most of them.

The following year, Gareth and I flew back to Osh and spent a month in Kyrgyzstan and Tajikistan, riding the Bartang Pass and reaching the snout of the Fedchenko Glacier after getting a bit lost amongst the boulders of a dry river bed.

After that, things started to go downhill. You see, Gareth is not normal. He tends to want to go to places most ordinary people steer clear of, and, because I'm often travelling with him, I'm involved. Which doesn't do my body or my mind much good but afterwards gives us lots to talk about. He had read about a small pass named after someone called Matt, 36ks long, that makes its bolder-strewn way across a remote mountain range in Tajikistan before joining the Langar-Kargush road. Naturally, he wanted to attempt it.

So we did. (Well, you read how *that* turned out in a previous article.)

After abandoning his bike in the mountains, we walked out. At our home stay in the small village of Langar, Gareth explained to the Tajik owner where his bike was and told him he could have it if he could get it out. Where we were concerned, the DR had come to the end of its days.

Having got my bike out, we rode two-up back to Muz-Too in Osh where we left my bike under the partial shelter of the corrugated-iron-roofed lean-to and flew back home.

Two little DR350s: mine left to gather dust for another two years until I flew back in 2018, replaced the wheel bearings and battery and rode it, with no other preparation, 20,000ks across Russia and back home; Gareth's, when we last saw it, forlornly leaning on its side-stand amongst the rocks and stunted high Alpine vegetation of Matt's Pass, partially stripped of a few bits and surrounded by a scattering of our gear that we abandoned after lightening our load to make it out on the one bike.

The next we heard about Gareth's DR was when a Kyrgh local working for MuzToo reported that the home stay owner and a bunch of his mates had made their way into the mountains and manhandled the bike out. How they did it we are not sure but, really, if you've got sufficient time, a large group of friends and determination, all three readily available in the remote mountains of Tajikistan, you can *carry* a bike, especially one as light as the DR, pretty much anywhere.

Gareth was philosophical: if they had the balls and the initiative to get it out, good luck to them. For him, the bike was gone, written off as one of the outcomes one has to be prepared for when travelling through the world's remote places.

It was a few months later that the next piece of news filtered out of the mountains. Inexplicably, and we've never been able to find out why, the local police turned up at the home stay, confronted the owner and confiscated the bike. It seems that all his hard work had gone for nothing. Once again, it was lost and, as the bike wasn't registered in his name, there was nothing the man could do about it. Chalk it down to experience, as Gareth had. And for the next year and a half, Gareth's DR, we assume, remained in some police shed in the Langar region of Tajikistan. The men who had confiscated it weren't riding it, the engine was seized; so, like my bike, it sat for nearly two years, gathering dust.

Some time in 2017, Gareth heard that the guys at MuzToo were leading a group of bikers into the mountains near Langar. Gareth phoned them, more in hope than expectation: Can you contact the police there and ask them if I can have my bike back? Please.

They did and, for some reason, the police agreed. The bike made its way back to Osh on the back of a 4X4 and was parked under the corrugated iron next to mine. I like to think they greeted each other: *Howzit, mate! Where you bin', man? Long time.*

Now at MuzToo they have a Russian mechanic who, in a Heath Robinson-ish, *'n Boer maak 'n plan* kind of way, can repair anything. (How long it lasts after he's repaired it is another story...) Gareth asked him to pull the engine apart and find out why it had seized. It turned out, as predicted, that the bolts holding the timing chain gear to the camshaft had worked loose. As a consequence, the valves were bent but, other than that, all seemed OK. Now, in order for Lazarus to be fully resurrected, all it needed was a repaired engine and someone to fly out to Kyrgyzstan to ride it back home.

When, in June this year, I flew out to collect my DR for my trans-Russia journey, I took with me new valves and left them with the Russian mechanic who, leaving off a few nuts and bolts here and there in the process, cutting stray bolts to fit and generally botching things back together, Lazarus was running again, peeking his nose out of the cave, smelling a little high and dangling soiled bandages.

And so, while I was half way across Russia, Gareth flew back to Osh. His ride home can best be told in his own words that I copied from a few social media posts he made along the way. It was, as you will see, somewhat touch and go for both him and the bike.

Sept 8th

Well, I didn't think I'd make it this far when I saw my bike for the first time in over 2 years. It's pretty battered. Made it across Uzbekistan and into Kazakhstan. The bike sounds like a bucket of bolts but it's still going. Now I'm waiting for the ferry in Aktau. 4000km to go.

Sept 9th

Fitted new rear wheel bearings and clutch plates while I wait for the ferry. There's no schedule so you wait for one to turn up, then it leaves when it's full. There's a hotel here but I'm the only one in it. £10 a night and the security guard looks startled every time I walk through the front door. He didn't mind me working on the bike outside the main entrance, though.

Sept 10th

Had some electrical problems a few days ago whilst still in Uzbekistan. I stop on the side of the road entering the town of Kungrad to investigate. Turns out a wire has shaken loose from a soldered joint on the back of the ignition barrel. The owner of a cafe comes out to see what I'm up to and indicates for me to wait as he gets on his bicycle and rides off. About ten minutes later he reappears and points at his bicycle for me to use and motions that I must ride on about 1km with the ignition barrel. I pedal off leaving my bike in bits on the side of the road. Up ahead, an old guy waves me down. I think he's hailing one of the taxis which are everywhere, and try to ride around him, but he steps into my path and points to a workshop just off the road. Inside the workshop he looks at the ignition barrel and then breaks out this soldering iron that looks like it was taken from Michael Faraday's lab shortly after he discovered electro-magnetic induction. He pokes the bare wires of the soldering iron into a socket and turns it on. After a time it gets hot enough to melt the solder that is already on the joint and eventually manages to re-join about 16 of the 24-strand wire onto the back of the ignition barrel. He didn't have any solder wire so the joint is a bit rough. In future I'll add a short length to my tool kit. Flux is your friend. He won't take any money from me for his work, just waves me off. I pedal back to my bike, put it back together and it fires up! I thank the cafe owner and ride off to see the stranded ships in the desert at the Aral Sea memorial at Moynak. One repair made with zero common language amongst any of us.

Sept 12 [th]

I had a few issues getting to the port when I arrived here a few days ago, which are probably worth recounting. I make it to Aktau at about 6pm. The ferries leave from the new port at Kuryk, another hour down the coast. By the time I get to Kuryk it is dark and I head to what looks like the port on the map after being followed briefly by a group of screaming children. It's just a pedestrian pier and someone points off into the far distance where I can see the glow of lights.

Looking again at the map, there is a track going in that direction so I follow it for about 15km when the track suddenly becomes new tarmac with no road markings on it. I can see a razor wire fence and the yellow floodlights illuminating an industrial complex that looks like it's preparing aggregate for the new road. A couple of hundred meters further on, a mound of stone blocking the road, with a No Entry sign propped up against it, looms out of the darkness, so I turn back to the industrial complex. Security guards appear and tell me to just keep going past the barrier, and going back to it, I see there is a dirt track leading off to the left into the darkness past the pile of stones.

It's pitch black now, and looking at my GPS, there are no roads or ports mentioned. My paper map doesn't even show the track I was on earlier. I can see the port lights and razor wire fence surrounding it, but I can't find a way in. There are dirt tracks criss-crossing the area, and I blunder around for about half an hour in the blackness until I stumble across a gap in the fence after coming over a small rise. I can see a ferry tied up, with railway wagons being rolled into its hold. It's the Professor Gul, *one of the Caspian Sea ferries that takes passengers. This is good news. Maybe I won't have to wait days and will leave tonight.*

I cross the railway tracks and ride towards the workers loading the ferry and they wave me closer and ask for my ticket. I have no ticket, and they look confused. A soldier comes over and also asks for my ticket and then wants to know how I got in here. I point to the gap in the fence and he looks aghast. He gets quite agitated and says something to the effect of: "This is a border control zone, get out!" He's got an assault rifle slung over his shoulder so I disappear through the gap in the fence sharpish. I can't risk too much scrutiny because my fingerprints are on record after stumbling into a restricted area on a previous trip.

After another 10 minutes of following dirt tracks, trying to stay close to the fence so I can find the actual entrance, brand new, unmarked tarmac abruptly appears again. It quickly leads to the main entrance where the barriers are lifted, and I'm waved past after security have phoned ahead. Later, I find out I missed the unmarked turn off to the new port on the main road from Aktau about 20km from Kuruk. I'm too late, the ferry is full and it leaves without me. The Merkury 1 *arrives three days later and I leave on that instead. (The* Merkury 2 *sank a few years ago.)*

Sept 16 th

The last few days have been fairly un-eventful. After docking in Alat in Azerbaijan, it took about 3 hours to get off the ferry and through customs. You pay for freight on arrival in Azerbaijan rather than upon departure from Kazakhstan. I had wondered why my fare seemed so cheap when buying my ticket - I had only paid for myself and not the bike. During the crossing I had snuck down into the hold to swap my Kyrg registration plate for my UK one. I had a brief moment during the customs check, hoping that no-one would notice the registration change between leaving Kazakhstan and arriving in Azerbaijan. The next day I crossed into Georgia after being given grapes and pastries by a Turkish couple waiting in the queue at the border with me. I skirted around Tbilisi and then took a southerly route through the Borjomi-Kharagauli National Park before crossing into Turkey. I made it across the D915 pass to Bayburt as the light was fading and found a cheap hotel for the night.

This morning, rain on a tin roof outside my window wakes me up at 5:30 and it's still 1200km to Istanbul so I decide to get going. I set off in the rain and about 20 minutes after leaving I'm on a dual carriageway doing about 80kph on a sweeping down hill right hand bend. Something has been spilt on the road and the next thing I know, the back wheel has lost traction and I'm sliding along on my back. When I come to my senses, I look up and see the barrier of the centre reservation fast approaching. My bike bounces off the barrier back into the outside lane, and I disappear under the barrier between the uprights. I jump up and try to pick my bike up to get it out of the road but my left arm hurts and doesn't work and my boots are slipping around on the road surface so I can't lift it.

I look around and my gear is strewn across both lanes - tent, dry sack, both fuel cans; there's a fan of gravel spread across the outside lane where my bike slid into the dirt by the barrier. I pick everything up and put it in a pile by the inside barrier, then shrug off my jacket to see what's wrong with my arm because it's quite sore. There are no abrasion marks on my trousers or jacket where I slid, not sure what has been spilt on the road but it is very slick. My left shoulder feels a decidedly odd shape and its range of motion is severely limited so I grab my left arm with my right hand to see how far I can make it move. I feel a pop and suddenly the range of motion is greatly improved so I manage to pick my bike up and get it out of the road. I notice my number plate is snapped in half and I find the rest of it in the ditch in the central reservation along with my tyre levers and spindle nut spanner. My bungee chords are snapped so I tie knots in them so I can strap everything back on my bike. Two trucks and a car have passed by this stage but no one stops.

I ride on but my left shoulder, elbow and wrist are very sore and I can't squeeze the clutch properly. I think I banged them on the barrier when I slid under it. After about 15 minutes' riding with my left arm resting on my tank bag, I stop at a roadside cafe and come across two French cyclists getting ready to head off for the day in the direction I have come from. I ask them for some Ibuprofen and sit drinking tea and feeling sorry for myself.

Later in the day, I get flagged down by police doing spot checks. They want to see everything: passport, visa, driver's licence, insurance, bike registration. The only thing they're not interested in is my snapped-off number plate. The other half of it is in my backpack.

Late afternoon I stop at a roadside stand where a guy is selling fruit and tea. He doesn't speak any English but shows me an old photograph of him and 3 friends with road bikes. He points to one friend and draws his finger across his throat indicating that he died *in an accident. When I leave he won't take any money from me for the tea.*

I stop at a motel on the side of the road as it's getting dark and my elbow, wrist and hand are very swollen. I ask the receptionist about a pharmacy but he does not understand. After showing him my wrist, he calls the owner who gets on his phone and about 15 minutes later a friend of his turns up in a car with a box of Ibuprofen! He won't take any money for it either. He speaks a little English and I mention to him how good the roads are apart from the slippery bits. He says he is ever grateful to Erdogan.

Sept 19 th

Through Serbia, Bosnia, Croatia and Slovenia. It's been nearly three weeks of almost relentless riding to make the distance in time and I'm feeling pretty run down. I stopped at Nis in Serbia to take a look at the Bubanj Memorial, huge fist-shaped sculptures erupting out of the ground, symbolising the resistance of the people despite the execution of thousands of men, women and children at that site. The following day I get in to Mostar in Bosnia at about 7pm. The roads twisting through the mountains are slow going. I had planned to do a section of the Trans Euro Trail towards the end of that day but it would have added another two hours' riding and I wasn't feeling well. I probably would have ended up getting a puncture and having to fix it in the dark. Had a look around the old town and the bridge then went to bed.

The clattering from the top end of the bike is awful so in the morning I check the tappets as a token gesture. Exhaust clearance is a bit wide but it still clatters.

The next stop was another WWII monument in Croatia, Monument to the Revolution of the people of Moslavina. I was hoping to get there before the sunset but it was a 620 km ride and my late start meant that it was dark by the time I got there. Was going to stay at a local hostel which turned out not to exist. The last thing I wanted to do was put up my tiny tent in the dark; I had no food or water and I wanted a shower. I found a hotel on my phone about 20km down the motorway. Something makes me turn and look over my shoulder and I notice my tail light is out. So I'm riding down an un-lit motorway with no tail light, a number plate reflector that's actually in my backpack, and a 4-candle-power headlight while being overtaken by trucks. The adjuster on my rear brake stop light switch is just a plastic thumbscrew that I move all the way over so my brake light is always on. At least I can be seen now. Hotel cost 60 euros but I don't care. Bought a new tail light bulb at a service station the next day.

Sept 22 nd

Made it home with the bike now called Lazarus, back from the dead. 8988 km in 15 riding days,

(By the way, if anyone's interested, I've got a lovely example of a 1995 Suzuki DR350 for sale. Recently had a new clutch, timing chain and exhaust valves. Well maintained, never abused.)

First published in Overland Magazine, Issue 26, under the title: "The Raising of Lazarus".

Excerpt taken from "A Pass too Far".

EIGHTEEN
The defensive towers of Georgia

I stare at the towers, imagining marauders on horseback, serfs crouching servile against these cracked stone walls, their bare feet muddy and calloused. Thin dogs wander at will; a horse makes its solitary way home. Against a stone wall an ox-drawn sled lies, constructed from logs, more practical in these rocky places than the wheel. Old carved doors, low and secretive, shut me out. There is a life lived here that I know nothing about; the towers, the small, square churches dating back to the eleventh century, hold pre-

Christian secrets about life lived in these isolated mountains that tug at my mind. I am allowed only the briefest of glimpses - the sights and smells and sounds that testify to an ancient people living lives to which I am only a transient spectator. The depth of history here humbles me, the timelessness of it.

Georgia greets us with a large billboard featuring a smiling young lass encouraging us personally to visit the local casino and lose all our money. Just behind the casino billboard is a church. I'm not sure if there's any significance in the order of placement and what that says about Georgia, but placing a church within a hundred metres of the border seems to echo the mosque placed an equal distance from the entrance into Turkey.

Tit for tat. The mosque is bigger.

But the Christian character of Georgia, distinct from the Muslim character of Turkey, is reinforced by the placement of crosses at the roadside entrance to and exit from most cities and villages as well as large crosses mounted on prominent hilltops. Even the Georgian flag features the bold, red cross of St George and, just in case you missed it, smaller *bolnur-katskhuri* crosses (like the German Iron Cross) in each quadrant. Five crosses for Georgia beats just one Islamic crescent moon and star for Turkey. It feels like the Crusades all over again.

The significance of the flag, though, is important to Georgia's history. The Jerusalem Cross can be seen on a fifth-century Georgian map and has been a prominent symbol of their identity for centuries. Until the Russians banned it, that is, and replaced it with the Red Banner in 1921. Like many other formally independent states, Georgians woke up one morning and found themselves suddenly absorbed into the Soviet Union.

But after its collapse, shortly before declaring independence in 1990, the hammer and sickle was banned and the centuries-old Jerusalem flag with its five red crosses was re-introduced. However the new president, Eduard Shevardnadze, refused to endorse it. It was only when his successor, Mikheal Saakashvili, succeeded him in 2004 after the Rose Revolution that it became, once again, the national flag of Georgia, coming full circle.

The first Georgian men we come across, because the weather is hot, are shirtless. Their bared torsos, the way they carry themselves, makes one think of strength and independence. They would need to be strong, these resilient Georgians, population just over four million, who, like many before, have dared to challenge the might of Russia and lost.

We ride through the lowland marsh-forests and swamps of the Black Sea coast near Batumi. Dense, sub-tropical vegetation encroaches onto the road; banana trees, vines clotted with purple grapes. Gentle-eyed cows claim the road as their own and all traffic is forced to give way. Briefly we turn inland and begin to climb; the air cools and is scented by eucalyptus trees that shed their bark to expose the smooth, blue-white skin beneath. Through Katumi, jousting with drivers who feel that traffic lights and white lines are merely gentle reminders, the obeying of which relies mostly on personal preference.

Back down again to the coastal wetlands, extensive and flat, the Black Sea on our left, lakes and swamps and estuaries on the right. The road is little more than a causeway raised above the level of a damp and sodden land. Pigs snuffle about in water-filled channels; ducks push their way through long grass but the cows seem to prefer the warmth and companionability of the road.

Finally, after Poti, we turn east, inland again, and towards the mountains. The road narrows, towns become villages and traffic fades.

Needing to discard our road tyres and fit the knobblies we have been carrying across Bulgaria and Turkey, we stop in the mid afternoon at a guest house. Hillda, the owner, is a small man sporting some gold teeth and a handful of English words which he practices on us. His wife, a homely-looking woman with white hair and a bulbous nose, fusses about preparing food. She wears sorts and slops and, like Hillda, has some gold teeth.

Hillda leads me into the dark interior of their house, a dilapidated, rambling, lived-in place that they share with a few paying guests. He shows me the bathroom, attempting to explain how to encourage the shower to work and the toilet to flush. On the wall, a Gorgon's head of wires sprout, eventually making their way into old-fashioned, porcelain contact breakers.

Once we have unpacked, the women tell us they have provided food. Their generosity is similar to that we have experienced from rural Russians on previous trips. Rough, dry porridge, bread, strong white cheese, bits of dry chicken meat and a bowl of tomato and cucumber are placed in front of us; we are encouraged to eat with gestures. Hilda provides glasses and offers an open bottle of his home-made wine. He smiles his gold-capped teeth at us and uses his handful of English words.

Rested and replete, we balance the bikes on rocks and spare fuel containers, remove the wheels and road tyres and fit the new knobblies. It will be a relief no longer to have to carry them. Later we shower in the antique bathroom, coaxing water from the pipes.

The next day the fun begins. The heavily-wooded foothills of the Caucasus Mountains enclose us, trees sometimes meeting overhead so we ride through a leafy tunnel of foliage. The road is tar and good; we are children again, playing. Gone are the days of enduring mindless roads through Turkey, the heat and rain, the clogged arteries of cities and coastal towns, the pain from stiff muscles...

The Rioni River follows the road (or perhaps it's the other way round), translucent and pale with sediment but it has none of the threat of the turbulent, deadly rivers that mark the track of the Pamir Highway. We reach Mestia by midday, a medieval town nudging its way into the 21st century. Bare-legged hikers relax in the sun drinking Cokes while old, bent women dressed all in black hobble their way past, living their austere lives seemingly oblivious of the changes happening around them. The town, too, exists in parallel universes: worn, lived-in, tumble-down houses made of stone and mud and hand-cut wooden beams rub shoulders with newly-constructed guest houses looking like Swiss chalets, and cafes soliciting the tourist dollar. It even boasts an air strip. And, dominating the town, ancient defensive towers stand like monoliths, hand-built standing stones, fifty foot high. This is a town so steeped in history that it asks to be explored; it needs time and patience for its secrets to reveal themselves.

But sadly we have neither. We relax briefly, pause for coffee. Then, eager to get on, we fill up with fuel, pump up the tyres and set off again, beyond the tourists, into the valley between the Caucasus and Svaneti mountains.

Later, on a small, deserted road, Gareth sees an abandoned bridge high above the grey turbulent waters of the river. We stop to play. Old bridges with missing and rotten timbers, like mountains, need to be crossed: because they are there. Not being stupid, we check the planks, rearranging some so that we and our bikes don't end up drowned. Gareth crosses first. I follow, but too close. His bike kicks a short plank loose and quickly I have to choose another line to miss the gap that has opened up, wide enough to swallow my front wheel. A YouTube moment just averted.

A short while later Gareth pulls over: puncture. I think the score is 6-0 to me. It's a six-inch nail. He must aim for them. The tube is ripped and cannot be patched. Hot and sweaty, sitting in the dirt on the side of the road, we replace it with our spare.

Finally we reach the dirt and life becomes interesting with some mud and rough stuff to keep us honest and we fly along the rutted track that still follows the river.

The mountains are sparsely populated; villages we come across seem desperately poor with many buildings abandoned and falling apart. And still the defensive towers, abandoned monoliths to a forgotten people defending themselves against a forgotten enemy. In one small village alone we saw twelve of them standing tall and silent, rising high above the roof tops.

We pause to explore deserted farm buildings built alongside one of the towers. There is something beautiful about its sad desolation. To reach it we must ride across a small wooden bridge and scramble up a steep earthen slope. It's like an old Norman motte and keep fortification. It appears that the enemy now is poverty. The rural way of life here seems more tenuous and insubstantial than the towers that have about them an eternal quality, mysterious and enduring.

In the late afternoon we reach the village of Ushguli, Europe's highest continuously inhabited settlement, a cluster of stone houses that have gathered themselves around the protective skirts of the towers. We find a guest house that we share with hikers and cyclists. On the horizon, snow-capped mountains beckon. Our host is an old crone, dressed in black. We enjoy our first beer in days.

Later, I walk out alone into the village. Instantly I am transported into the twelfth century. Rocky paths too narrow for vehicles make their way between rock-built houses, roofed with great slabs of rough slate the size of tables, randomly piled. Gentle-faced children smile and greet me as I pass. The sweet smell of horse dung fills the air and, far off, a cock crows. Rough-cut wooden picket fences lean and sag, separating the path from overgrown plots of land. Above me the ancient towers loom, speaking of olden times. They are all empty, holding their secrets, their ornately carved doors barred from within. With my face pressed to the cracks, I can feel the cool air inside, smell the damp earth. I find one door unbarred and crouch my way through the low entrance. Inside it is as dark as an underground tomb, the rough stones thickly covered in ash. Under my feet it is soft with a deep layer of dry cow dung. Outside again, old, black-garbed women go about their business acting as if I am not here. To them, I am inconsequential, an intrusion into their anachronistic lives.

The sun is close to the surrounding mountain peaks. The air grows cold. Cows make their slow way home across the opposite valley, following well-worn paths. In the distance, the higher mountains are capped with snow. In the clear evening air they seem strangely close. The day settles to quietness. All about is the sound of flowing water. A cow bellows from somewhere far away. Shadows creep across the village but the high snow is still bright with evening light.

Clouds darken, threatening rain. I glance up and, in front of me, the ancient towers take me back again to swords and bows and arrows and frightened people hiding in upstairs rooms, staring out pale-faced from the narrow slits in stone walls; of cloistered monks offering up silent prayers from their narrow monastic cells.

I follow the path further into the village. A woman sits on a rectangular wooden stool and milks a cow by hand into an enamel bucket. Other cows breathe their hot, impatient breath, nudging each other, waiting their turn. In the houses, children are being put to bed. An old woman, shawled and hobbling with a stick, makes her way home. On her feet, heavy boots. There is the smell of wood smoke in the air.

In the sky, high above the mountains, a jet aircraft catches the last of the sun's rays and glows like a light. It is centuries away.

At first sight, I took the defensive towers to be the steeples of old churches. But there were too many. For that many churches, there needed to be a population living here that would fill a city. Clearly this was not so.

The towers, I discovered, are defensive, not religious. They were built between the 9th and 12th centuries as protection against aggressive neighbours - the northern Caucasian tribes on the other side of the mountains and the Ossetians to the east. For centuries the Svans, this isolated tribe with their unique language and its distinctive script, lived in fear of invasion from their neighbours, as well as attacks nearer home caused by blood feuds that often took place in these communities. Instead of building large fortresses or castles with defensive walls to protect the whole community, each Svan family constructed their own tower, five storeys high, with a gently tapering profile. The towers had entrances twelve foot above the ground with a ladder or staircase that could be quickly removed if they were attacked. Inside, heavy, flat stones were kept close to the ladder holes, ready to block the entrances.

Each tower was attached to a large two-storey, rock-built home that provided shelter for the extended family and their livestock, especially during the long, harsh winters. While many of the towers have fallen into disrepair and collapsed, in this village, Ushguli, at the head of the Enguri gorge, more than 200 towers have survived.

The next morning I wake early, get up and head again into the village following the muddy, rocky paths frequented at that time of the morning by cows and farmers' wives carrying wooden stools and milk buckets. I need to be absorbed once more into the medieval atmosphere of this place before we leave and pass on into the future. I find myself accompanied by a large, hairy dog who lightly bites my hand when I stop petting him. Faithful brief friend, he sticks by me even though every dog through whose turf we trespass attacks him. I am faithful too and fling stones. We make it through together.

Cows stand about with yearning in their eyes, waiting to be milked. An old crone, stooped and, as always, dressed all in black, scoops up cow dung with a spade and flings it on a compost heap. Women, their cheeks pressed against the warm flanks of cows as they milk, smile at me as I pass. The metallic *hiss-hiss* of the warm milk frothing into the bucket blends with other early-morning sounds and the warm smell of cow dung.

Then it is time.

Back at the guesthouse, a friendly cow, tethered to the back of a truck, leans on us as we pack the bikes. The owner scrubs a large, cleanly cut log under a block and tackle attached to a metal frame. He had told us the previous day that he needed the block and tackle for "some business" and both Gareth and I assumed it was to lift the engine out of a car. However, the tethered cow and its desperate neediness sparks a thought: It isn't an engine that is about to be sacrificed to the block-and-tackle gibbet - it is the cow.

We are sad. It's a friendly cow. But such is life (or death, if you will).

Breakfasted, packed and loaded, we set off into the mountains. Immediately I can feel that my bike is out of sorts. Gareth notices my rear wheel bouncing repeatedly on the stony road. We stop and check the tyre pressures. And then I notice I've blown my monoshock.

It's not terminal. I'll just have to bounce along for the next few thousand kilometres.

How can I best describe the day? Playing?

What did we do? Well, we rode. It was like four hours of solitary enduro riding - rocky tracks; undulating tracks; muddy, slippery tracks; the mountains and the rivers and the trees our silent companions.

Occasional villages surprise us, tucked away deep in the mountains, picturesque, I am sad to say, in their rural, tumbledown poverty. The beauty of decay. Here the villagers cling to survival; only the very old and the very young and their parents seem to live here. The teenagers, the young men and women, seem mostly absent. They -

the old ones left behind - watch us as we pass, a fleeting intrusion into their struggle for existence.

We pass oxen pulling wooden, log-built sleds laden with hay; black and white spotted pigs in the roadway; small, straggly crops of maize; dusty streets; logs cut and stored against the high-altitude cold of winter; hay filling barns to their roofs, forked there by men standing on the top of loaded wagons. Desolate and abandoned houses seem the norm, not the exception. The most vibrant life in these villages seems to be the trees that often cover the road completely, pooling it in shade. High up, the air is cool. Stream water is blue and clear and icy cold. We pass the remains of a glacier left un-melted in a mountain cleft close to the road. The ice is dirty and brown but with traces of the aquamarine blue that characterises old, glacial ice. Outside a small village we meet about twenty men in the road carrying what I at first think is a coffin. Closer, it turns out to be a large black-and-gilt Madonna and child being ceremonially carried on a wooden bier.

But all good things must end and we begin to descend into the heat of the more populous lowlands. The road still dirt, the villages through which we pass still poor.

Having been warned that the province of South Ossetia has closed its borders and won't let us through, we head further south to Kutaisi, the road now good tar switch-backing between valleys in the Great Caucasus Range, almost traffic free. Loving the freedom of good tar, we ride... well, not idiotic fast; not even stupid fast; perhaps *silly* fast would best describe it - that speed when you have to think a little before each bend to get the speed and line right, especially if there might be a rock fall in an unfortunate place on a bend to make life interesting. This wasn't back-wheel-slipping, knee-scraping stuff - just good, old-fashioned fast riding that brings a smile to one's face, for about an hour.

And then I had what Gareth calls my "encounter with death" when a suicidal cow skittishly galloped across the road in front of me. I couldn't stop in time so accelerated hard to get past it, heading onto the grassy verge just ahead of the cow, and then scrambling back onto the road before I hit two large rocks in my path.

We rode a little slower after that. (Just a little.)

First published in Overland Magazine, Issue 15, under the title: "The Beauty of Decay".

Excerpt taken from "A Pass too Far".

NINETEEN
The banja

*O*n *our return journey through Kyrgyzstan, Gareth and I spent the night in a typical ex-Soviet hotel which served no meals and had no working plumbing.*

Dirty from long hours in the saddle, we badly needed to wash. The only option was to visit the local banja...

A large rectangular concrete building, *Soviet Chic* in style, squatted alongside the road with *BANJA* in Cyrillic letters across the front. We crossed the street to investigate.

Inside the entrance was a large, empty, undecorated space covered with brown ceramic tiles; set into one wall was a small metal grill; behind the grill, a woman.

We mimed taking a shower and said, *"Douche?"* but she insisted,

"*Nyet - banja -*" and pointed to a card with a printed tariff of fees. Evidently, for $2 each we could enter and do whatever one did in there. In an adjoining bare room, a few young women lolled about on wooden benches and Gareth wondered aloud whether the *banja* doubled as the local brothel.

Clutching our towels and soap, we opened a door feeling very much like the new members of the golf club who didn't know the rules. We gingerly entered a humid and airless room, about three metres by ten, floored with the same brown tiles as the entrance. The only furniture, a row of rather battered lockers and some wooden benches upon which reclined two naked men. The first was small and almost hairless - bald head, bald torso, almost bald pubes; the other, almost by deliberate contrast, was large and hairy. He reclined on one of the benches lengthwise, like a male nude posing for a portrait, chest like a gorilla's, hirsute face, dangly bits ... well, dangling.

We stripped off, somewhat self-consciously, and entered room No. 3. It was so hot I felt as if I were breathing hot water and wondered if I might drown. Another naked man stood before a concrete block, about navel height, soaping himself.

The floor was mostly smooth terracotta tiles but filled in with cement where these had broken and come away. In the centre of the room was a drain hole partially plugged with gunk and hair, smelling like your drains do when they've been blocked for so long that your wife threatens to leave unless you call the plumber.

The naked man was using a black plastic bucket to slosh water over his head and body from taps attached to the concrete block. I looked around through the steam and saw a number of these buckets lying about so, following his example, I took one, set it down on another concrete block and felt each pipe to find the hot one; I filled my bucket and, hoping it wouldn't kill me, quickly poured the contents over my head as I had seen the hirsute man do.

It was so hot it took my breath away. Breathing in the liquid air like a fish drowning, I soaped myself all over. Then I filled the bucket again with hot water and sluiced myself again... and again... and again. It was a strangely erotic experience.

Knowing that if you're Swedish or Russian or from northern climes, you're supposed to leap into an ice-covered stream after being in a *banja*, I then filled my bucket from the cold tap and, taking a deep breath, poured it over my head.

Whooo! Is this rebirth?

I filled the bucket with hot water again and dumped it over my head.

Whooooo!

Then cold.

Whooooooo!

I could get to like this! My skin was beginning to pucker.

I glanced over at my hairy friend and he was scrubbing away at his skin with what looked like a strap full of nails. Well, plastic nails. Lying about the floor I saw several of these things but realising they were probably clogged with the dead skin of previous masochists, I decided I'd give that a miss.

At about that time I heard an ominous *Flap! Flap! Flap! Flap!* coming from another room. My immediate thought was that the sound, clearly involving naked flesh being beaten, had something to do with pain and sado masochism. I looked about the steamy room and saw yet another door set into the wall. Glancing about to make sure that no one was watching, I tip-toed to it. The *Flap! Flap! Flap!* was clearly coming from behind that very door. Tentatively, I opened it a crack and peeped in.

The heat hit me in the face like a bully. I reeled back, gasping. But I had caught a glimpse of a narrow cell of a room, about three metres by five, a naked man sitting on the top rung of five wooden tiers, alternately beating his back and his chest with a bunch of leafy twigs.

I shut the door quickly. Whether it was the heat or the naked man, I'm not sure - probably both. But if I was to experience the full joy of this *banja,* I knew I had to enter the Fourth Level, face it like a man. While I stood outside the door trying to pluck up courage, the flagellating man exited, leaving me alone.

Next to the door, I noticed some bunches of what looked like leafy oak twigs tied together with string. I picked one up, telling myself to man up... I can do this. I breathed deeply, screwed my courage to the sticking point, opened the door and stepped inside, closing it behind me.

The heat inside that dark, concrete cell was truly frightening. Determined to experience it fully, I made my way up the slippery wooden bleachers and sat down at the top. My head was close to the ceiling and I gasped, genuinely afraid that I might pass out. Claustrophobic bare concrete seemed to press in upon me, compounding the effect of the damp heat that threatened to drown me, stifle me, overwhelm my senses. I was being waterboarded without the use of a towel over my face.

But what was perhaps even more frightening (considering the exposed electric wires we had seen on the streets and in buildings throughout the 'Stans just waiting to kill anyone who ventured too close) was the loud buzzing sound coming from directly beneath the wet, wooden bleachers, emanating from some massive, primitive source of electricity being used to heat this awful place, so powerful that one would imagine the lights of Kyrgyzstan dimming and flickering when it was fired up. It felt like there was something alive hiding in the dark beneath me. And to think that everything was wet: my body, the floor, the wood, condensation dripping from the walls and ceiling whilst right there, in the room, underneath where I was sitting, was enough electricity to electrocute the entire world buzzing loudly to itself, waiting...

Frightened I might die in there, I gave myself some tentative blows across the back and chest with my *vihta* and then wimped out, making my way carefully down the wet, slippery bleachers and then out into Room 3, which felt positively cool by contrast. Gritting my teeth, I filled a bucket with cold water and quickly poured it over my head.

Whooooo!

I poured a few more buckets (this was becoming addictive) then pressed the buzzer to be released. We dressed and emerged like troglodytes into the sunshine, our flesh clean and tingling.

An alcohol-smelling, toothless woman latched onto us the moment we entered the outside foyer and dragged us off to a "cafe" situated just behind the *banja*. She led us through a door into a back yard filled with junk, piles of cardboard, broken children's toys, a dead car on concrete blocks and other waste. At a table, a woman was stuffing sheep's intestines with meat to make sausages; in a basin next to her, a sheep's stomach stank.

We thanked her politely but decided we would not patronise her establishment for our meal that night.

Excerpt taken from "The Wakhan Corridor - A Motorcycle Journey into Central Asia".

TWENTY
This is real

After crossing the border into Kyrgyzstan, Gareth looks up from his map and says, "There's a small pass over the mountains."

Anyone would have thought that, after our 2014 experience, he'd have learned his lesson. A "small pass over the mountains" indeed...

Shortly after Bishkek, we leave the main road and enter more rural areas, edging closer to the mountains. Twice we are warned that it will be cold up there, once when we buy petrol from a woman who has a stock kept in plastic bottles locked in a metal bin around the side of her shop and again when we buy sweet corn and bread to supplement our meagre emergency rations. They look puzzled that we intend to attempt the pass. I look at the vodka on the shelves and think briefly of purchasing a small bottle - just for the cultural experience, a barrier against the cold, medicinal purposes?

We ride on, into the mountains, the road narrowing and becoming a track. We haven't seen anyone for a while. Not even herdsmen, sitting on the backs of their patient horses, driving their sheep over the mountains to find new grass as the cold begins to set in, scrawny dogs ranging about, getting in the way. There are lots of hoof prints where the track is muddy. No car tracks, though. There hasn't been a vehicle up here for a while.

The setting is idyllic and we have it all to ourselves. In fact, we see no one at all between filling up with fuel and the occupants of a smoky yurt we come across in a narrow, sheltered valley the following morning.

I'm concerned about my rear shock. Empty of oil, my rear wheel tramps whenever I hit corrugations or rocks and I lose traction. On corners it sidesteps alarmingly. I wonder how it will cope in loose scree on a steep, rocky slope.

We begin the pass and it is beautiful. Fir trees cover the lower slopes and a clear stream meanders between grassy banks, softly coloured with flowers. We climb and the trees fall away, exposing rock. Although the mountain range ahead is covered with snow, there is little of the fear I felt the previous year. Perhaps the difference is in the lack of heat. Or maybe the condition and length of the road. At this height the air is cool, the track pleasant and meandering. The bikes are not being hammered. If the mountain defeats us, the return journey won't be so arduous. Maybe it was the knowledge last year that, if we didn't make it, we would be faced with a five-day detour; here it would only be a number of hours.

It's getting high and the pass gets steeper and more rocky. The winters here must be bitter. I look at the thick snow on the peaks ahead of us and feel sure that this will be a repetition of last year's failed attempt.

Then we reach the snow line. Occasional tongues of snow creep over the road but they are easy to cross. Once I miss a turn and find myself in deeper snow. I struggle to get out. My back wheel spins without traction. I know then that if the road higher up is covered, we will not make it.

As we climb, the track becomes more rocky and neglected; in places snow covers the entire surface but the tyres break through easily and find grip underneath. As we climb, the track becomes more neglected. In places, snow covers the entire surface and begins to build up on the edges, leaving a stony path only a foot or two wide.

I miss a turn and get stuck. Gareth rides on and up, leaving me. I manage to extricate myself and set off after him. Thank goodness for a light bike. Snow over loose shale, a steep slope and motorcycles don't mix well.

Then I am in front. I ride into mist. Or is it cloud? Everything seems insubstantial. The track, narrow now and rocky, takes a sharp left and disappears somewhere higher up the mountain. It's steep and covered with snow. Not thick, but enough to have you over.

Of course, there is no barrier. We are high up now but the slope on the down-hill side is not precipitous; if we go over the edge, with luck the bike might lie down and slide to a stop. Of course, if it begins to tumble...

Unlike the previous year, there is no turbulent river writhing and knotting itself down an almost vertical slope; just a clear, friendly stream; no clinging to the throttle with clawed hands here. I feel more relaxed, more confident. *We nearly made it*, I think to myself, knowing deep down that we wouldn't.

So close. Beaten by the mountains again, just like last year. Back then it was scree. But that pass was for livestock anyway, not vehicles. Now it is snow.

It isn't a serious problem. We can turn back, head for Bishkek and take the road to Osh normal people take. It had been a scenic diversion anyway. But I'm not sure I want to ride up that misty track ahead, rock-strewn and covered with snow; no barrier between me and the mist-dimmed slopes below and to my right. I don't relish the idea of sliding off the track and tumbling down this mountain.

I'll wait for my son, I decide, let him give it a go, get stuck half way up in the snow and the mist and the slippery, wet rocks, manhandle his bike around (I'll even give him a hand, ease his broken rib). He'll laugh and tell me it was fun giving it a go and we'll back track down the pass, back to the road, to people. I'll act as if I really wanted to tackle that slope - but discretion, you know...

I hear his bike puttering up the pass through the mist. I get the GoPro rolling. He takes the corner wide, missing a thickish drift of snow and keeping to the loose, raised rock on the edge. (Why didn't I think of that?) He then continues up the track, his momentum taking him across each drift of snow onto the next patch of rock, up and up, disappearing into the mist and around the next corner. He keeps going until I can't hear his engine any more.

Damn. Now I have to do it...

The mist and snow deadens sound. I can't hear his bike any more and I am alone with my uncertainties. I fire up the engine. Give it a go and see how far I get. I am sure I'll come across Gareth a short way past the bend in the mist ahead stuck hub-deep in snow or with his bike lying on its side somewhere. Hopefully he'll be OK.

I let the bike run back as far as I can to give me a decent run up, drop the clutch and kick it into second before I reach the snow. Momentum, that's the key. Just like in sand. The track narrows, cut in half by encroaching snow, pushing me ever closer to the edge. It's rocky but not too bad. Despite my blown rear shock, I am still getting traction. Then I hit the section entirely covered with snow. I can see Gareth's track passing through; it isn't too deep. All is going well with the sharp switchback to the right approaching. I expect to see the road ahead wiped out, but as I make the turn, the snow disappears; ahead of me is a stony track, steep but clear.

This section of the mountain is facing the sun, the section below in shadow. The snow has melted. Relieved, I press on. And then, deep in the mist, I see Gareth's bike parked. It's the summit. The last ten metres is deepish snow but the bike's momentum carries me to the brow and I switch off.

We've made it - just. Not "just" in terms of difficulty but in terms of snow. Had we attempted to cross just a few days later, we would not have made it: a snow storm completely blocked the pass.

After a brief pause to take photographs, we set off down the other side. Below the mist, a vista of mountains, lit by the late afternoon sun, spreads out in front of us. The road switchbacks its way down, at times snow-covered but never a problem. As the sun dips close to the mountain peaks above us, casting long, purple shadows into the valleys, we pull off the road onto a flat piece of land covered with finely-cropped grass and make camp. We are still above 3000ft and in the shadows the air is cold. We erect our tents alongside a rough stone kraal, ten metres across and deep in powdery dried dung. The rank smell of sheep is strong in the still air. Further back are two smaller rock-walled structures, like the makings of a Lesotho mountain hut for shepherds. Just metres away an icy, clear stream runs, filling the air with its noise. Tents up, we search about for firewood. The night will be cold. There is little wood, probably enough for twenty minutes, but dried sheep dung will help. A fire is always good; you can't camp without the companionship of a fire.

Gareth removes links from his chain which has stretched beyond reasonable adjustment. He tries to remove his spark plug but it is jammed in the head. He leaves it; good judgement because later, in Osh, when he tries to remove it, it breaks off in the head.

We are all alone with the rocks and the grass and the sound of the stream. Unlike in Africa, no little heads pop up from behind rocks, creep close and sit and stare. Above, a gibbous moon hangs from a clear sky. There is an icy chill in the air.

We light the fire and pull on all our clothes. Smoke wreathes about us and over us but we crouch close, accepting its warmth. Earlier, looking for fire wood, I had fallen into the stream. My trousers and socks are wet. I wring them out and arrange them on rocks around the fire to dry.

Shadows lengthen; the snow on the mountain peaks flares white and yellow and then the sun is gone. The world turns grey and a bone-deep cold enters the air. We crouch next to the fire, feeding it small pieces of wood and sheep dung, absorbing the last of its warmth. Perhaps I should have bought that vodka. Eventually the fire dies; even the stubs of sticks have burned away. My socks have almost dried. I pull them on damp and take a long walk in the twilight, putting off the inevitable moment of crawling into a cold tent.

The next morning is icy cold. We pack up quickly. There is no breakfast. Gareth's bike won't start but with a run downhill the engine takes. A short way down from where we spent the night we come across a yurt, smoke seeping through its roof and pooling about a small herd of horses steaming in the early morning sunlight. The air is clear as if it has been washed. Colours seem brighter. The road follows the stream and we come across more horses cropping long grass next to the water. It's like riding along a South African farm road or in the foothills of the Drakensberg Mountains. More yurts; even more horses. Large herds of sheep block the road, the air hazed with the rising dust of their hooves. Water is channelled from the river along small canals, flowing busily next to the road.

At last a village. We pull up at a small general store. They have sachets of coffee and a kettle. We point and smile, raising two fingers. On shelves, tinned food, vodka, electrical goods, clothes, hardware, make-up, shoes, ice creams, flour in 50kg sacks, plumbing. While we wait for our coffee, a man walks in and buys vodka.

On again, past fields of wheat being harvested by old tractors. On recently reaped fields, horses and cattle graze. From a distance they look like wildebeest on the Serengeti. Barns are piled high with hay. Bricks made from mud and straw dry in the sun.

We ride for hours through a high alpine valley, fertile and extensively cultivated. Mountains loom over the valley on both sides like some elemental barrier. We are sad to be leaving this place. It is remotely beautiful. We feel honoured in being allowed to pass through.

Yet another hour riding steadily and gently downwards, the road still small and almost unused, the landscape quaintly rural. We pass through a number of villages; then, while still in touch with the mountains at the top of a pass, we stop at a gypsy-type caravan on wheels to ask for coffee. The Kazakh woman with high cheek bones tells us she only has tea. She goes outside with a hammer and breaks lumps of coal from a single piece the size of a large dog, stowed under her caravan. We wait while the water heats in a samovar.

Inside, on the table, is a chipped enamel plate piled high with dried fish. We ask if we can have some. The woman places two fish on plates for us and dry bread in a yellow plastic bowl. We sit at a wooden trestle table covered with a plastic cloth decorated with bright red poppies and pull the flesh off the fish bones with our fingers and drink smoky tea from handle-less china cups. While we eat, she cleans yesterday's ash from a welded iron stove, chimney passing through the roof, three enamel kettles on a shelf to one side.

We ask for more tea. She smiles shyly and fetches the teapot.

This is the way it should be, I think to myself while licking the fish fat off my fingers, smelling the cold ash and yesterday's smoke. Not a meal prepared for tourists; just eating what ordinary people eat, where they eat, truck drivers and sheep herders and everyday passers by. This is the Kyrgyzstan we have travelled so many long, hard miles to experience; to taste and see and smell the essence of life here, just briefly as we pass through. And it's times like this that make it all worth while.

"This is *real* -" Gareth says as we get on the bikes again.

He can sense it too. The moment is palpable.

Originally published as "Never Give Up" in Overland Magazine, Issue 16.

An extract taken from "A Pass Too Far"

TWENTY ONE

Road of Bones

The Road of Bones runs for over two thousand kilometres through one of the most remote areas in the world, north eastern Siberia, connecting the cities of Magadan and Yakutsk. Every kilometre of the road was constructed by forced labour - at first by inmates of labour camps, but later by prisoners held in the gulags that were established throughout this region.

Many prisoners died during the long journey into the wilderness by train and ferry, and once set to work, thousands more died from overwork, exposure and starvation or were shot by guards for not working hard enough. The temperatures here are extreme: 40C in summer and minus 60C in winter - and prisoners laboured for 12-15 hours a day, surviving on a diet of little more than porridge and bread. Any worker who died was "buried" where he fell, to become part of the log foundation because, as the road is built on permafrost, digging new holes through the ice seemed impractical. Survivors' reports indicate that bodies were as common a sight as fallen logs. Because of the number of bodies buried just below the surface, the road is treated as a memorial to this day.*

"It's the biggest cemetery in the world," a woman who lives in one of the dying towns along the route of the road commented. "At least twenty five people died on that road every day and nobody knows who most of them were. Bones are always breaking through the surface."

I wake at 3... 4.30 and then again at 5.30, as if my brain is unconsciously counting down the hours. At six I get up and make a cup of tea then load up my bike while sharing a little more blood with the mosquitoes who have also decided to make an early start. I fire up the engine and, while it's warming, check the tyres - pressures still holding.

A short ride through the early-morning, rain-washed streets of Yakutsk to the bank of the Lena River. The old ferry is loading and I ride straight on but, like African taxis, we wait a frustrating hour for the ferry to fill. The sky is overcast but not threatening. Three gnarled truck drivers gather around the old DR, staring. Then come the usual questions: *"Otkuda?"*

"Anglia," I reply.

They shake their heads, absorbing this. *Where you going?* one asks in Russian.

"Magadan -"

They shake their heads again.

"Adgin?" holding up one finger and pointing to me.

"Da," I confirm, admitting that I am, indeed, travelling alone.

"Ochin delico." (It's very far.)

"Da," I agree. *"Ochin delico."*

At last I detect some movement from the crew manning the winch of the massive barge-like ferry that will take me across the wide Lena River to the beginning of the Kolyma Highway, the legendary Road of Bones. Then, with a loud clanking, the anchor is raised followed by the loading ramp. We pull away from the bank and swing into the stream as the current catches the battered steel hull.

At last I am on my way...

A raised causeway across flat swampy land - not the usual taiga where trees predominate and thousands of small ponds and lakes gentle an otherwise uniform landscape; here it is mostly water and reeds and mud and the dead, drowned bowls of trees. Mosquitoes cloud the air and descend upon you if you are unwise enough to pause, immediately attacking any exposed flesh.

Later mid-afternoon clouds turn threatening and dark, roiling against the skyline of trees and I know a bad one is heading my way. I stop to don my cheap waterproofs and then the rain hits me like a bucket of warm water poured over my head. Instantly, the road becomes a river, every depression a deep pond; both my feet are wrenched repeatedly off the pegs by the force of water flung back from my front wheel.

And then, just as suddenly, it is over. I ride on along a rain-wet track until a wide river blocks my path. Moored to the sandy bank, loading ramp down, is another metal barge, this one attached to a rusty paddle-wheel tug, its riveted plates dented and worn. No one is about. I ride up the ramp and park against the railings. I am the only vehicle here. I know the wait will be long when I see a crewmember emerge from a metal door carrying a fishing rod and a worm-tin full of wet earth.

Leaving the ferry, I explore the sandy bank, twelve foot high and deeply undercut. Under the dark sky and the endless presence of trees that I know continue uninterrupted for thousands of kilometres in every direction, the slow moving of water and the old paddle steamer waiting and still, I am transported elsewhere, to an older, unpeopled world separated by space and time from the one I am used to. I can understand why during Soviet times, this place was deemed so suitable for establishing penal work colonies. The extremities of space and climate make fences and walls redundant; you don't need them when there are thousands of miles of forest between you and freedom: mosquito-infested swamp in summer, frozen solid in winter - although, even in these remote places, prisoners were kept penned behind barbed wire with crude wooden guard towers constantly manned.

Darkness comes. The banks of the river merge with the trees. The mosquitoes have gone to sleep; a deep calmness settles over the land and the river surface turns to silk. At last the man who has been fishing pulls up his line, drags the chain across the ramp entrance and, with a clatter from the winch, the heavy metal ramp is raised. The ancient paddle-wheel tugboat nudges us into the flow and we set off up river. I stand on the stern watching the huge paddles churn up the water, the empty riverbanks sliding by on either side, and feel like Huckleberry Finn looking out on the wide, slow-flowing Mississippi long, long ago. The river is so deep that at times we pass just a stone's throw from the low, pebbly riverbanks and in the evening stillness arctic terns dip and weave just above the water, showing off.

* * * * *

There is a small rise in the road ahead of me and it is only as I crest it that I see the river. Of course I was riding too fast, I don't deny it. Perhaps it was because I just wanted to reach Ust'Nera before I started growing mould. It isn't a particularly big river but it is flowing strongly, has a stony bottom and I have no idea at all how deep it's going to be. I hit the brakes but, probably because they've been wet all day, nothing happens and in a moment I am calf-deep in a strong, icy flow amongst the rocks, and the engine dies.

Suddenly, except for the rushing of the water, all about me is silent. Mountains surround me, shrouded in mist and rain, and I feel very alone.

I give it a moment or two for the heat of the engine to dry the electrics and to allow me to gather my thoughts. I'm not in any real danger but I recognise I'm in a predicament where riding alone is not wise. I'm a very long way from anywhere, there've been no other vehicles on the road for a while now and I have no big son to leap off his bike, wade into the flow and steady the bike while I try to extricate myself. I tell myself that drowning the engine is simply not an option. Not out here. (Not anywhere, really.) Lifting a laden bike in the dry and on a firm surface is bad enough; lifting it, alone, when half under water and being resisted by a strong flow will be well nigh impossible. Well, it would be for me. Fast-flowing water is a scary thing and if I get my body trapped under the bike I could drown...

* * * * *

I wake to a strange light in the room. The sun is shining.

All is forgiven.

I pack up quickly, strap my panniers onto the bike while beating off mosquitoes and fire up the engine. The road shimmers ahead of me like hammered silver in the low sunlight reflecting off its wet surface.

For about an hour I ride in a state or relative bliss until, yet again, the sky closes down and rain begins to fall, intensifies to another deluge that lasts, without cessation, throughout the day. Once again I ride along mud-slick dirt roads, mostly in good condition; the rivers and streams are swollen now and deluge across the track, seeking lower ground, the clouds heavy and low, partially obscuring the mountains and trees all about me. For hours the road follows the meandering valley of the Indigirka River that boils and swirls below me, carrying with it tangled knots of trees that spin and cartwheel in the mud-yellow waters.

What strikes me about this 395km section of the Kolymer Highway between Ust'Nera and Susuman is its desolation; even more desolate than the first 1,000ks, if that's possible. Throughout the day there is nothing but the muddy road and swollen rivers under a leaden sky, and trees. Possibly there are some people living here; I have no doubt that they do. But I don't see any and the only man-made structures I ride past are wooden pylons carrying dipping cables into the mist, broken wooden bridges across swollen rivers, the occasional settlement - one quite large, almost a small town - but, in every case, as I look more closely, I become aware of broken windows, doors ajar like the open mouths of dead people, the wrecks of cars and the usual detritus left behind when a family or community is forced by circumstances to abandon their homes, their places of work, everything they used to call dear as if suddenly, one day, by mutual decision, every one just closed their doors and walked away.

* * * * *

In a brief hiatus in the rain, I come across yet another ghost village and leave my bike to explore. When planning this journey it was my feeling that the most obvious place to get mugged was when exploring the mouldering buildings of an abandoned community just like this but now that I am here, I feel quite safe, just sad. I am all alone, walking down a muddy street with small wooden houses on both sides, some of them looking as if the occupants have just stepped out to visit a friend and that, if I were to peep inside, I would feel a still-warm kettle on the stove and coals glowing in the hearth. But, other than the mosquitoes, there is no one here except for two large dogs that appear from somewhere, investigate me with intelligent eyes and, after a cursory bark, job done, they continue on their way to wherever.

And for the next twenty minutes I walk about this village, its streets waterlogged and overgrown with tall grass, weeds taking over the front gardens that used to be so carefully tended, broken toys, a single boot, an old crash helmet, worn car tyres, bottles and rusting cars standing outside the houses as if waiting for the occupants to return with their keys. Walls bulge and tar paper peels away from roofs in long strips. Vegetable patches in back yards are overgrown with weeds; a telegraph pole leans to one side, its wires hanging - there's no one here to speak over these wires any more. The wooden cottages usually rot first and some are already beginning to lean but some stand firm and whole except for broken windows.

I feel ill at ease walking through the sad memories of others' destroyed lives, like a voyeur or one who pauses to stare at a traffic accident, but I need to see this, to pay my respects, as it were, for this is the evidence of the dying of Russia's far-off rural communities.

And then there is a man. He has about him the creased look of a rough sleeper and he plods along the muddy road towards me following the out-thrust keel of his grizzled beard; he passes within a metre of me without any acknowledgement, as if he hasn't seen me. And then he is gone. It seems somehow right that the only life in this place are feral dogs and a man more at home within the disturbed workings of his own brain.

Then with the wind still gusting between these silent walls, the rain comes, not hard, but annoying - and I don my waterproofs and ride on through a wet and muted land.

* * * * *

On the high passes, snow lies thick on the ground; many of the rivers are ice-bound - and still the freezing rain falls. My little bike, never a friend to water, begins to hesitate and falter and, each time it happens, my gut clenches at the prospect of standing on the roadside in the freezing rain, hundreds of kilometres from anywhere, hoping one of the few trucks on the road might stop and help. But after each stutter, each heart-stopping hesitation, she picks up again and continues, unhappy but strong. I talk to her as one would an exhausted pony, even patting her, encouraging her as if she were struggling to keep going just for me, "Come on, little bike, just keep going, just another two hundred kilometres. You can do it..."

I must admit to a certain desperation creeping into my voice.

* * * * *

On the third day my rear tyre punctures and I sit flapping mosquitoes and miserable in the roadside mud and repair it, alone, my bike balanced precariously on a piece of plank. At last the spindle slides home and the job is done. I ride on through the pouring rain, reaching the outskirts of Magadan in the late evening, soaked to the skin and numb with cold.

* * * * *

It is the unknown that always engenders fear, the dark presence behind the bedroom door that threatens until the light is turned on. Once the dressing gown is revealed, the fear disappears.

So it has been for me with the Road of Bones. It was an unknown and I was fearful. But now that I've ridden it, albeit in atrocious conditions, it is no longer an unknown and the fear is gone.

Now for the return journey to Yakutsk: another two thousand kilometres of wilderness. It is early morning and I am confronted in the kitchen by a very hung-over young man, his head shaved clean as a spoon. He digs a hole in a raw egg and offers it to me to suck - "Give Russian strong!" he assures me. He wants to compare tattoos, flexes his biceps then adopts a boxer's stance before embracing me as drunken young men do.

And so, I set off with a light heart, confident that my little friend has the fortitude to keep going until the end; my tyres are good, the tubes new (with four spares) and I am ready for anything.

I ride at a sedate pace towards Ust-Umchug along a narrow dirt road with the encroaching trees that threatened me so earlier in this journey. I am enjoying the isolation, the silence, the sense of solitude as snow-patched mountains pass by and the road weaves its way towards the west. I am on my way home.

In the mountains I come across deep snow high above a long scree slope, pull off the track and switch off. The silence is crisp and pure as I strip off my riding gear because of the heat and begin to climb. Sharp rocks slide and tumble as I struggle upwards, clinking like metal being struck on metal, sharp in the still air. Reaching the snow, I sit in its cold softness and look out over the tree-covered mountains; I take a handful of snow and put it in my mouth...

Much later, tired and dusty, I reach the small town of Ust-Umchug in the heat of the mid-afternoon. As I ride through its dusty streets, I am reminded of one of those places where, after the world as we know it has come to some violent and apocalyptic end, angry, flat-eyed men range about looking for people to hurt just because they can. Its very name, the sound of it, *Ust-Umchug*, hints of violence and deviance. The battered *khrushchyovka* apartment blocks, ranged like battlements, are difficult to distinguish from the abandoned buildings on the lonely roads of the Kolyma.

I ask directions and follow a man through mouldering tenements along an atrocious road. *Sing-sing,* I think to myself, feeling as if I am entering that notorious prison where amoral men with tattoos smudged like bruises on their bony limbs commit atrocities on other men in the showers. Mothers push babies in prams along dirt streets; children play in a brightly-painted playground; a truck trundles past, spraying water to lay the dust; old women sit on crude benches outside their tenement doors, watching life pass by; from a hundred identical windows comes the mutter of radios.

Wait here, the man gestures.

A group of young men in their twenties begin to gather, stray-dog-looking men with shaven heads and bad teeth, wet lips and muscles on their arms like bicycle tyres, their trousers loose on their hips - the kind of men who make you wish you were somewhere else or, at the very least, had your back to a wall and only a little money in your wallet. They greet me, smiling their ragged smiles and gathering about, examining the bike.

"Vy Anglichanan?" one asks in Russian. *"Na Suzuki?"*

"Da -" I nod. They look at each other blankly as if I have told them I come from outer space.

Later, on the steps outside my apartment, four stories down, three old women wearing shapeless dresses lean towards each other and talk. Their voices float up to me like the chirrupings of birds. They have gold teeth and wear scarves tied about their heads.

Outside of town, the river runs shallow and dimpling and clear as ice. A woman lies on the stony bank in her bra and pants, exposing her pale fat to the evening sun. An old UAZ 4X4 on the other side engages low range, slithers down the gravel bank and drives deep across the river. An older man with red whiskers and no upper teeth approaches me; his open shirt reveals a livid scar from abdomen to his sternum. He seems to be asking for money and I demonstrate that I do not have my wallet with me but he negates this with his hands, asks me where I am from and when I tell him he clasps my hand and then hugs me to his bony chest in a tight embrace.

Three men in their early thirties sit on a river-washed log in front of a fire close to the water. Their voices tell me that they have been drinking. I approach them and we shake hands. One has rotten teeth and his grip crushes my hand. They are shirtless, their torsos lean as whippets. One, called Sergei, pale-skinned and unshaven, has a tattoo of a skull gripped in a fist on his arm and the Madonna and child across his stomach. They ask if I'm American and I tell them I'm British and they smile and exclaim. I sit with them on the smooth-skinned log, white-bleached from the sun; they offer me vodka in a crumpled plastic cup. I accept, stressing *malenkie* - small! They pour me a cup full and break off a piece of stale bread. We toast Russia and England and drink. They offer me more but I decline and they don't insist. Instead, they fill their own plastic cups and drink deeply, as one would water. It's going to be a drink-yourself-motherless night, I can see. I leave them to their drinking and walk on.

These are the young men who will die young; pencil tallies on a statistician's sheet; lads with vodka in their veins and tar in their lungs and eyes filled with an empty desperation that this throw-away place in the wilds of eastern Siberia will be unable to fill.

When I return to my apartment block, two young ladies, a little worse for the wear from alcohol, blow me kisses. In my room, there are dead things in the sugar and my bed feels as if there are a number of knot-headed dwarves living inside the mattress.

* * * * *

I had set my alarm for 3am so I could break the back of this 600km stretch to Khandaga before the heat could lay its heavy hand on us.

I awake with a start. The room is light, have I overslept? I look at my watch and it tells me *Ten*.

In the morning?

Then my brain begins to function and I realise that it's still night, still the day before, as it were, the same day as yesterday, or today. Whatever. I'd slept for three hours. But then, *What the hell*, I think to myself, I'm awake now, let's just *do* it.

I pack up quietly so as not to wake the other sleepers, load the bike while the mosquitoes are still resting, and set off into that strange half light of a northern summer where a book can be read outside at midnight without the need for light. Mist hides the bowls of trees on either side of the road so that only the dark froth of their leaves and upper branches are visible. The road is a pale narrow ribbon through the sepia light and I ride through a silent daguerreotype world. This is fortunate because my headlight has blown and all that is left to illuminate me, rather than the road (in case I meet a truck in the dark on a mountain bend), is the pale glimmer of my park light. The sky is pale and low under the horizon, holding still the last flush of the sun. The air is still warm, trapping within its molecules the intense heat of the day and the dry smell of dust from the road.

Occasionally I ride into cold pockets of air that taste of the night and the swamps and muddy ponds hidden between dark trunks of trees that glint silver in the twilight as I pass. I ride carefully, favouring my worn tyres, happy that the engine is being properly cooled; it really doesn't need the added burden of 37-degree heat as well as the multitude of other stresses I have thrust upon the poor little beast during this journey. But now she purrs sweetly in the eerie half dark and I begin to relax, revelling in the strange sensation of riding all night.

And it is beautiful! Mist gentles the landscape, rising like a veil above the ponds and swampy places on either side of the road, the rivers reflecting the bloody colours of the sky; there is a softness about the landscape lost during the heat of the day, when colour is leached from the air and things are harsh and blunt. In this light, even the dirt of the road, the very stones, seem softer, more welcoming.

It turns cold, suddenly, as if the last exhaling of warm breath from the day has lifted, begun its rising that will form the ballooning dark clouds of the next day and the afternoon rain. I begin to shiver but console myself with the thought that it's better me too cold than my engine too hot, and I hold my now zip-less jacket about me with my left hand to preserve some body heat and ride on.

* * * * *

Some time after 3am I begin to fall asleep. I wake to find myself, oddly, riding my bike somewhere along a dirt road amongst the rocks and mountains of a strange land. I tell myself that I have been sleeping, momentarily, in all probability - but asleep nonetheless. I shake my head and ride on. It happens again, this time as I approach a corner. I wake and find myself on the wrong side of the road, confused and disorientated. Stand on the pegs, raise my visor to let the cold air beat against my skin, sit and fall asleep again. Even in the act of forcing my eyes open, I feel the weight of the lids dragging down, and down, and with a jerk I wake again. I know I should stop, lie in the roadside dust with my jacket as a pillow and sleep, know that sleep-riding off a cliff or into the forest in this place is not to be contemplated. If I died here, deep off-road in the mountains amongst the shadows of trees, if I were to break a leg or my back, no one would ever find me. I would join the statistics of those who have disappeared without trace here in the Russian far east. But I don't. I stand up on the pegs, bash my hand against my helmet, slap my face *hard*, shout and sing - and keep on riding.

The drowsiness passes and I am still alive. But then the hallucinations begin. It's a strange experience. I see a rosy-cheeked woman leading a rosy-cheeked child on a reindeer. They are very real; they could have stepped out of a tourist brochure for Lapland. I tell myself that what I have just seen is impossible, that I am hallucinating, but then their dog chases after me and I'm not sure any more. Pale-barked logs on the roadside take on living forms, get up from their slumber and walk about, stare at me; I see animals moving amongst the trees and people who stand mutely and watch as I pass. They have about them a disturbing reality that flutters between wakefulness and dreams. And then, strangely, I find myself outside my body looking down at myself riding.

At about four in the morning the sun finally breaks free of the horizon; it is behind me so I catch only glimpses of it in my mirrors as it emerges from behind a mountain, an intense red ball, mist-occluded, radiating little light and no warmth, covering the world with rust.

I begin to count down the kilometres in hundreds: into the 5's, into the 4's, now the 3's...

The low sun begins to draw webs of mist off the surface of water, the lakes and ponds and wide, swift-flowing rivers, mist that hangs trapped in the branches of trees. Stones in the road cast long shadows and the sepia landscape begins to take on colour.

My rear tyre is wearing fast now, I can notice the difference each time I stop, a little less left on the knobblies, more bits ripped off the edges, star-shaped cuts where a rock has penetrated but not quite punctured the tube. But now I am into the tens, 90, 80, 70... All is well with the world. Nearly there. I'm going to make it. After this, just one more day, a short one at that, just 450ks and then the wide Lena River and Yakutsk and the train and Omsk and a hop, skip and jump to Europe. 60, 50... Nearly there.

By now both front fork seals have burst and a fine spray of oil covers everything, even smudging the glass of my instruments. My boots are bright with oil, my jeans yellow to the calf where dust has clung to the wet.

40, 30, 20... Oh, the relief! Bed, some food.

The engine dies.

Without warning, without hesitation or stumbling, it's gone. My speed quickly drops, a Doppler-effect of despair as I fumble with a petrol tap, flip it onto reserve in the vain hope that my fuel is low, waiting for the hiccough, the stutter as fuel runs through, but there's nothing. My wheels come to a stop on the side of the road, in the dust, amongst the stones and the trees, the silence pressing down on me, the heat beginning to rise from the road.

(A passing car tows me. After hours of frustrated searching, I find the fault: side-stand cut-off switch.)

Later the room begins to lie on its side and my knees give way. I brace myself against the wall, head hanging, and wait for the world to come back but my lady host has seen me and guides me back to my bed. I hear her on the phone and, shortly afterwards, a nurse with Mongolian features appears. She takes my pulse and makes questioning noises so I get my phone out and type on the translator: *I'm just tired. 3 hours sleep, rode bike 12 hours and no food since yesterday.*

She gives instructions; the Russian man sharing my room makes me sugary coffee and my lady host prepares *borscht* and fusses about me like a mother...

* * * * *

Last day. Trucks blunder their way past me, filling the air with swirling clouds of white dust so thick that all visibility except for a few metres in front of the wheel is obliterated. Slow down and you risk being killed by a truck coming from behind; in that obscuring cloud of dust, no driver would see you until he felt the crushing of your bones under his wheels.

It is two long hours before the road begins to improve and I ride in the heat through a land bleached of colour, an atmosphere paled by dust and the smoke from forest fires that plague the taiga each summer. By now I am filthy with a layer of dust covering my clothes, sand in my teeth and my eyes, oil from the blown forks spewing onto my jeans and boots which absorb a thick layer of sand only to be coated with oil again. The heat is enervating and by midday I can feel my body weakening...

...A ferry is about to disembark. I ride up the metal ramp, park my bike between two large 6WD Kamaz trucks, kill the engine and drag myself wearily off the bike. A group of men watch me. I approach them and ask, pointing across the river, "Yakutsk?" It's a stupid question but I don't want to make a mistake when so close to home.

"Da," they nod, taking in the state of me with their eyes.

It is done.

I strip off my gear and stand at the bow of the ferry, willing the water to rush by and wondering how many times over the past two weeks and 4,000kms I have thought about this moment, the time when I would have completed my solo, double crossing of the Road of Bones and am now safe, carried along peacefully by a battered, rust-covered ferry. I relax and watch the water move across her battered plates and feel in my bones the throb of her engines.

First published in Overland Magazine, Issue 26, under the title: "The Road".

Excerpt taken from "Two Fingers on the Jugular".

TWENTY TWO
True bikers

To most of us bikers who live in more affluent countries, setting out over the weekend to ride our iron steeds is little more than a fun activity, a fairground ride to break the tedium of daily existence. Our shiny and cosseted bikes are the grown-ups' toys we always wanted, the passport to a few stolen hours when we Easy Riders feel the wind in our hair and imagine ourselves unencumbered by the baggage of life that has begun to tie us down.

And before you remind me, yes, I know there are many who use their bikes daily to commute, but mostly this too is a lifestyle choice; we ride our bikes to work because we want to, because it's fun, not because we *have* to. It gives us a delightful sense of pleasure and - let's be honest here - superiority when we gently filter between those long, nose-to-tail, stagnant queues of stuffy cars that have trapped their frustrated drivers in the inevitable traffic jams of life.

But when we travel to some of the poorer countries of this world, those that are synonymous in the mind with dusty, pot-holed roads, stick-limbed children and the yellow, mangy dogs that range the edges of the streets looking for road-kill, motorbikes are seen as something quite different. In these countries, generally, if you want to get to work, you walk - or, if you've got a little cash to spare, you catch an overloaded bus held together with rust and bailing wire. If you're *really* wealthy, you own a donkey, the poor man's pick-up truck, often loaded until its knees buckle and kept moving with the cruel encouragement of a stick.

Or you own a motorbike.

Now I'm not talking BMW 1200s here. To buy one of those would take the entire salary of an extended family a few lifetimes to accumulate. Instead, think of something with two wheels and a small engine. Boots, helmet, protective clothing? I don't think so. Flip-flops and shorts and, for the well-heeled, a Barbie-and-Ken plastic hat-thing balanced on the head. And if it rains, you can buy a plastic poncho in pink or blue, made in China, for under £1.00. Rolled up, it fits into the palm of your hand.

Recently, I spent a month travelling through some of the more remote parts of Vietnam, a country with, well, just a *few* scooters. Ho Chi Minh City, so they say, has eight million citizens but manages to squash 8.5 million motorbikes onto its already congested roads. In fact, roads are so cluttered with motorbikes that some enterprising soul has decided to make a virtue of necessity and sell t-shirts to tourists adorned with pictures of the scooter-chaos on city intersections.

But it's not really the HCMC/Hanoi scooter commuters I want to write about here, those nifty, noisy little things ridden by *everyone* to get from a to b, the 50cc screamers that clog the roads and pavements and hotel foyers and cafe entrances so tightly that if you dropped your bike it wouldn't fall over because of the press of other bikes on either side; where personal road space is measured in millimetres; where the predominant rule of the road is: There are no rules; where everyone understands that, in Vietnam, size really does matter so that whoever is largest will always dictate the terms of engagement. It's a madhouse out there, a Darwinian nightmare where the small is devoured by the large. On a bike, when you hear the strident blaring of a horn you know a large truck is about to run over your back wheel and you get off the road sharpish.

That's the way it is there. Get used to it or die.

A few days' riding those roads made me understand why Vietnam is regarded as the second most dangerous place on earth for motorcycles - just after India - with approximately 40 traffic fatalities a day. Perhaps it's understandable then, that, near the end of my trip I found myself in hospital with a crushed foot inside a bloody boot with a large hole in it. But that's another story.

Doing a little research before I flew out to Vietnam, I came across this:

PRACTICAL ROAD USERS' ADVICE FOR VISITORS TO VIETNAM

- On the road there are no rules, so make sure you ignore any traffic rules you know. This should help to achieve a fine balance between two-wheeled fun, beautiful landscapes and complete and utter chaos.

- Remember that larger vehicles have the right of way.

- Traffic is like a river - flow with it. Riders will find a way to move forward.

- If you kill a dog or a chicken, don't stop, cry or feel sorry. It's not your fault. Slow down when you spot these animals and don't hit water buffalo, cows, pigs or horses - simply they are too big.

- If the police stop you, just keep talking in any language you know (but not Vietnamese or English) or whatever you want and they'll soon let you go in less than five minutes.

But this is supposed to be an article about third-world bike riders, not the chaos of Vietnamese roads, I hear you say. I'm coming to that.

Traffic aside, the land is beautiful, its remoteness away from the tourist centres enticing. Here there are more animals than people: water buffalo make their ponderous way along the hard shoulder, the grey fluff on their fat stomachs looking soft as a cat's, heads strangely tilted back so that their horns lie flat against their shoulders; pot-bellied pigs snuffle about, so cute I'd like to take one home as a pet; ducks and fowls scratch and forage near any homestead. It's a land seemingly lost in time. I pass wooden-wheeled, medieval-looking carts weighed down with bamboo as thick as my arm, laboriously pulled by water buffalo, the Montagnard owners sitting on the load and allowing the beast to make its own way. Roadside stalls selling sugar cane cut into precise lengths by old women, their faces shaded by traditional conical hats. Deep in the surrounding bush, stilted houses nestle, their wide verandas and open-plan interiors speaking of communal living and restful afternoons lying in strung hammocks. On cleared fields, engine-driven cultivators break up the soil ready for planting and between steep-sided valleys, conical hills meld and smudge into the distance, bush-green and verdant, like mammalian clouds facing the sky.

Even after just one day of riding, I begin to accommodate to the rules - or non-rules - of motorcycle riding in Vietnam. No quick, sudden movements; ride with gentle assertiveness. Anything goes. Plastic tape marking off road works? If you're on a bike, just lift it and make your way through. Miss an exit ramp on a motorway? Just turn and retrace your route using the hard shoulder. Toll booths? There's a special lane, just narrow enough for a bike, that allows you through. No fee.

I see a young woman on a scooter negotiating traffic whilst cradling an infant against her breast, steering with one hand; a middle-aged woman rides, talking into her mobile phone, a toddler standing in the foot-well, holding onto the handlebars with both hands. Riding in shorts and flip-flops is the norm.

On the road, trucks and the inevitable clutter of scooters mill about in seemingly random directions. Scooters carrying impossible loads - a wheel-barrow, handles leaning against the rider's back; a large wooden wardrobe; a pink pig, trussed up in a metal cage like a sausage, piggy snout protruding from a metal ring at the end of the cage as if sniffing the air; multiple smaller pigs, layered like fish in a tin, trotters and snouts and tails and tits hanging through the bars; windows and large panes of glass held in the bare hands of pillion passengers; kitchen cupboards; a full-sized fridge...

I come across scooters rigged out as shops: If the customer won't come to you, you must go to the customer - on a scooter, piled high and wide with displayed produce: pots and pans, vegetables, meat, balloons, plastic goods, cool drinks and crisps. Live fish carried in waterproof canvas tanks, gasping and thrashing in six inches of water while a small mounted pump, taking its power from the scooter battery, blows bubbles into the water. As I watch, a scooter carrying another scooter, balanced at right angles, sails nonchalantly past, the rider holding it in place with one arm draped carelessly across the seat while he controls his bike with the other hand. Cages full of ducks and chickens, eyes closed, loosened feathers dancing in the wind. Scooters carrying hundreds of kilograms of scrap iron, recycled tins and plastic bottles, logs...

Here, the motorbike/scooter is not a toy, it's a necessity; riding a bike for most of the population in Vietnam has been woven into the very tapestry of life. I wouldn't be surprised if some children hadn't been *born* on a motorbike.

I pass a man on his scooter, a true entrepreneur, who has fitted a wood-burning stove onto the back, spare stock of wood to keep the fire going, large pot bubbling away over the fire, ingredients and stuff packed into a cabinet fitted to the other side and a loudspeaker connected to the bike's battery advertising his wares. He rides along in front of me, smoke billowing out the back of the bike from the fire, steam seeping from beneath the lid of the pot, loudspeaker blaring. I'm not sure Health and Safety plays a significant part in the lives of people over here.

Now, bear in mind that these are not the un-killable Ural + sidecar, the Soviet poor-man's ute/bakkie/pick-up truck seen on the back roads of Russia and the 'Stans; these are scrappy little things, the buzz-bikes we used to scream about on the roads when we were kids. It is these plastic toys-with-engines that have become the work-horses of the rural poor and which fascinated me during my time in Vietnam.

And now, finally, I come to the point of my article, how so often we in the more opulent West treat our over-priced, over-polished bikes like the expensive toys they most often are, while hidden away somewhere in places that most of the world has forgotten, struggling their way across pot-holed tracks, a back-drop of snow-capped mountains or the sun-baked Sahel, small, hardy men with thin arms and skin burned to leather by the elements, pilot their cheap, iron steeds, fighting the roads and the weather and the geography of their world in an attempt to make a living.

And it was some of these men that I met on a remote dirt road in the mountains of Central Vietnam near the border with Cambodia that made me realise just what posers most of us modern bike riders are, adorning our bikes with all the bells and whistles in a vain attempt to attract an admiring glance.

It happened like this:

I had been attempting to find a more remote section of the Ho Chi Minh Trail close to the border with Cambodia but was struggling. Wide rivers barred my way; then it was a downed bridge that, if I understood correctly, had been destroyed during the Vietnam War. In a small, dusty village a polite policeman turned me back and, later, down yet another small track, a soldier at an army checkpoint stopped me: I had strayed into a restricted Border Area.

Eventually, I discovered another track heading east and decided to give it a go. Immediately it was clear that this was something different. The broken tar soon gave way to a dirt track deep red in colour, covered with a layer of bull dust that at times must have been all of six inches deep. Soon the bike, my clothes and luggage were stained red with a fine layer of dust that gathered in the corners of my mouth and eyes and clung to the sweat of my skin. The further east I rode, the more the road deteriorated - rocks, steep dips and gullies, hard-shouldered tracks worn through the surface that threatened to have me over. The going was slow.

But at last, as I left humanity behind, the litter thinned and disappeared. It was as if the land had wiped its hands clean of the smudge of humanity and suddenly it was beautiful again: a stark, remote beauty, hot and dusty, a land of trees and rocks and ragged shrubs that mute themselves into the smoky haze of the horizon, the cloudless sky above wide and white with heat. I began to enjoy the challenge of the road again, the feel of the tyres slewing and undulating through soft sand. I stopped and removed my helmet and gloves, strapped them on top of my luggage and allowed the hot wind to touch my skin.

Small Montagnard settlements began to appear, the stilted houses no longer quaint and picturesque, surrounded by the deep green of bamboo and banana trees; here they were ragged, covered like everything else with a fur of red dust. Men lounged in the shade, their clothes worn, faces and limbs gaunt as if just keeping alive in this place was a struggle. Each ragged settlement seemed to be engaged in slashing and burning so that the air was acrid with smoke. In places I rode through a scrubby landscape that was still on fire and I felt the heat of the flames against my skin. The earth was grey with ash and stumps continued to smoulder long after the fire had passed. I didn't see any ploughed fields, though, just a burned-out land.

Logging continues in this place, harvesting what is left of the big trees that once covered this ground with a soft, wet canopy, a concealing camouflage of foliage, now destroyed. It's not large-scale logging, rich multi-nationals with expensive machinery, bulldozers with linked chains ripping up the land. This was more low tec but, in the end, just as devastating.

Pausing to strip off some riding gear before my flesh melted in the heat, I noticed something strange making its way towards me along the dusty track. Its motion was slow and rolling, like a small boat on an undulating sea. I switched off the engine, watching. The thing approached with a ponderous heaviness, another behind it and, even further back, yet another.

When the first was close enough, I realised that each of these things was a small motorbike, pressed-steel body, 50cc engine; strapped across the puny frame at right angles were two heavy poles, 6-9 inches in diameter to create a carrying frame. Strapped onto these were four massive split logs, seven or so metres in length, two on either side of the seat. The rider would have to step *inside* the two sets of logs in order to control the bike.

How these small motorcycles do not collapse immediately under a load so preposterous I have no idea. The weight and length of the logs protruding metres in front of and behind the wheels made for the wallowing motion over the rough track that I had noticed. How small men, wiry though they are, can keep the bikes up, how they manage to escape having their legs crushed by the logs if - and when, surely - they fall...

Perhaps they don't; perhaps the bikes do fall apart, the logs do crush their legs in a fall but no one cares.

I watched until they disappeared into the trailing cloud of red dust they left behind then rode on, filled with a deep admiration for these men and what they are able to achieve with so little, for their resilience and skill.

A short while later I came across a small settlement where four of these laden machines were parked on the side of the road, their dusty riders resting under the shade of a Montagnard stilted home drinking coffee. I stopped, dismounted and checked out the bikes. I needed to know how toy motorcycles manufactured for teenagers are able to carry such heavy loads without breaking apart, being crushed.

On closer inspection I could see that double rear shock absorber mounts had been welded onto the frames, which had been further strengthened with pieces of flat bar and reinforcing rod roughly welded across the stress points, but the basic pressed steel frame, like the exoskeleton of a beetle, was unchanged. Any engineer would condemn them immediately as inherently unsafe, would predict metal fatigue, cracking and frame collapse. A Health and Safety officer would take photographs, impound the bikes and start taking names.

And yet the little bikes were nodding their awkward, lumbering way along that execrable track day after day, delivering massive, hand-split logs to the highway where they could be picked up by large trucks and taken to wherever. And these stick-limbed Vietnamese men, gaunt and smiling, rode them like un-funny circus performers desperate to make a living.

Seeing me scrutinising the bikes, four men left their coffee and the shade of the veranda and approached me. They were hardy, rough-looking men yet the welcome in their smiles removed any momentary concern I might have had for my safety. We had no shared language at all, not even a word, so I pointed to the welded struts holding the frames together, the dilapidated state of them, to the massive logs strapped onto their bikes and laughed, throwing my hands into the air and shaking my head in mute disbelief. They laughed too, understanding. They invited me to have coffee with them but the sun was low on the horizon and, sadly, I needed to press on.

Much later, tired and dirty, I reached Ea Sup, a small town in the middle of nowhere; time to look for a cold one, I decided, and, perhaps, something to eat that wasn't rice noodles.

And later, sitting on a small plastic chair on the pavement, beer in hand, I realised that my journey - and others before this - had been all the richer for those rough, beaten-up tracks: the heat, the bull dust and the brief encounter with a small group of hardy men who, although riding small-engined machines, are *true* bikers in every sense of the word.

Excerpt taken from: "By Motorcycle through Vietnam - Reflections on a Gracious People".

TWENTY THREE
Ford Fiesta Desert Crossing

"Do not be misled by distances on the map. Your mobiles will die today. Refuel at a brown petrol station on the right of the road to the border. There is a track to the Mauritanian border which takes ages, largely as they are not used to this kind of traffic. You will have to buy Mori insurance, have your passport inspected and people without visas are buggered. Your car will be inspected and maybe after 3 or 4 hours you are free to go. Beware of land mines that are unmarked and can kill. Do take a guide. I did not and had to U turn, having got lost. Sadly there are few good guides. Nothing you can do about this but explain that you want the 2WD route, not the 4WD route. Your guide will take you on the piste to Nouadhibou; expect a little soft sand. Please help each other. Most cars will get stuck here,

it's guaranteed! Crossing the iron ore rail line is an experience as there is no formal crossing point. Your guide will take you to a campsite in town.

ABOUT SAND

This will probably be your first experience of desert driving. When you get stuck (and you will) you will need a piece of wood for your car jack. Best to let your tyres down. Drive too slow and you get stuck, too fast and you do unspeakable things to your suspension and exhaust. Just remember not to ride your clutch but do rev the nuts off the engine as you need power to get through soft sand. Keep the steering pointed straight ahead in loose sand, more than a touch of steering input and the tyres act like dozer blades and you come to a stop. Guides will deflate your tyres to below 10psi/0.7 bar; they do it by eye so be careful not to roll a tyre off the rim."

(From the Plymouth-Dakar/Banjul Old Bangers' Challenge Roadbook):

Our last day in Morocco. The slower vehicles - like the fire engine (they had decided not to join our group after all), - had left the previous night to give them a head start on the 350km drive to the Mauritanian border. Others began leaving at about 6.30 in the dark; tucked up in the warmth of my sleeping bag, I could hear the engines start and the muffled sound of voices as the cars were carefully packed for the desert crossing. It was all I could do to keep from leaping up and waking Charlie! I forced myself to wait another half hour then got up in the bitter cold and made coffee. Because we were reasonably fast, we finally got away by 7.45, aiming to catch the rest of our group on the road.

We pressed on, covering the 320kms to the Mauritanian border without any problems, driving steadily across mile after mile of desolation, the wind howling (as it has done now for the past three days) sand being blown across the road so that at times it is completely hidden as if under a swirling mist. Even the sky has turned white with dust and sand. What this place must be like in mid summer does not bear thinking about. I have travelled quite a bit in Africa and yet I have never been in a place so desolate, so far from anywhere, so empty of anything - people, animals, birds, vegetation or water. If we were not travelling as part of a group, this place would be very scary; I would hate to travel it alone.

We finally reached and passed through the Moroccan border before midday - and immediately the tar road ceased to be. There was a rawness to the land very different to what we had experienced in Morocco. The track heading towards Mauritania, through an extensive minefield that no one had bothered to map properly, was rocky and potholed with sneaky stretches of soft sand and soon the unwary and inexperienced began to get stuck. We came to a three-way fork and Mark, who was leading and who had done this route a few years before, insisted we take the right fork. Bad move! We struggled along for about 7kms at just over walking pace, scraping over rocks and carefully choosing the best track, stopping and standing on the car bonnets to try to see something - anything - that would indicate we were on the right track.

Then, ahead of us, the road suddenly stopped. It had been deliberately blocked by a 7ft high wall of bulldozed earth which stretched away on both sides of the road for about 30 metres. There was no way round because of very soft sand. By now we were sixteen vehicles all lined one behind the other, blocked by this massive sand barrier. We emerged from our cars, stiff and tired, eyes slitted against the blown sand and the harsh white glare of the sun. Much agitated consultation took place. Mark was adamant that this was the right track; some wanted to turn back; others suggested digging partly through the barrier and making a ramp, using all our combined sand mats and ladders and manpower to manoeuvre the vehicles over.

And, laughing and running about like children let loose on a new and exciting playground, this we did! With great spirit and camaraderie, spades and sand mats were dragged from under our piles of equipment, stores, spares, water and fuel, unbolted from roof racks, distributed and laid out on the sand. Everyone who could get hold of a spade started digging. We were desert adventurers! Nothing could stop us, least of all huge barriers of sand deliberately pushed across our road to spoil our fun. In thirty minutes we had dug about half way through the barrier and redistributed the sand into ramps on both sides. Then, one by one, we drove, ramped, stuck, pushed, tried again, pulled with the 4X4 until all cars were through. We then all waited while the Trabant's exhaust system, which had been ripped off, was repaired.

However, just as we were finishing the job, over the horizon appeared a number of soldiers, shouting, waving their hands and running towards us. Quick debate: Should we make a run for it? Bluff it out? Offer a bribe? Saner minds prevailed and we waited, more than a little fearful, for the arrival of a rather annoyed group of soldiers. They strode up to us and, with much gesturing, bad French and sign language, they managed to inform us that the border between Morocco and Mauritania had been moved a number of months before. We should have taken one of the other tracks from the three-way fork we had passed about 7kms back, and this abandoned road had been blocked by bull-dozing the wall of sand across it. We had, therefore, entered (*accidentally strayed into*, we would have said) Mauritania illegally.

Fortunately, they were understanding and let us go. Happy smiles all round, the soldiers included. We had no option but to turn round, ramp, pull, push, drag the vehicles over the wall of sand again, bounce and bump our way back to the fork. Then, for a frustrating hour we milled about this featureless, rocky plain, not really knowing where we were going (and all of this in a mine field - although we scrupulously stayed on the tracks at all times). And all about us the wind howled, filling every exposed orifice with sand. Then, finally, as evening was settling over the desert, we reached the Mauritanian border - five hours after leaving Morocco.

DESERT DAY 1

Your guide should arrive at about 7.30am (God - this sounds like the Thompson's rep!) and you leave town the way you came in - parallel to the iron ore railway. The going is firm but sandier than Kempton Park. After lunch you may make Desert Camp 1 next to a tall dune. There is a hut and a shagged Merc, with no plates. The locals may kill a goat for you but the flies are epic. You can stay the afternoon here waiting for stragglers and it's a good night stop."

(From the Plymouth-Dakar/Banjul Old Bangers' Challenge Roadbook):

And so, into the desert. It is difficult to find words to describe the sheer joy of our first spell of desert driving. Again and again throughout the day both Charlie and I exclaimed to each other with a delirious sense of wonder - *we are in the Sahara! We are crossing the desert!* Hour after hour of nothing but sand and rocks, mostly trackless, for about 200kms without seeing a person, a goat, a camel - anything!

This is what we had come for; this is what we had dreamt about for so many months.

Our guide, a wizened old man whose skin seemed to have been toasted to the consistency of biltong from years of desert living was waiting patiently next to the cars when we crawled out of our tents in the semi dark of a cold, still morning. He carried all his belongings - clothes, bedding, cooking utensils, food - for the three-day crossing in a small plastic bag which he stowed on the back seat of Mark's car. He climbed into the front passenger seat and waited wordlessly, filling the car with a musty, earthy, smoky odour. He spoke no English at all. Anything that needed to be communicated was done by sign language. Throughout the desert crossing he sat crouched in the front seat, leaning forward and peering into the middle-distance with studied concentration, directing us this way or that with small flicks of his bony hand.

The morning started inauspiciously with two cars getting stuck in the soft sand of the camp site, one car not starting because sand had got into his distributor and worn the cam flat, effectively closing his points. Then another car discovered a leak in its petrol tank. With much running about, borrowing of tools and spares and a number of bodged repairs, we eventually got everyone ship-shape and ready to go. We had all filled our tanks the day before and bought bread and supplies for the next three days so, once the guides had arrived, the cars, in small groups of five, set off.

With our guide squashed into the front seat of Marc's car, we headed out on a newly-constructed road towards Nouakchott. After a frustrating hour, we finally turned off into the desert proper, following a rough track whose surface alternated between very stony and very soft. Almost immediately cars began getting stuck as drivers encountered really soft sand for the first time. Without saying a word, the old man got out, crouched next to a tyre and began letting the air out. He judged the pressures by eye, noting the bulge at the base of the tyre. I worked with him on the other cars and, when he was satisfied, he climbed back into the car and we set off again, the cars rolling with a strange motion as if the ground was moving beneath us as the soft tyres flexed and spread over the yielding sand. Now, with ten of us in our 5-car group, many willing hands and the tyres let down to about 0.7 bar, we were always able to extricate ourselves.

Then, finally, there were no tracks at all. We found ourselves driving across the desert proper, five little old cars, in one of the most remote places in Africa. The Western Sahara! The Sahara desert! The surface was infinitely changing, stony, rocky, pebbly, soft fine sand, long stretches of black nuggets of iron ore covering the ground, the occasional acacia tree, stark and thorny, clinging to life, tufts of dry, yellow grass, each with its own little sand dune trailing off behind. These were dreadful to drive through because each was about the height of a brick and, when hit by a wheel at anything above a brisk walking pace, felt like driving over a pavement at speed. At first we shuddered and grimaced at each other each time we were careless enough to hit one, feeling as if we had ripped the little Fiesta's suspension apart, checking in the rear-view mirror for bits of car left behind in the desert, but after an hour or so we became quite nonchalant about it and the poor little car pounded its way along at a jolly pace. How its suspension survived and wasn't ripped out I just don't know. At one stage, though, we noticed that Mark's car was no longer behind us so, after waiting a long time in the stillness of the empty desert for them to catch up or find us, one of the cars drove back, following our tracks, to look for them. It turned out that their car had broken an engine mounting which, with ingenuity and Mark's "happy box" - his collection of miscellaneous spares, bits and pieces to cope with any eventuality - they managed to strap up. Fortunately, although broken, the engine still rested on a cup-shaped depression in the mounting. We slowed down somewhat after that.

While we were waiting, I walked away from the car into the desert towards a low range of rocky hills alongside of which we had been driving. It was so beautiful, austere, pure and clean, just nature in all her harsh beauty - a very special time of quiet contemplation.

At other times the desert surface was smooth and firm and we made our own tracks, sometimes driving at 80 kph in line abreast across the featureless, endless desert plain. It was then that we were most happy, sliding the back wheels a little, making doughnuts in the sand, passing cameras from car to car while driving, racing each other, cutting each other off like teenagers trying to impress their mates, sitting outside the doors and hanging onto the roof, ramping up the sides of small dunes. A glorious, delicious time!

We were supposed to be driving not more than about 80ks into the desert on this first day and then, hopefully, meeting up with other groups to camp the night alongside a large dune. But our guide decided on his own to take us where *he* wanted to go and, after about 280ks we realised there was a problem. It was getting late and the old man suggested leading us to the beach and camping there. We were not particularly happy but what could we do? I think he then got completely lost because we drove about in a random fashion, this way and that about the desert, up and down dunes and dry water-courses for another hour, getting stuck when we stumbled into patches of very soft sand and having to push each car out until it reached more firm ground and generally going round in circles.

Finally, as it was starting to get dark, he led us to the base of a beautifully shaped barchan dune about 25 ft high and indicated that we would be camping there. One of the lads had a GPS and discovered we were still 15kms from the coast and a very long way away from Nouakchott (only about one third of the way, in fact. It seemed that our guide had become just a little lost) but if it had allowed us to spend more of the day driving through the desert, who were we to complain?

The campsite was absolutely delightful, pure and untouched. George, usually so introverted and serious, rushed up to the top of the dune and leaped and rolled down like a little boy! We got our sand mats out and tried to sand-surf but they dug in and flung us off, rolling and flailing down the steep dune sides. Then, calming, we put up our tents and made a fire with very dry wood we had collected throughout the day. I decided to sleep under the stars.

Later that evening, after the sun had set over the stillness of the all-surrounding desert, the wind - which had been blowing for the past 5 days - finally died and the ten of us, nine men and a woman, sat around a warm crackling fire and chatted about the day, nibbling olives and sipping whiskey from a bottle passed round the group; above us the sky was black and clear showing millions upon millions of stars so close you felt you could reach out and touch them. Across the flat vastness of the desert I could just make out our old guide, a darker smudge against the dark night, crouched in front of his fire, as still and timeless as the desert itself.

DESERT DAY 2

"This is a hard, hard day with lots of pushing and digging; some will wish they'd never left the UK. There is soft sand and the guide will be in the lead car, route-finding. Cars may die and be abandoned. If so, don't worry about the car having been written in your passport as the guide will handle this in Nouakchott (hopefully!). Cars will die from smashed radiators, stuffed clutches and blown cambelts. The softest sand is near the coast but when you reach the coast the worst is over. From this point, tides permitting, it is possible to take the beach to Nouamghar. It is a bit further and there are fishing camps along the way where you can get fresh fish. Your guide may want to cut across the peninsular but the beach is oh so much easier for 2WD. If things work well you will drive on down the coast, pass a dead bus in the water and then camp above the high tide line. Tides govern when you can drive down the coast..."

(From the Plymouth-Dakar/Banjul Old Bangers' Challenge Roadbook):

My decision to sleep under the stars was, in retrospect, unwise. Soon after bedding down, the wind picked up again and, no matter how I tried to cover up, sand blew into my face and hair. The constantly moving grains rattled on my groundsheet like thousands of little insects crawling all over me. And it soon became freezing cold so any thought of getting up and attempting to erect my tent in the dark was quickly dismissed. I did eventually get to sleep, though, and woke just before dawn. The night was perfectly still, the moon very bright, casting an other-worldly, pale silver sheen over the desert. I could have been looking out on another planet. The sky to the east was just beginning to lighten so, feeling rather cold and uncomfortable, I got up and made myself a cup of tea. Seeing I was already up and dawn was clearly imminent, I decided to walk out into the desert before any of the others woke - just to experience and savour this amazing landscape all on my own without the distraction of any one else around. I set off over the sand dune that was sheltering our camp site and made my way towards the rose-tinted sky where the sun would rise. Just over the dune I noticed a number of tiny tracks in the sand, obviously made during the night: birds, beetles and, most exciting, the paw prints of a four-legged animal about the size of a dog, probably a desert fox. Amazing how, even in this featureless and apparently waterless desert, life is abundant.

The desert landscape in the pre-dawn dark was beautiful, deathly still and completely silent as if the whole world was holding its breath. I walked on for about two miles, crossing another two long dunes and a high ridge of rock. Every few hundred metres I looked back to maintain my orientation and made sure my footprints were always clear in the sand. Each time I reached the top of a dune or ridge, there was another just ahead luring me on and which I just *had* to explore. Then, finally, the sun rose and I sat on the knife-edge of a dune crest and watched it, feeling the earth roll under me and tip. The strange silver tint which had covered the land leached away, the sky took on colour and long shadows appeared on the ground.

Realising that the others might have started to rise and begin to worry about where I had got to, I reluctantly stood and began to head back to our camp site hidden still in the lee of the large dune, carefully following my trail over the undulating sand. When I finally crested our dune, I could see down below a few of our group had risen and were beginning to break camp...

Our second day in the desert was a delightful repetition of the first. We left late after necessary vehicle maintenance and then drove on through the desert for about another 100kms. At one stage the old man stopped and let our tyres down even more because the land between the desert proper and the coast is made up of very soft sand and some quite high soft ridges. At times the tracks we were following were so soft and impassable that we branched off and headed through low scrubby underbrush, which had appeared as we neared the coast. The small bushes provided some traction for the tyres and this, with speed and momentum, kept the cars moving forward. We had to drive as fast as the terrain and soft sand permitted because, if any car bogged down, we all had to stop and it took at least six of us pushing and shoving to get the bogged car moving again. Although we were all becoming more confident driving in soft sand, cars were regularly getting stuck and progress was slow.

Finally, at about 1 pm, we reached the coast. The tide was fairly low exposing a firm, wide beach so we set off driving just above the water line. The wet sand just after a wave had broken and sucked back was most firm and we flew along, soon becoming more confident and spraying through the waves as they swirled up the beach. As the day progressed we became more daring, sometimes driving through the water which sprayed right over the cars. People hung out of windows, sat on bonnets, clung to roof racks, skimmed their feet in the breaking waves as we flew along.

Finally, just after four in the afternoon, we lugged our way up the soft sand above the high tide line and made camp. During the afternoon other groups straggled in until about 20 cars had battled their way up a very soft bank of sand above the high-tide line. Some of us stripped off and had a welcome though icy bath in the sea while Mark and George headed back along the beach to a fishing village we had passed about twenty minutes before, returning just before dark with ten fresh sea salmon and a Dorado which we gutted and char-grilled over a driftwood fire. The dusty bottle of whiskey miraculously appeared again, a bottle of red wine was dug from the depths of some car, I contributed a pot full of new potatoes, someone else donated a plate of couscous, another some tomatoes and onions, someone else chapatis and we all sat around the fire, peeling back the charred skin of the fish and eating the delicious white flesh with our fingers, with baked potatoes and tomato and onion chapatis on the side. A very special moment which I will never forget: A wonderful still evening, the dying embers of a fire, good food and a very close and companionable group of diverse people, united around a common goal of adventure travel.

Excerpt taken from "The Plymouth-Dakar Old Bangers Challenge".

TWENTY FOUR

Qu go' fish ling-ling?

"Vietnam slow-slow, good," my diminutive guide tells me, laughing. He points at his dilapidated scooter, making a virtue of necessity. His name is Mr Dong, he tells me. "Fast-fast bad," he insists, making sure I understand. I think he means when crossing the road as well as riding on it because we trundle along at just over walking pace through a depressing drizzle that mutes the harsh angles of the cluttered streets.

Then his aged Honda breaks down. We pull off the road. "Twelve year," he tells me.

"So I see," I reply as he crouches over the engine and fiddles. He thinks I am giving him a compliment.

Finally he coaxes the engine to life and we set off again into the traffic. He leads me to a Vietnamese cemetery, the white headstones disappearing into the mist. We park our bikes on the roadside and enter through an iron gate, glistening and wet. The cemetery is large, a few acres in size, the gravestones set in neat rows, a telling contrast from the tangled jungle where most of the interned men would have died, man's need for order and uniformity smoothing out the unpleasant wrinkles of history that we prefer not to confront, the horror of the battlefield gentled into neat graves and precisely carved names, turning mangled victims into heroes.

In front of each grave, bright artificial flowers have been placed; the garish colours jar somewhat with the sombre feel of the place.

"Many people -" he tells me, again stating the obvious but attempting to fulfil his role as guide with the limited number of English words at his disposal. But he is pointing, not to the neat rows of graves that stretch before us in linear ranks like men standing to attention, but at a number of raised, grass-covered mounds to one side. Only then do I realise that he is drawing my attention to a number of ragged, overgrown mass graves which evidently hold the body parts of multiple victims ripped into unidentifiable bits in the many bombing raids that devastated this place.

Carved into almost all the grave stones is the same phrase. I ask what it says.

"Martyr," Mr Dong translates, bringing his hands together, palms down, overlapping, then spreading them wide. "No name."

He explains, and I understand with some difficulty, that American soldiers wore aluminium dog tags and, because of this, their bodies could be identified even if found years later when everything else had rotted away. Vietnamese soldiers had no such means of identification but some used to write their names on pieces of rice paper, sealed in small bottles to keep them dry and kept in their pockets. But often the bottles were shattered along with the bodies that held them and the rice paper would quickly disintegrate in the wetness of the climate, so many bodies remain unidentified. As most of the North Vietnamese and Viet Cong were fighting far away from their homes and communication was, at best, primitive, families could be left for years not knowing that a son or husband had been killed. Usually they had to wait until someone who had survived the battle came home and could tell them in person what they had seen.

"Missing in action..." a dreadful phrase with all the heartache and lack of closure it implies. The 2,265 American m.i.a. have exercised the conscience of the nation since the end of the war but little mention is ever made of the 300,000 Vietnamese soldiers who are still missing, their lost bodies long since rotted away into the jungle soil.

Mr Dong's voice pulls me back to reality. He sweeps his hand over the massed graves and says one word, "Hero." Then, with chopping movements aimed at his arm and legs he adds, "Dead -" and a disturbing image of dismembered bodies enters my mind. "Me -" he continues, pointing to himself and miming a gun firing and himself running away. Then he smiles: "One year..."

"Me too," I assure him, acknowledging that I too would probably want to run away if confronted by heavily-armed soldiers intent on killing me or aircraft dropping cannisters of Napalm that will melt my flesh.

He explains that he was fourteen when the war came to his village. The fighting continued all around the area in which he was living until he turned eighteen and he was called up. He served one year in the NVA, the North Vietnamese Army, until the war ended.

There is a special irony in this war cemetery: whether intentional or not, I couldn't make myself sufficiently understood, but Mr Dong tells me that it has been built right on top of the site of a major US army base during the war.

We cross the road in the rain, careful not to get killed. Mr Dong assures me that there is the wreck of an American tank in the undergrowth close by. We make our way along a muddy path through grass and weeds beaded with rain drops. Partly hidden by overgrown bushes is the rusted hulk of a tank. We clamber up and stand on the hull; the turret and barrel have been blown off and lie half hidden in a tangle of weeds. I wonder why more has not been made of it, why it has been left here slowly disappearing into the undergrowth.

He takes me to the old bridge across the Ben Hai River, 22kms north of Dong Ha. The riveted, metal structure has been painted blue on the northern side and yellow on the south. Now kept as a memorial, the rusted bridge is a reminder of the physical and ideological separation of the two halves of this long, narrow country. It is falling apart now and vehicles are prohibited from using it; the wooden slats that make the roadway are rotten and expose the river far below.

Mr Dong points to a statue on the northern bank and tells me it is in memory of a young woman who lived near here and who relayed information about American troop movements to the North Vietnamese forces by radio until she was killed by a bomb.

In a small building are photographs and artefacts from the war, amongst them, of course, photographs of Ho Chi Minh.

Seeing me looking at his beloved Uncle Ho, Mr Dong stands at my side and says, "No family. Us children," pointing at his chest where his heart lies. "Fighting... freedom..." and these words are enough for me to understand.

On our way home, Mr Dong stops at a fish market at the edge of a calm inlet where red-and-blue painted fishing boats bob in the rising tide, their heavy planking curved sweet as birds' wings.

Stick-thin women crouch in front of their shrimp and fish, resting back on their feet, knees spread wide beneath their skirts, balanced in a way impossible for us Westerners, used all our lives to sitting on chairs. They greet me with sweet smiles, call me over to inspect their wares even though they know I will not buy. Mr Dong buys a large fish and straps it to his bike's seat so it will hang between his legs as he rides. It's for his family's evening meal, he tells me.

Pointing to the fish, he asks me in his heavily-accented Viet-lish, "Qu go' fish ling-ling?"

My brain takes a few seconds to translate but, having spent the day with him, my ear is attuned to his accent and vocabulary. "Yes," I assure him, "we do indeed have fish in England."

He smiles and mounts his little Honda.

Excerpt taken from: "By Motorcycle through Vietnam, Reflections on a gracious people".

TWENTY FIVE
Old biker still riding

After riding the Road of Bones in the Russian far east twice, solo, on an old DR350, Lawrence Bransby trusted his bike to the Russian railways. It would take a month, he was told, to get the bike from Yakutsk to Omsk. Time enough to explore some of the Russian rivers to the north on an old barge of a ferry,

"Be here by seven," the crewman tells me in Russian, holding up stubby fingers to confirm his words. He stands on the rusty deck of a large vehicle ferry that has been pushed against the riverbank, its heavy ramp wedged deep into the sand.

The next day I wake early and walk the two kilometres through empty streets of Kargasok inhabited only by a herd of brown-skinned horses and some cows that crop unkempt grass tufts on the side of the road. Nothing on the ferry stirs so I sit on the stony beach and wait. Clouds of midges conspire to make my life miserable.

I notice that on the ferry are twenty or so motorcycles that hadn't been there the day before. Time passes and the sun lifts itself off the horizon; on the barge, a few of the bikers emerge from what looks like a railway carriage without wheels on one side of the deck and that must be used for accommodation. I approach one of the bikers and he tells me that they're on a joint expedition to a small town 1,500ks further north and above the Arctic Circle.

They are friendly. I explain that I, too, am a biker and I tell them of my journey and why I'm now bike-less. *Deja-vu*, I think to myself, remembering meeting up with the Black Bears Club eight years ago north of Archangel and their welcome.

I catch the word *"Anglia"* - a group of bikers is looking at me with smiles on their faces. One makes a *You got shafted, mate!* gesture with a crooked right arm and they laugh. I assume they are referring to the Football World Cup so, before thinking, I flip them the bird and, as I'm doing it, I realise that this, perhaps, is not the wisest thing I've done of late. The biker who made the gesture is massive and tattooed, his stomach bulging over his trousers like a sack of piglets, his neck and shoulders seemingly fused. He walks up to me, slowly, and I think *Now what?* - but then puts his arms around my back and crushes the breath out of me. The watching bikers applaud. I am relieved - sometimes you're not quite sure of the response you'll get when using the old middle-finger salute but, when delivered with a smile amongst fellow bikers, it's usually taken in the spirit that it's given.

If I'd had my bike, I could have joined them. I have no doubt it would have been a *"'sperience"*, as the husky-voiced Malvina murmured to me on the first evening after joining the Black Bears on their camping trip to the White Sea coast. There, too, I was bear-hugged by massive, tattooed Russian bikers who welcomed me into their fraternity like the brother that I was.

Finally, at ten in the morning, the ferry engine rumbles to life, a crewmember casts us off into the fast-flowing, dark waters of the Ob River and we begin our 24-hr journey downstream towards the north west. It is so good to be on the move again after a three-day hiatus at the road-end town of Kargasok in northern Siberia.

My cabin, which I share with three middle-aged women, is painted green onto which has been pasted bright green wallpaper decorated with pictures of apples and oranges, whole and sliced. It's a little tight - 2.5m X 2.2m in size and designed to sleep four. In fact, the whole ferry functions in this utilitarian way: it's little more than a massive, unpainted, floating platform with a flat bit at the back and a slopy bit at the front for ramming up against the riverbank. An old railway carriage has been secured to the metal deck for sleeping; a shipping container houses a simple *magazin* with some wooden tables and benches for customers; inside, a large pot of *borscht* steams away on a gas stove. That's it - transport up and down this remote river for people and vehicles, sleeping and eating with the minimum of fuss; old-world pragmatism like the trans-Siberian railway.

I place my camera, wallet and glasses on the small table between our bunks; a bit later one of the ladies taps me on the shoulder where I am lying and tucks my belongings under my pillow, whispers something behind her hand and gestures down the corridor to where the bikers have gathered. I want to tell her that I would trust those bikers with my life but I can't; the barrier of discordant language is too high. I thank her instead.

Later I walk down the narrow corridor and meet the bear-like biker who gave me the shafted gesture before; as we pass, he hugs me again. It seems that man-hugs amongst bikers are acceptable here.

The river slips by. We travel fast downstream. I find a sheltered spot behind a truck and lie down on the sun-baked deck. Close to me, a number of bikers sit on aluminium panniers detached from their bikes; they pass the extended tube from a hookah from one to another and pour vodka into plastic cups. For the moment I am alone, isolated, but at peace with the world.

Then it comes, as I expected it to: *"Hey, Englishman!"*

I sit up. The group clustered around the hookah beckon me over. One makes room for me on a pannier, a cup of vodka is thrust into one hand, sunflower seeds into the other. Introductions are made. They are from various bike clubs throughout Russia, coming together for what they have called the "Arctic Circle Expedition". They are happy, excited; a few work on their bikes as the riverbanks slide by.

Like the Black Bears so many years ago, they, too, have their "fixer", the hard man who, if necessary, will sort out any problems they come across along the way. His name is Max, an ex-soldier of numerous campaigns, mostly Chechnia, Dagestan and the other Balkan republics who fought so hard for independence but failed in the end, although they exacted a heavy toll. Max is massive, his chest muscles like firm breasts. He shows me scars on his hands, his head (he has a metal plate inserted, one of the others tells me) and he points to his knee - another ragged scar.

"Motorcycle?" I ask, pointing to his knee.

He shakes his head. "War."

Despite our struggles with language, they make me welcome, tell me that I could join them on their journey north if I had my bike. And I am sad that I can't. What an adventure it would have been!

It's time for a ceremony; all line up at the railing and the sergeant-at-arms dips water from the river in a small bucket tied to a piece of rope. Each member of the group drinks from this - like the shared drinking of sacrificial blood in some obscure pagan ceremony, a bikers' rite of passage. I stand to one side, watching, but they insist that I join the line, drink river water from the bucket and ritually seal my inclusion into the brotherhood. Then vodka is produced - we all must drink. I am told, after swallowing my large mouthful, that it is home made and very strong. Almost immediately it hits my stomach and the whole world begins to melt. I remember the warnings: never drink home-made spirits in Russia, you don't know what horrors have been used to produce it - but it's too late now. The concoction flows warm through my veins and loosens the edge of my vision.

A small boat pulls up alongside, keeping pace, one man in the front holding onto the side of the ferry for balance. Smoked fish are offered; money is passed down to waiting hands and a bag of sturgeon passed up. We all gather about a pannier table and bits of smoky flesh are pulled off the bones and eaten. I am offered a skull to gnaw but I decline - like offering the choicest cut, a goat's eyeball, to the honoured guest. The biker who has offered it smiles, takes a bite, crunches the skull between his molars then flexes his biceps.

The day passes slowly; with it, the low, sandy banks of the river slide by, lined, as always, with the wall of taiga forest blurring darkly to the horizon. The river is broad and calm, flowing deep and dark towards the Arctic Ocean. The wind dies until only a light breeze disturbs the club flags that have been zip-tied onto stanchions and poles on the sides of the ferry. Like the riverbank, the hours slip silently by. Conversation has slowed; vodka is sipped instead of gulped; the hookah pipe is passed from hand to mouth; sunflower seeds are nibbled, the husks eddying as hot gusts of wind tug them about the deck. I sit with the bikers and we talk - one speaks passable English and he translates for the others. They ask me how much money I spend each day and I tell them about $30; they exclaim that I am a rich man, tell me they spend about 1200 roubles a day ($12) - the difference, one says amidst laughter, is the price of a Russian woman.

"What is your name?" one asks. He has braided hair, a darkly tanned torso with the body of a naked woman tattooed across the whole of his back. I am confused because they already know my name. The translator attempts to explain: Not my birth name, what is my *name* - my biker's name, a name given by my mates to reflect some attribute of my character, something I have done. (Like "Killer", I think, the name given to the Black Bears' *fixer* who beat the drug dealers to a bloody pulp on the White Sea shore and who showed me his hands saying with a wry smile, "Blood - not mine!")

They seem delighted when I tell them I don't have a name and begin making suggestions; eventually *McCloud* is settled on.

"Why McCloud?" I ask, not then being aware of Dennis Weaver in his eponymous role in the 1970s detective series.

"It means you are still living," our translator tells me - then he ponders a while, realising this explanation is less than flattering. He tries again, "Still living - in a *good* way. Like McCloud - an old biker still riding..."

I thank them, deeply moved, then feel liquid being poured over my head. I look round and, surrounded by their laughter, I am baptised with vodka into their fellowship by the leader of the tour and they shake my hand all round.

I am McCloud, still living - and it is one of the most special moments of my life.

At intervals throughout the afternoon battered motorboats set off from isolated - very isolated - settlements along the banks of the river, keep pace with the ferry while transactions are concluded: money passed across while dried and smoked fish, sometimes bottles of home-brewed alcohol, are passed up. Then the bikers all gather, the fish is cut up with sharp knives and handed around, nibbled with white teeth and chased with vodka drunk from plastic cups.

Next to me, a biker called Oleg asks me what it is about Russia that has brought me back so many times. I try to express the vastness of it with my arms spread wide but he captures my meaning with just one word: "Majestic -" he says, looking out into the endless sweep of taiga against a sky heavy with cloud, the fecund smell of the river in the still air all about us, the throb of the engine rising through the rusty metal deck and the wide, slow river making its way north between islands thick with birch trees.

The sun sinks low over the trees, setting the dark sky alight; the wind rises again, blowing spray across the deck. I join a group of bikers clustered around a pannier, watch as they continue to cut strips of raw, un-smoked fish off the bone with sharp knives, lifting their heads and feeding the fishy strips into their mouths like spaghetti and chasing it with vodka.

"Russian whiskey!" one says to me, catching my eye and raising his plastic cup. I decline both the fish and the rocket fuel, despite their urgings, and they laugh good-naturedly at me, confirming, I am sure, in their minds the weakness of British men and the superiority of the Russian spirit. No matter - I'd prefer to be regarded as weak and live a little longer.

A damp coldness descends on the decks; the riverbank is a pale line of sand now against the dark trees and sky. The bikers have congregated in the shelter of the eating area; their voices are loud in the confines of the room with its few small tables and wooden benches. The lady in charge reprimands them and they respond like chastened schoolboys. I don't understand what she is saying but its meaning is clear: *This is a place for paying customers only so settle down, buy something or get out!* But she's taken a liking to me and her face softens and a smile forms on her otherwise severe face when I come in and she gives me biscuits for free with my coffee and refuses my offer of payment. She either likes the look of me or she feels sorry for me - I presume the latter.

* * * * *

The next morning dawns bright and clear and soon the bikers are up, seemingly unaffected by the alcohol consumed the night before. They fire up the hookah as the low sun warms the metal of the deck and throws long, dark shadows over the river. Water is boiled and coffee brewed. A steaming cup is put into my hand; one lifts his cup to me and says in broken English, "Good coffee... river..." Trying to express his feelings with the few words he knows, he points to the blue sky above us and adds, "Friends -" and I can only agree.

The landscape surrounding us is unchanged. Very little alters here - except the weather and that, I feel, is enough to make up for all the rest. I look out at the river twinkling past, bright in the early morning sunlight, and try to imagine it frozen over, the dark trees white with snow, the river an ice road, plumes of smoke rising vertically from the chimneys of small, log-built houses tucked away between the trees, the occupants huddled inside. What do they do all day throughout the dark winter? How difficult is it for young people way out here to find a mate? How do widows cope when their husbands die? What do they do when someone falls seriously ill or has an accident? How long does it take before the lame dogs of society in this wilderness die?

And again I am aware that I am little more than a voyeur passing through a majestic land and its people and, in all reality, I know very little about them and the lives they live. But more than I did before, I suppose, and that makes all the difference.

Excerpt taken from "Two Fingers on the Jugular".

TWENTY SIX
The Dempster Highway

Excessive speed is always a factor when you come off your bike. But as I baled off my V-Strom in mid air, I didn't have time to think to myself: *You know what? You could have chosen a better place to*

leave the road off an eight-foot causeway into swampy tundra just a few hundred miles south of the Arctic Circle.

Twenty three miles east of Dawson City, Yukon, that iconic town that became synonymous with a brief period of madness in the 1890s when half the world seemed to be overtaken by gold fever, the road splits: take the right fork and, 500ks later, you will end up in Whitehorse; but if you take the left, you will follow a gravel road that, for the next 900 or so kilometres, will take you along a route that loosely follows the old Royal Canadian Mounted Police trail of the early 1900s. In those days this was a three-month-long journey by dog sled in mid winter from Dawson to Fort McPherson in the far north. This is the Dempster Highway, named after Inspector William J.D.Dempster who made the dangerous winter patrol more than any other officer and who, in 1911, led the search party that found the bodies of the Lost Patrol, a group of four RCMP officers who had lost their way in the snow and died of starvation and exposure after having run out of food and eaten all their dogs.

I had ridden the Dalton Highway a week or so before, the Ice Road Truckers' highway that seemed to have drawn every adventure biker in North America to Alaska just when I decided to ride it. Despite its Ice Road Truckers' fame, I felt that the Dalton just lacks a certain something in the adventure biker stakes despite the fact that "doing the Dalton" seems *de rigueur* for many US bikers, a sort of right of passage. Certainly, the Dalton is not the Road of Bones. I found it rather too civilized, to be honest, and, anyway, much of it now is tar.

I was looking for something a little more challenging in my long trip around the US, Canada and Alaska so headed south and east, back into the Yukon, across the Top of the World Highway to Dawson. After a brief pause to catch my breath, I took the left fork and set off along the Dempster Highway towards Eagle Plains, my first day's stop, 580ks to the north, where I had been told there is fuel. With careful riding, I could just make it on one tank but was carrying an extra five litres just in case.

The gravel track is far better than I thought it would be; I had expected a pretty rough track this far north but then, Canadians in my experience just don't do bad roads. It's not part of their psyche. Unlike the Dalton, there are no sections of tar here at all, just good dirt, which is all a biker can ask for. Sadly, sharing the track with me are a number of camper vans trundling along, filled with happy, smiling occupants who somehow destroy my attempt at feeling adventurous. It's always difficult taking "Look at me, I'm riding the Dempster!" selfies with a Winnebago in the background.

Hemmed in on both sides by spruce, balsam and aspen trees, I follow the gravel road across the Klondike Plateau then on between the low North Klondike and Snowy Mountain Ranges. It is only when one reaches the Tombstone and Ogilvie Mountain Ranges that the road begins properly to climb, the trees fall away to reveal the vast wilderness that diminishes into a blue haze of distance in all directions.

The road, still good, smooth dirt with occasional stretches of loose gravel and embedded rocks to keep the rider focused, climbs up the North Fork Pass, at 1,328m, the highest pass on the Dempster, and then up Windy Pass onto the Blackstone Plateau. This is the northern continental divide: rivers to the south flow into the Yukon River watershed that ends up in the Bering Sea far to the west; rivers to the north flow into the Beaufort Sea via the Mackenzie River system.

The road follows the Blackstone River, beginning as a small stream and, as the miles fall away northwards, it grows steadily into a strong flow across a land of rock and Arctic tundra, high and cold and windy, and once again I feel as if I'm riding across the top of the world and looking down. This whole region is permanently frozen and has been so for thousands of years, insulated by a thick layer of moss and lichen. In places, the permafrost here is 1200ft deep but so delicate that if the surface covering of vegetation is removed (or disturbed by road building or driving a vehicle across it) the ice melts, turns to mud and does not re-freeze. The damage is permanent. Because of this, the Dempster is built on a raised berm of gravel which protects and insulates the permafrost beneath.

Although the road is basically good, the constant vibration over corrugations, the bumping and, I suppose, the added concentration required not to slide off on the gravel and occasional stretches of mud, tire me and by early afternoon I am flagging. I find myself wanting to fall asleep but manage to keep going until, at last, the small (very small) settlement of Eagle Plains appears, wind-swept and exposed. A helicopter stands silent next to a fuel station and garage; then there is the hotel and, well, that's about it. I park alongside a handful of laden adventure bikes, switch off and drag my leg over the seat. In the hotel foyer I enquire the price of a room, shudder, then follow a small track off the road and pitch my tent amongst the trees. At least the rain is holding off and there don't seem to be any bears about.

It is evening. I have sneaked a shower inside the hotel and am clean. (The mosquitoes seem to like that.) I sit on a rock looking out over range upon low range of gently rolling hills, one, two, three, four I can make out in the late evening haze, each more pale as distance softens and blurs its outline, lower on the horizon, merging into the clouds until I can no longer discern sky from land. The sun is a copper disc, smudging and reappearing as the clouds are shuffled and nudged by high-altitude winds. Across these hills I can see the dull yellow track of the Dempster, coiling its way north along the ridges. It is silent here, except for the wind; a silence of empty spaces and the emptiness between spaces. And it is beautiful in a way that no man-made thing can be beautiful. Strangely, although I am alone, I am not lonely, that gut-wrenching aloneness I felt last year on my trans-Russia journey has gone. Perhaps it's time's healing hand that is slowly wiping away the pain of my wife's death; perhaps it's also because I feel more at home here amongst English-speaking people, those of my own heritage. Perhaps it's because on this trip I feel less fearful.

Even in far eastern Siberia, throughout the remote taiga, there is always evidence of man, the small, log-built settlements, most abandoned now; the remains of factories and mines; abandoned vehicles and industrial materiel; and the living ones too, those lonely outposts of human occupation where people live out their lives amongst the trees and the snow.

Not so here. Yes, people have lived here for millennia, First Nation inhabitants who have, and still do, eke out their existence close to the rivers and the land. But their impact was, and is, so slight as to be considered of little significance. They built no permanent structures, itinerant hunter-gatherers who lived in shelters made from caribou skin that they carried with them when they moved to areas where berries ripened, fish spawned or caribou migrated. So, other than the remains of their fireplaces, they left no permanent mark on this land that probably looks, as I stare out in the late-evening silence, just the same as when glaciers nudged and burrowed their way across here thousands of years ago. A sense of awe and deep, almost spiritual, joy fills me as I look upon this ancient, untouched land that encompasses me.

* * * * *

After a comfortable night in the woods, I fill my tank and continue north along the Dempster, the road initially treacherous with a deep layer of loose, marble-like gravel that wants to have me over; but then it smooths and firms for most of the way to Inuvik. A joy of a road that crosses the glacial outwash channel of the once mighty Eagle River, now just a small stream. I cross the Arctic Circle again about 25 miles north of Eagle Plains, then the road begins to climb into the Nicholson Mountains. At the top of the pass I leave the Yukon and enter the Northwest Territory. The road drops onto the Peel Plateau and then a further drop of 853m to the Peel River. Leaving the tundra-covered mountains far behind, the road continues north through boreal forest, poplar, birch and spruce, a land covered now with lakes, many of which have been formed by pingos. These are caused by large, mushroom-shaped domes of ice which are forced to the surface by the expansion of freezing; when these eventually melt, the land collapses inward to form beautiful, round lakes, clear and blue and still, reflecting the sky and the clouds and the surrounding trees as if inviting one to look deep into the earth's soul.

At the wide, slow-flowing Peel River I wait for the cable-stayed ferry to cross and take me and a few other vehicles to the other side. During the winter freeze, there is an ice bridge crossing the Peel here, once the ice is thick enough to carry the weight of a vehicle. Then on, ferried over the Mackenzie River in a sudden downpour of rain; across the river, on a far bank and hazed by the rain, is the settlement of Tsiigehtchic (population 192), home of the Tetlit Gwich'in tribe, their wooden houses and the white-painted church starkly clear against the dark storm clouds behind.

Finally onto the Makenzie River delta, a vast, flat land over 50% water with lakes and swamps glinting between the trees. And then, at last, in the late afternoon, I reach Inuvik, Canada's largest settlement above the Arctic Circle. Built in 1955 as an administrative centre in the Western Arctic, its name means "Place of Man".

Here, I stay with a tall, thin young man called Jared, his long, straight hair tied back in a pony tail. Lonely in this remote posting as an air traffic controller at Inuvik airport, he welcomes passing travellers into his home, offers a warm bed and hot vegan meals in return for good conversation and a friendly face across the room.

North of Inuvik is the Tuktoyaktuk Highway. Officially opened in 2017, it is the only public road in North America to reach the Arctic Ocean, the final section of the long road north from Dawson, begun in 1959.

Having made it to Inuvik, rested and fed, it's only logical that I make one last push to the Arctic Ocean. So, after lingering over yet another cup of coffee in the warmth and comfort of Jared's home, I fire up the bike and set off on the final 160ks north towards Tuktoyaktuk (locally known as "Tuk", population 962) under a cold sky, dark with clouds that threaten rain. The road is atrocious, badly corrugated and covered with a deep layer of loose gravel ridged by heavy vehicles to trap the unwary. Numerous times over the next four hours I have to wrestle control back from wildly oscillating bars that threaten to shake the bike, and me, into an early grave; a couple of times I come very close to losing it.

The land is flat. Only from the tops of occasional low, rounded hillocks can I see the Mackenzie River threading its way through a maze of sand bars towards the coast. Soon the last remaining scraggy, stunted trees die away, giving up the battle against the cold and the dark. The now bare landscape reveals hundreds of lakes so that, at times, it looks like the aftermath of a battle where scattered bomb craters have settled and filled with water across a sodden and devastated land.

An icy wind blows from the Arctic and my fingers and face begin to freeze despite my protective gear. More lakes appear and what look like estuaries probing in from the sea until I am surrounded by more water than land, the road threading its way across the Arctic tundra on ridges of dry land raised above the waterline. It is strange to think that, once, long ago, at a time when the level of the ocean fell, the whole of this sodden land including the Bearing Sea was dry, covered with grassland, and people and animals from north-west Russia walked across to populate north-east Canada.

At last, in the distance, some man-made structures appear and, amongst the rusting wrecks of cars and bleached, storm-tossed logs piled high onto wind-swept beaches, the first small, clap-board houses appear on either side of the road. All are built on piles or raised above the ground on blocks of wood; most are surrounded by a scattering of junk: disembowelled Skidoos, old boats, a bear skin loosely nailed to a wall, wooden sleds, junked cars. Most of the inhabitants are Inuvialuit, descendants of the most northerly indigenous people of North America who have lived here for thousands of years. In the old days, they survived the long, cold winters by constructing their homes underground, insulated with sod as there are no trees here to provide material for above-ground houses. In the summer, they lived in caribou-hide tents.

I follow the rough, gravel road between these small houses; chained dogs bark at me in lonely, bored voices as I pass by. The gravel road ends. A sign tells me I've reached the Arctic Ocean. The water is uninviting, cold and grey and wind-ruffled, spume fluffing in dirty brown lines on the beach. The air smells of dead fish and the wind lifts grit and tosses it into my face. On a far shore, ridges of ice still dully reflect a grey, lowering sky. It's a cold, desolate, ragged place and, except for the dogs, seemingly empty of outside life.

I find somewhere for coffee, sit at a plastic table and shiver into my jacket. "It's so *cold* out here!" I observe to the young lady who serves me.

"No, it's lovely!" she exclaims, looking with a smile out the window at the pale, cold fingers of sunlight that try to penetrate the low covering of cloud.

If you live much of your life in the snow and the darkness, this weak attempt at sunlight could be described as "lovely", I suppose. It's all about perspective. The sun does not rise above the horizon here from November 28th to January 13th and June, July and August are the only months in the year where the temperature rises above freezing.

After making my way back from Tuktoyaktuk to Inuvik and another companionable night with Jared, I gird my loins for the long ride back to Dawson. Other than flying, there is no other way. If you decide to ride the 886ks of the Dempster and Tuktoyaktuk Highways, you have no alternative but to turn round and ride them back again.

At the small settlement of Tsiigehtchic I take the ferry away from the main road south and ride onto the riverbank under the high bluff upon which the picturesque old Catholic church has been built. A woman cuts newly-caught fish into long, thin strips with a razor-sharp *ulu*, the sharp, half-moon-shaped blade that is also used for skinning animal carcasses. A large dog barks at me, although he keeps a respectable distance. To one side of the rough plank table at which she works is a structure made from a pole frame wrapped in sheets of plastic; smoke leaks from gaps and the smell of fish and wood-smoke is pungent in the cold air.

The woman has the round, flat face so typical of indigenous people of the sub-Arctic and, while I watch her work, she tells me she is preparing smoked fish for winter food and also to sell in Inuvik. Inside the makeshift smoke house, fish strips and whole fish, whose flesh has been diced whilst still on the bones, hang on sticks above a fire smouldering in a tin drum. The woman plucks off a piece and offers it to me; it has the consistency of biltong and tastes fishy.

I leave the woman and ride up the hill towards the houses and the church. The settlement is made up of about thirty wood-framed houses and a few administrative and commercial buildings loosely strung out along a circular gravel road. I leave my bike and walk. In front of each house is a chained dog who does his duty by huffing and barking at me as I pass.

A man hails me from a window, gesturing for me to come. I climb the steps to the raised front door. Inside are three men, the one who hailed me, his father and his uncle. A little later, his two sons arrive. They are in their early twenties. All five of the men, in varying degrees, are drunk. It's midday.

"I'm a good carver," the old man tells me, "the best."

"He's a good carver," his son agrees.

Inside, the house is warm, utilitarian, untidy; there are no feminine touches.

"I'm the best carver in the whole district," the old man assures me and his false teeth drop loosely in his mouth. He bites them back into place.

"He can carve a naked woman," the uncle adds his bit, his eyes sliding towards mine in the manner of someone covertly offering a dirty postcard. "When you look..." He is unable to complete his thought but I get the drift.

One of the young men, who has insisted on shaking my hand and seems reluctant to release it, tells me his sister is pregnant. He swears. "Your grandfather, your grandfather..." his father plaintively reprimands him. The boy ignores him.

The other son offers me food. He turns to his father, "What food you got?"

His father seems not to hear him, sits in his chair and stares at the wall. I want to accept just so I can gain a greater insight into life lived in this isolated place. The grandfather tugs at my arm. "I can carve a naked woman..." he insists and his teeth drop again, exposing his gums. The son stares at his father a while then rummages in the deep freeze. He takes out a large frozen salmon, looks at it speculatively then puts it back.

I decide to leave. The father walks me out, breathes alcohol fumes onto my face and says, "He's the best carver..."

I wait on the beach for the ferry. It takes me back to the main road heading south to Eagle Plains and Dawson.

About seven hundred kilometres to go. I fire up the bike and ride on. I have nearly made it to back Eagle Plains when the road and I part company.

Of course I was riding too fast. I have this stupid compulsion to ride at a speed that is just slightly lower than what the road conditions dictate, which is all very well until things suddenly change. Then there's no margin of error.

The day is overcast and cold; the weather dry although there had been rain and the track is wet but not slippery. I stand on the pegs and look about me at this endless, empty land and feel blessed indeed. The road is good, the gravel smooth and grippy, and I accelerate even faster, loving it. There are, I must admit, short sections of wet, black clay and, when I hit these, the bike slews about but, because they are small sections, almost like elongated puddles, grip soon returns and the bike straightens up. I should, of course, have taken this as a warning, but I didn't; should have paid attention to the sign warning me that the speed limit on the Dempster is 50kph. I must have been doing about 100 when I hit the long section of mud.

Nemesis always catches up with the unwary and the over confident. Before I can react, it's there, that black clay, the kind that makes wet glass feel grippy, clogs mudguards and causes motorcycles to fall over. The bike slews to one side, I correct briefly then she slides again and heads for the edge of the causeway. I bale off whilst still in the air, hear that awful sound of breaking plastics before I hit the ground and roll to the bottom of the bank. Thankful that nothing is broken, just a wrenched shoulder and ankle, I get up and look at my bike lying on its side with the front wheel buried in a water-filled ditch. A closer look and I can see that the front fairing and mudguard are pretty badly smashed up, the instrument panel glass broken.

Bollocks. In this empty landscape I am pretty much on my own but know that, if I can't get the bike out, someone will come by sooner or later. First things first: remove panniers, top box and tank bag. Turn the key, broken instrument cluster comes to life, a hopeful sign. Lift the bike, drag the front wheel out of the water and work the gear lever into neutral; press the starter, she fires up. So, if I can get her out of this swamp and up the steep side of the causeway, I can still ride her out. Rocking and lifting, spinning the back wheel, I manage to make a few metres towards what looks like a more gentle slope up the side of the causeway about twenty metres further on. But I soon realise it isn't going to work. The deep holes, high tussocks of grass and bushes that catch and snag are too much for me. There's no way I can get it out on my own.

I stand, somewhat forlornely, on the side of the road and wait. It's not long before a 4X4 arrives. Inside, a young man who works in construction; in the back of his SUV, a tow strap that could lift a Sherman tank. We attach it to my front wheel and, while I struggle to keep the bike upright, he drags the V-Strom out of the swamp, up the bank and onto the road.

Loaded up again, I make my way, more slowly now, to Eagle Plains. A few bikers are there. They tell me that heavy rain is forecast for early next morning, predicted to last the whole day. I decide to eat and then ride on, complete the Dempster in one day instead of two and beat the rain by riding through the Arctic night.

This I do - and it is strangely beautiful. As the hours crawl towards midnight, the whole world seems to pause and catch its breath; warm smells from the muddy ground rise into the air, the scent of grass and wild flowers and, occasionally, the acrid tang of woodsmoke. The sun does not set, just sinks ever so slowly towards the tops of the mountains as it travels across the sky, becomes a red ball behind low clouds, the colours reflecting off still lakes and ponds and rivers as I ride by. A surreal light suffuses everything; the land and the mountains take on varying shades of blue and purple and indigo and there comes upon the world a mood of fairytale magic, hour upon hour.

Eventually, tired but exhilarated, I reach the outskirts of Dawson at 2.30 in the morning and take a small road into the woods. Desperately thirsty, I walk about the woods in the eerie half-light, looking for a river or pond but there is nothing. I retire to my tent thirsty, sleep well until the dawn.

760kms and one accident. Seventeen hours' riding. Makes me think of my all-night ride on the Road of Bones,

First published in Overland Magazine, Issue 30, under the title: "The Dempster".

TWENTY SEVEN
Death Valley and Vegas

Death Valley draws me like moth to flame. With a name like that, who can resist?

Whilst the famous Highway 101 heading north up the California coast beckons, it is the solitude of the desert that exerts the stronger pull and, after dipping my toe into the steamy pool of Vegas just a few hundred miles to the East, the cleansing wastes of Utah, Wyoming and Montana will await, offering atonement.

Why Las Vegas? I hear you ask.

Because it's there, I suppose. The juxtaposition of natural desert, hot, dry, hesitant for millennia to share its space with living things, and Vegas, man-made temple to the lusts of the flesh, have got to be worth experiencing. The two contiguous extremes of the American psyche: the desire for ostentatious, unearned wealth in the midst of pure, open plains and desert. Bling vs *Little House on the Prairie*.

But what do I know? I'm just passing through, testing the cliches.

The Mojave Desert comes suddenly after the high mountain passes of the Sierra Nevada. The wind is hot and dry, picking up sand and grit from the salt flats and the semi desert and flinging it about; powder-fine dust rises high and turns the sky a milky white. Cacti hunker down and endure and the olive-green leaves of sagebrush flutter in the wind. My teeth and eyes are gritty, the bike tugged and buffeted about by pockets of hot air whipping across the desert. From out of the scrubby plains, ridges of bare mountain rise, dust-smudged layers of red and black and pale yellow and brown.

The road descends to Badwater Basin, the salt flats shimmering in the pale light. 282 ft below sea level, North America's hottest and lowest point. Occasional storms cover the flats with a thin layer of water but with an average annual rainfall of 48mm and an evaporation rate of 3,800mm, it is soon sucked dry.

Later I leave my bike on the edge of the Mesquite Flat sand dunes and, still wearing riding trousers and boots, stagger my way through soft sand. The bleached limbs of dead trees, no longer able to withstand the encroaching dunes and the lack of water, protrude from the sand and remind me of the high Namibian dunes of Sossusvlei. The heat drives me back.

And then, out of the desert, the first signs of a human presence: large billboards advertising ambulance-chaser lawyers: "Had a fall? Give Bill a call" - smooth-skinned, come-hither faces of 40-something white men with snowy teeth and lying eyes, fake tans and pampered hair. "Had a wreck? Need a cheque?" another billboard shouts at me as I ride by. "After 911, call 411". Behind them, the sagebrush desert and the low mountains and the wide sky, empty of cloud lie quiet as an intake of breath.

I struggle my way through a hot snarl of traffic to the outskirts of Vegas where the poor people live, down a street of boarded-up motels and bus shelters where indolent, bony men loll in the shade and stare at nothing. There I find my hostel.

Inside my shared dorm, two men stand at the window. They nod a greeting but otherwise ignore me. One is tall and smooth-skinned, spare of flesh. His hair has been straightened and plaited into short pig-tails, the ends tied with different coloured rubber bands. His friend says little. It is the tall man who is speaking, a rapid torrent of words so in keeping with my preconception of the language of Coloured men from the South that I am compelled to take out my phone, surreptitiously press record and leave it on the bed while I unpack:

"These big-ass niggers come out to Vegas," he is saying, "mother-fuckers rentin' condos payin' twenty-two, twenty-three hun'ed dollars a month they don't hardly stay there - they rentin' 'em for the bitches. For the bitches, man! Jerry Springer, all these celebs come out here, go to the gym, pay the bodyguards, you don't know they bodyguards, these big-ass mother-fuckers in the gym, big-ass niggers, you know what I mean?"

"Mmmm," his friend agrees, nodding. He's older, shorter, darker skin. Head shaved bald.

"Know what I'm sayin'?"

"Yeah -"

"That's not average American shit, know what I'm sayin'? Big-ass niggers workin' as bodyguards. An' the broads up there an' all. That's a 24-hour business an' shit. Come on, man! Know what I'm sayin'? Big-ass motherfucker. I'm in the gym and they're everywhere. Escorts everywhere! An', look, when you're gamblin', they jus' walk up to you - 'Wha- wha' numbers you play?' I say, 'Why you talkin' to me?' - She wants the money. They walk up, they see you playin', you win a few big ones, they start talkin' - they want the money."

"Yeah."

"If you ain't about no money out here, it's a waste of conversation, man."

"Yeah."

"You make it on with a few bitches an' shit, that's cool, but, like I said, once that money starts a' surfacin', they gonna be there. Start to lose, they goin' away. 'Cos they wan' the money. That's what they come out here fo'. This niggah, he say, 'I'm movin my girl to Vegas.' I say, 'You movin' your girl to Vegas?' He say, 'Yeah, I'm movin' my girl to Vegas.' I say, 'You move your girl to Vegas, don' lose your job, man'."

"Heee-ya," the short man says, understanding.

"I say, 'Don' lose your job, man. Don' lose your job or be locked up'."

"No."

"I met a nigga' here, from Michigan, big dude. Hooked up with this broad and moved in wit' her. Two weeks later he went to jail. 'Cause he got broke. Light-skinned nigga'. He went to jail. I say what you gonna do? He say she goin' to wait fro' me. I say you crazy. Well, not long, she got tired o' that nigga'."

"She wan'ed that place fo' herself. Do her thang," the short man says.

"Sho. She di'n't wan' no nickle and' dime thang. She wan' 'bout three hunnerd a week, three-four hunnerd a week, but that's enough, that's twelve-sixteen hunnerd dollars a month, for her, that ain't really shit, but she gonna get a little food and stuff and, for a female, that's enough for her to get a car, know what I'm sayin'? And then move around like she wants to. She ain't got time for that nigga' no more. She only used that mother-fucka to pay a coupla' thousan' dollar now she say, 'You gotta go'."

"Yeah, man. That shit. An' this hotel is shit. After a bit, ya know, I'm goin' home."

"Yeah, man. I ain't goin' to fuck wit' no broads out here. All they want is the money, know what I mean? Shee-eet, whooo!"

* * * * *

It's the next day. Every weirdo in the world has come to live in Vegas because this is the only place they seem normal; just the short walk from my hostel to the bus stop is a surreal experience. I have entered another world, different to the one I thought I knew.

No wonder the desert keeps its distance.

An old woman, eighties, large, pendulous breasts hanging to her navel, sits in a wheelchair on the pavement, nipples covered with duct tape. She holds up a sign: "Retired stripper, all tips welcome". She grins yellow teeth at me as I pass.

A young woman sits on a low wall and smokes a spliff; on her upper thigh is the tattoo of a sunset forest. Tattoos are *de rigueur* here, exposed flesh splashed with colour, an American Holi Festival with ink instead of powder paint.

A tall, stick-thin man dressed in suit and tie walks the pavements with a stiff, old-fashioned formality, addressing the phantoms in his mind. He approaches me, greets me politely, proffers his hand which I take. He has the face of an aesthete. Melanin bleeds from his skin into the whites of his eyes like tobacco juice. I can see the angles of his bones under his skin.

"Hitler tried to take on the world," he informs me in a voice that is close to a shout, "but the Russians fucked him up. Leningrad,

Stalingrad, they fucked him up. You a married man, Suh?"

"My wife died eighteen months ago," I tell him.

"Oh, I'm *so* sorry, Suh," he says in a sane voice. He takes my hand in his, soft and cool and smooth-skinned, stands silent with his eyes downcast for a long time. I take my hand back and he allows me. "Kids today," he segues onto a new tack, lifting his stained eyes to mine again, "they get married and then want to divorce after six months. Now what's that about? Hey? What's that about?"

When I leave him, he continues to address the human-shaped space in front of his eyes, his voice loud and carrying across the road, explaining about Hitler and the war. Words flutter like moths in the empty cupboard of his mind.

On the pavement a woman lies sprawled in the manner of recently dead people; pedestrians pick their way around, ignoring her, their voices bright chirrups in the hot, diesel-smelling air.

A random man on the pavement says to me, "How ya doin'?" I am looking at a poster of The Beatles looking Sergeant Pepperish and don't realise that the man is addressing me. "Great, huh?" he adds, as if we are friends. It's the American way.

"I'm from Manchester," I tell him, not sure what else to say and thinking that might be appropriate. "England," I add when he looks perplexed.

"They doin' well?" he asks and I assume he means Paul and Ringo. Not having spoken to either of them in a while, I smile blankly.

"They're comin' here next month," he tells me. "I got tickets. Paul's voice is gettin' a bit - you know -" and he rocks his hand. "But then, he's gettin' on now, what, 78?"

I nod my agreement that Paul's seventy-eight-year-old voice is a little - you know? and we part. I am beginning to come to an understanding of the American habit of initiating intimate and unsolicited conversation with anyone, anywhere, any time, a trait somewhat disturbing to British people.

A man, his skin tanned to the consistency of leather, palms his wheelchair along the pavement. He has red tattoos of lightning bolts across both cheeks.

A man says, "How you doin'?" as I walk past him.

I look about, yes, he's talking to me. He sits on a bus-stop bench; alcohol, it seems, is coursing through his veins. There is foam drying in the corners of his mouth. I expect him to solicit me for money but he doesn't, he's just being American.

The bus to "The Strip" is waiting. I am early. I climb the steps and feed dollar bills into a slot to get my ticket. The bus driver, a middle-aged woman wearing a uniform that strains to contain her generous flesh, watches me from her seat.

"Makes it easier," I say to her to fill the silence. "No hassle with change..."

"Stops us gettin' robbed," she corrects me laconically, her eyes flat.

A roar outside and a pack of Harleys goes by, the riders un-helmeted, wearing bandannas and wrap-around sunglasses, easy-rider foot-pegs and ape-hanger bars, wife-beater T's with the sleeves ripped off exposing flexed biceps.

It's all Harleys here; none of the rice-burner garbage that I'm riding. No self-respecting white man would ride a Jap bike in this place, it seems. It's Harleys or nuttin', bud.

The bus driver fires up the engine and we set off. We pass cutie-pie chapels advertising weddings (Elvis impersonators to officiate, no extra cost). There's a shop selling $10 wedding dresses next to a drive-through wedding chapel. Bail Bonds by Phone. Then a large neon sign winking its message: LUST KILLS, JESUS SAVES across the road from an Adult Superstore, "Come in and Browse". Another sign offers "Beers, Bets and Burgers" so fat people don't have to leave the establishment to replenish their calories while they throw their money to the wind.

Opposite a gambling emporium, a pawn shop. When you've lost your last dollar, you can pop across the road and pawn your wedding ring, your car, your wife for a few more spins of the wheel.

My phone beeps: it's a message from my Couchsurfing host in Salt Lake City: *Just to let you know, my partner, the woman I live with, likes to smoke some pot in the evenings. Just thought I'd let you know in case it's a problem.*

I reply: *Consenting adults can do whatever they like in the privacy of their own homes, unless they want to kill children, I suppose.*

We reach The Strip and I get off the bus. The heat is unpleasant, the sun's glare piercing my eyes. Caesar's Palace, Country and Western music playing. My daughter told me that if I sit at a table and play the slots I'll be offered free drinks. I decide to watch instead.

Xtreme Jackpots, Golden Century, Mighty Cash, Dancing Drums, Gold Stacks, lights flash and flicker and blink, happy lights and sounds of joy to lure the star-struck, to raise the beat of your heart, to numb the senses: *BOOM, duh, BOOM, duh, clicketty-clicketty, dum-te-dum-te-dum, tratra tra, deedle deedle dee, tickety-tickety DUH, duh, tickety-tickety, SQUARK, ting-ting-ting, DUH, tickety-ticket-tickety, SQUARK.* Flash-flash go the lights, fire burning, flames rising higher. Phew, it's hot in here. *Tickety-tickety-tickety BOOM!*

"Player 3, *a WIN!"* a woman's canned voice calls at a table around which no one sits. Her voice is followed by a round of ecstatic applause. She's a doll-faced creature on a large screen with open, trusting eyes and innocent, pouting mouth. Child's face atop an adult woman's body. This way pleasure lies. (Lies indeed.) *Flash! a*nd a cascade of bright stars fills the screen on the table. The doll-woman rests her hand on an out-thrust hip and rolls coquettish eyes. The sound of a telephone ringing, Oh, yes, she's calling *me!* She jumps up and down like an excited child and claps her hands then leaves them together under her chin momentarily, as if in prayer. Sweet praying hands; sweet, innocent child-woman who is just *longing* for you to play with her. The phone rings again and she rolls her eyes, clearly disappointed that I've turned her down.

A woman, the skin of her face stretched tight as a drum, sits at a gaming table, cigarette caught between the last two joints of her index and middle fingers. The smoke flubbers briefly, as if on a string, and then is absorbed into the warm fug around me. She could be 38, or 60.

"Oh, come *on,* man!" a young man with tattooed arms mutters at the screen when the barrels settle on two dragons and a seven. A young woman in a short, black skirt with a cigarette tray around her neck walks past: "Cigarettes, sir?" I smile at her and shake my head. Next to me a woman vapes. *Ding-ding, ding-ding, ding-ding* goes her machine as she feeds it coins. At another table, a woman of a certain age, dressed all in black, sits in front of the Hot Stuff Wicked Wheel, stares at the barrels through her winged, diamante, sixties-style glasses and prods the button again... and again... and again...

My brain turning to mush, I manage to find my way out of this labyrinth of pleasure back onto the street. On a pedestrian crossing, I lightly bump a man, brush him with a loose arm. He turns, gives me a full-in-the-face look and says, "Sorry, man! I apologise for that."

Everything is bigger here, even the apologies. Like at gas stations, you don't just get a *Thank you*, when you pay for your fuel; here, it's, "Thank you *so* much! You have a safe trip now!" with eye contact that seems to imply that, somehow, you're special, that you've conferred a blessing on the establishment by just *being* there. This is America.

I consider deliberately spending a day on The Strip without placing a single bet - as a statement, something like that. But because that might seem more an act of censorious piety and, also, because I feel the need at least to have experienced the act of throwing away my money, I enter another bright, buzzing casino, approach a bar tender and ask him how these things work, nodding at the slot machines. He walks with me to explain then adds, "Cash is king in Vegas, Sir - good luck!"

I feed the machine a one-dollar bill. It sucks it up quickly, before I can change my mind, and deposits it into one of the vast concrete vaults, piled high with money like Scrooge McDuck's (or was it Richie Rich?) that have been hollowed out under each of the casinos in Vegas, piled high with money. Mine is a Dragon's Luck machine that has a picture of a large panda eating bamboo shoots. I select the 1c button, assuming I will now have the pleasure of one hundred button-presses, each with its little frisson of excitement. I can already hear the clink and tumble of coins as they cascade into my trembling, outstretched hands. I press the button: *whirr-whirr,* I lose.

Press again: *whirr-whirr,* I lose again. Just as I am about to press a third time (98 to go, *whoop-whoop!*) an electronic voice tells me that my money has been used up and I need to insert more. It seems that the panda eats dollar bills as fast as it eats bamboo shoots.

Well, that was fun.

Next to me, an annoying machine makes *Yee-ha! Hey-hey! Giggle, yo-ho!* noises and a voice says, "Use your joy stick to find a mystery prize!" *Pop, squeak, boof! Yee-ha! Oooooh!* If I could find the annoying little man and my joy stick, I'd be tempted to use it in a way he hadn't intended. *Doof, doof, doof, di, doof, doof, doof, yee-ha! Doof-di-doof.*

I need to get out of this place before I break something or die of nicotine poisoning. I look for the entrance but am lost in a labyrinth of tables and flashing lights. I pause to watch as a kind-faced croupier named Ron guides a young woman wearing false eyelashes and long, white-painted false nails into the mysteries of the crap table. He plays sleight-of-hand tricks with her chips like an annoying uncle discovering coins in a child's ear. She places three $25 chips on the number six, throws the dice and loses. Boo-hoo. I just lost $1, so I know what it feels like.

"Oooch, that's *bad!"* Ron says with a wry smile and sweeps up her chips. She nods and places another chip on a different number and loses that too.

Next to the crap table, a pretty lass cries out, "How much did I win?" I glance over her shoulder in a surreptitious manner and hear the machine tell her: "Ten free *pla-ys!"*

"Who-hoo!" she cries and pushes another coin into the slot.

No money, then?

At another crap table are four men, early thirties, wearing baseball caps and gold chains. They look like guys auditioning for the role of drug dealers. Two Chinese women croupiers work the table with Oriental stoicism while a white man who looks strangely like Robert Downey Jnr looks on. His name tag calls him Savet.

"Yo, man, how you pronounce your name?" one of the guys calls.

"Steve," he says, unsmiling.

I watch the table; it all happens with mind-numbing complexity. One of the men *tap-taps* the dice on the table for luck then throws. Chips are moved and exchanged, hooked off the table and replaced by others, winnings scooped up and added to rows of chips held in convenient slots around the edge of the table.

A bill is passed across to the man called Steve who presses it through a slot with a wooden spatula where it drops into that 1000-ft-deep underground vault filled with money and tears and broken dreams. I notice that it's a $100 bill.

Tap-tap and the dice are thrown again: double three. "What'd I *tell* ya? What'd I *tell* ya?" the dice thrower cries out, high-fiving the guy next to him. "Keep 'em rollin', man! Keep 'em rollin'!"

A cute girl in hot pants offers me a drink. Sadly, it's not for free but then, I've only spent $1.

Outside, on the pavement, a woman wearing jeans and flip-flops stands, covered in a bed-sheet. She nibbles on a biscuit, oblivious of the happy people passing by. Later I come across two men asleep on pieces of cardboard lain on the pavement. It's ten o'clock in the morning. I pass a wanna-be biker whose T-shirt declares: *Gnats, flies, cops, the aggravation never stops.* A tall man dressed as a Wookiee stalks past. He has long grey hair and, except for the Wookiee outfit, could pass for a college professor. People greet him as he strides by and he replies with dignified condescension, in keeping with a visitor from the star-system of Kashyyyk. Then there are two smiling young ladies wearing skimpy black panties, high heels, ostrich feathers and nipple caps: pose for a Happy Snap, only $5. One has stretch marks across her stomach. A Chinese-looking man walks the pavement with a neck harness holding his i-phone so he can check it hands-free wherever he goes. Ahead of me waddles a very fat woman wearing nothing but a bikini and a see-through wrap. No-one seems to notice her or feels that anything is amiss.

I make my way past the Eiffel Tower, a fairyland castle, a pyramid and the Sphinx. Who needs the world? It's all here in Vegas.

I lift my eyes for a moment above the crenulated walls and peaked towers of the fairy castle and there, just there under a wide, blue sky and the stillness of palm trees, lies the desert and the pale rocks of the Spring Mountains. I pause and rest my eyes on them for a long, long time as the strange river of humanity passes me by.

Back to the pseudo reality of The Strip I see a young man sitting on the pavement; around his neck, hung on string, is a cardboard sign that says: "US Army Vet, anything helps. God Bless you." He is reading a Jesus tract.

Then there are three more women wearing bikinis, their breasts large and pendulant. Elvis passes me wearing a white jump-suit heavily embossed with rhinestones and spangles. He's riding a mobility scooter.

I am reminded of H. Rap Brown's comment that America is the ultimate denial of the theory of man's continuous evolution...

A young man stands bare-headed under the sun, American flag hanging limp above him; he holds a large sign saying: "Trust Jesus" and hands out tracts held in a fanny bag. Another young man walks past him wearing a T-shirt stating: "God is DOPE". They pass each other without noticing.

A sign invites me to savour the pleasures of "STRIPPERS, nude daily". I pass by: not today, but thanks for the offer. Another young man's T declares: "I already hate our next president". Then there is an old man, dancing. His arms and legs jerk as if tugged by strings. Propped on the pavement, next to his donations bowl, a sign says: "Dancing Grandfather, 72". Next to him a twenty-something back-packer stands patiently behind a sign that says: "I just like holding cardboard". He has a wry smile on his face and a donation bowl at his feet.

Back at the hostel, my room-mates have gone. Found a needy bitch to share an apartment with, perhaps. In the street outside I notice a blood bank. They are touting for customers and I need to augment my meagre funds. Inside, a large uniformed man stands guard. He has a pistol on his belt. Sitting around the wall on plastic chairs are five guys, all young, early twenties, Hispanic and Coloured, clothes loose on their bony limbs. They eye me warily as I enter; I look about for advice on how the system works, then take an empty chair next to a guy with jail-house tattoos leaching out under the skin of his arms and tear drops inked under one eye.

"You gotta fill in a form, man," he tells me and I take a piece of paper from a large lady behind the counter. It tells me that I will be paid $75 for my first pint of blood, then $50 for the next three and $75 for the fifth. Whooo! Donate a pint a day and I could live here forever.

But my eye scans down the page and I see that I must be a US citizen and have a fixed residential address.

So that's a no for selling my blood, then.

TWENTY EIGHT
Two lads and a Ural

It is cold in the mornings now before the low sun warms the air. Increasingly thick boreal forest casts deep shadows across the road. Old men sell honey from the bonnets of their battered Ladas and tea from crude roadside stands, the smoke from their samovars hanging still in the early morning air.

At a truck-stop cafe I drink black coffee, thick as syrup, and fill my stomach with the warm, fatty, doughy things called *Piroshki,* always available on the side of the road throughout Russia, poor man's comfort food for 45p and shared with the earthy company of truckers.

Later, passing an interesting-looking village in the middle of nowhere made up of a few dirt roads lined on either side with unpainted wooden houses, on a whim I decide to pause in my headlong dash east, slow down and experience something of the reality of life lived in rural Russia. And within twenty metres of leaving the main road onto the narrow, muddy track between the log-built houses, I come across two young men, early twenties, working on a battered green Ural outfit under the shade of a tree. And with a deep sense of shame, it strikes me: In every village and town I have passed so far, mindlessly focussed on the straight road in front of me and unconsciously counting down the miles, there is *real* life being lived on every corner, in every home, and I am missing it all.

I pull into the long grass on the verge, switch off and remove my helmet and gloves and greet them, shaking their greasy hands. Because of the heat both of them are shirtless, their torsos pale and milky white, their forearms and heads burned dark from the sun. One lad has crudely-drawn tattoos on the pale flesh of his upper arm and shoulder. They have that tough look about them that marks the bodies of people brought up hard, but there are none of the indelible marks that substance abuse or a villainous spirit etches into the contours of a face.

After a brief handshake, they turn back to the Ural; they are not here to entertain me and there is work to be done, but they are quite happy to allow me to stand and watch. The Ural's gearbox has been replaced with another, the old one lying in the grass covered in oil. Like the young lads, it has clearly lived a hard life; amongst other bumps and scrapes, some metal thing has come loose and scored away the casing in a deep circular pattern. I notice a heavy truck leaf spring, about two metres long, bolted to the fixings between the Ural and its sidecar. On one end a thick piece of flat bar has been welded, a hole cut through it with an oxyacetylene torch and I realise that it is a roughly fashioned tow bar for a trailer. Tools, nuts and bolts, and greasy spares are scattered on the floor pan of the sidecar.

I turn my attention back to the lads. One is whacking at the rear spindle with a large hammer; eventually it comes free and he pulls it away, releasing the back wheel. Both tyres are smooth, the edges heavily ridged with tread like those you find on tractors.

I so want to talk to these young men, ask them about their lives: do they have jobs? What do they use the Ural for? What is it like living in this Siberian village so far from anywhere and how do they cope in the winter? Do they have girlfriends or wives? What do they hope for in the future?

But, of course, I can't and it frustrates me. *This* is the real Russia, not a ribbon of tar and truck-stop cafes; not a mad dash across umpteen thousands of kilometres in the vain pursuit of a random point on a map.

In the end, all I can do is thank them and ride away, knowing that I am missing some elemental thing here. Reluctant to hit the main road again, I ride slowly up and down the narrow dirt streets of this anonymous village deep in the Siberian taiga: wells surrounded by low palings on street corners for those houses without running water; a man pulls a large milk churn full of water down the road on a small, two-wheeled cart; wooden duck-boards have been laid along both sides of the roads, rotting now and with weeds and long grass pushing through; an old woman, her back so bent that her head faces the ground, carries four brightly-coloured plastic buckets in her arms. As I pass, she looks up with difficulty to reveal, momentarily, a large, bulbous growth across her lower jaw. Quickly, she lowers her face again, hiding the deformity in the folds of her jacket. A broken-down truck with opened bonnet and flat tyres stands amongst engine parts in the grass. Small children play on the street verges; ducks paddle in a pool of muddy water; a woman enters a small, dark shop about the size of a double bed. The air smells of cow dung and the sweet smoke of fires. Rough piles of wood, still yellow from cutting, show early preparations for the winter cold. The duckboards suggest that they must have a snowy time of it here.

And then there are the pretty wooden houses, always with brightly-painted window surrounds, carved and shaped into geometric patterns, and matching wooden shutters, small touches that reveal a pride in ownership no matter how crude or basic the construction of the houses; and these touches are to be found too in the pretty flower beds and window boxes and neat rows of potatoes and beets and carrots cultivated in small back gardens. Outside, between the houses and the street, rusty cars, tractors in various states of disrepair, farm implements; cows mouth the long grass; picket fences lean.

And it is with a sense of shame that I come to the realisation that this journey across the continent of Russia has become for me an end in itself; that the goal of reaching Magadan, the compulsion to put miles beneath my wheels, has taken over the initial concept of this trip, whatever that was. What, I wonder, has happened to the dictum that the journey is of greater importance than the destination? Each day I fire up the engine of my little bike, put my head down and ride, the comforting sound of the engine in my ears (and the lurch of my heart when it hesitates), feeling the vibrations through my body, the road a black ribbon ahead of me undulating through endless horizons of taiga as I count down the miles that creep with frustrating slowness across each fold of the map.

And getting off the main road to explore this small village has enabled me to pause a moment and reflect: Why am I doing this? What is it about Magadan that has taken upon itself such arbitrary significance? Yes, I want to claim that I have ridden alone across Russia; and the more people I meet along the way who tell me I shouldn't do it, has turned the journey into a personal challenge; that to fail would be tantamount to an admission of inadequacy.

Am I trying to prove something to myself? To impress others? Perhaps it is all of these things. I suppose I am doing it because I am doing it. I do it because it defines me, who I am. And not to do it would negate something of myself. Perhaps.

But meeting the two young lads working on their Ural has revealed to me the essential falseness of my journey. I have come to realise that I am riding *over* this country and not *through* it. I am, essentially, passing by the people I ought to be meeting, allowing their lives to become a part of my own. My journey through this world has become the tableaux of my own little drama.

D.H.Lawrence was right when he wrote mockingly about us stepping out of our own self-centred, imaginary little lives into the real world of the bar tender with thin arms and tired eyes whom we ignore because we are so immersed in ourselves. And my experience of Russia seems to have become little more than a narrow track of tar between trees, of sleeping in truck-stop motels, drinking coffee in road-side cafes, all conveniently situated along the route. I don't get to enter the villages, interact with the real Russian people and my tar-road, trucker's perspective of this vast country is, essentially, a false one.

Reluctantly, I leave that place and, once again, take to the road, heading east...

Excerpt taken from: "Two Fingers on the Jugular".

TWENTY NINE
A thin red line

It was still dark when we turned off the main road that leads south across the arid coastal plain towards Nouakchott, Mauritania. The sun, still just below the horizon, cast a pale pink glow across the desert sand. The small village of Bou Lanouar seemed deserted as we made our way along the sandy tracks between crudely-made, square, breeze-block houses. The noise of our engines woke some dogs who followed us, barking.

There is a track that roughly follows the Mauritania iron ore rail line 350ks east into the Western Sahara - before turning north at Choum; it begins somewhere around this village but we didn't know exactly where. We had been warned not to ride too close to the line itself because of the many bits of metal and discarded sleepers lying about in the sand, so the plan was to make our way into the desert then turn north until we bisected the track.

Easy, although the sand through the village turned soft and deep, especially where it had banked up around the houses, and I felt my back wheel sink and lose grip, the engine of my stripped-down KLE500 begin to labour. I accelerated hard, broke free and struggled my way onto a small rise. Here the sand was firm enough for me to pause and look back.

Mike was struggling. He was in deep sand, still in first gear, back wheel flinging up a rooster-tail of pale, almost white sand. His forward motion slowed and the rear wheel began digging itself in; he took his feet off the pegs and began paddling, urging his DRZ400 through the sand one, slow foot at a time.

The revving engines had woken some kids who emerged from the huts and ran towards us with the dogs.

Eventually Mike got his bike onto firmer sand and pulled up next to me, switched off his engine. The sun broke over the horizon and the shrill cries of the children came to us across the early-morning silence like the shrill chirpings of birds.

"How you doing?" I asked, concerned about his obvious difficulty coping with soft sand. He opened his visor. What looked out at me in the pale desert light were eyes that spoke as clearly as if he had said the words himself: fear, despair, exhaustion; the dawning realisation that he wasn't able to do this.

* * * * *

But let me step back a little. A year ago my son, Gareth, with whom I have ridden extensively over the years, rode the track to Choum solo. I wanted to give it a go but lacked the courage to attempt the desert crossing alone (or, perhaps, I'm just not that stupid). My fears were fourfold: I'd injure myself badly and die before anyone found me; the laden bike would fall on me, trap me under it; I'd break down somewhere and have to attempt to walk out and, finally, I'd blunder into a steep-sided depression filled with powder-soft sand and, alone, not be able to get my bike out.

These were the things nightmares are made of. I needed someone to ride with me, an extra pair of hands when things got rough; a second bike if one broke down.

I put the word out and got a message from Mike Vitkovitch: Yes, he'd join me. We'd only met briefly once before. He seemed just right: a mature rider with 48 years' experience; five Morocco trips beneath his belt (although, he pointed out, he'd always turned back once he encountered soft sand); a skilled mechanic who had, on a previous Moroccan trip, got three bikes up and running again after they'd been completely drowned in a wadi when sudden flash flood caught them unawares.

Over the next two months we prepared our bikes for the trip. Two things were paramount: lightness of load and the ability to carry sufficient fuel, water and food for the two-day desert crossing. Mike acquired a 28-litre Safari tank and added a 10-litre plastic container "just in case"; my KLE couldn't take an after-market tank so I fitted two Rotopax 6.6-litre fuel containers to my pannier rack and would carry the rest of my fuel in four 2-litre cool drink bottles in my back pack. Add to that six litres of water each and we were already pretty heavy.

So, early in the year and before it got too hot for desert travel, we crossed from Portsmouth to Algeciras on the ferry, followed by a long two-day ride across Spain. Watching The Rock slowly disappear into the mist, we crossed the Gibraltar Straits to Tangier; then on through the fertile north Moroccan plains with the Atlas Mountains, snow-capped, a distant purple on our left until, eventually, we reached the coastal plain and the long, long road south. Wheat fields and olive groves disappeared to be replaced by sand and rock; sheep gave way to goats and the occasional camel which observed our passing with the disdain one has come to associate with the breed. Agadir, Sidi Ifni, El Quatia, Tarfaya, Laayoune, Dakhla, the road at times blurred for hours as we rode through dense coastal fog or, on other endless days, the dreaded Harmattan howled from the east, carrying with it a wreath of desert sand so thick that the road itself seemed fluid, eddying and swirling, settling into small tongues of sand that grew and threatened to swallow it all up silently, as the desert does.

We rode hard, ten hours a day, marking our progress in frustratingly small centimetres across the map. Finally the border: Morocco-Mauritania. No-man's-land was like something out of Mad Max: hundreds of wrecked and abandoned vehicles dumped among the dunes, the track between border posts a moonscape of rock and sand. Brushing off touts like sticky flies - "Change money? You want Mauritania? Dollar? Euro...?" "I take you, just five minutes. Otherwise one hour. Fifteen dollar. Give me passport. You want?"

Sweltering in the heat, we made our laborious way through a bewildering maze of bureaucracy, entering obscure offices, windows taped over with cardboard, where bored officials stamped forms and held out pale-skinned hands for our passports. A fat, uniformed official tapped the pocket of a Mauritanian man standing in the line in front of us; the man took out his wallet and opened it. The official fingered through, selected some notes and dropped them into a drawer. Next to his desk, on the floor, an old man crouched in front of a photocopier and copied documents. Our tout, whom we hadn't been able to shake loose, tugged at my sleeve: "Ten dollar. You must pay," pointing to the fat, uniformed official behind the desk.

There was no use arguing, even if I had known the language. Our money too went into the drawer. "Am I going to get a receipt?" I asked sarcastically and was ignored.

Mauritania, Nouadhibou. We were entering sub-Saharan Africa now for real and it showed. Julian Nowill, un-organiser of the Plymouth-Dakar Old Bangers Rally, calls it "...an outlaw town run by criminals. What can I say, this place feels like Somalia."

We shouldered our way through the snarl of carts pulled by donkeys, cars and trucks newly resurrected from the scrap heap (driving here on one side of the road only seems optional). Few tyres have any tread on the vehicles in this town, lights are optional and cracked windscreens *de rigueur,* doors and boots often held closed with rope or wire. On a dusty pavement, two goats ate a cardboard box; a camel, trussed up like a turkey, bellowed his anguish at passers-by, exposing long, yellow teeth.

At a petrol station we met a French biker arguing with the attendant, a black youth wearing shorts and an open shirt. *"Impossible!"* the Frenchman insisted. The youth was charging him for more fuel than the capacity of his tank could hold and the dial on the pump was blank.

Later, despite having been thus forewarned, we got done as well: first, we made sure we knew the local price of a litre of fuel; then, at the service station (and before any fuel was pumped), we agreed the price with the attendant and wrote it on a piece of paper. Only then did I allow him to begin filling my tank. When full, I pointed to my Rotopax containers but, quick as a flash, he shut off the pump. I looked at the dial; it was, of course, blank. The youth had a glint in his eye. But Mike had noted the amount just before it shut down. One-nil to us. I instructed him to now fill my spare containers that I *know* are 6.6-litres each - I mean, it's even moulded into the plastic. I watched carefully. The dial registered 6 litres, then seven and, somewhere after eight litres, it was full.

He got me. I laughed ruefully and paid up. I would imagine fuel pump calibration inspectors are a little thin on the ground in Mauritania.

Mike and I took a day's break, our first, to rest up and prepare for the desert crossing. Fuel, water, some food. Check the bikes. Go through all our stuff and leave behind anything unnecessary - we'd pick it up on the way back.

I set the alarm for 5am. Neither of us slept much.

* * * * *

Back to the deep sand and the dawn sun flooding the desert surface with a glow of pink and the deep disillusionment in Mike's eyes.

"I don't think I can do this," he says to me.

Those who have ridden across or through long sections of deep sand will know that the key is speed. The faster you go, the more the tyres rise to the surface. Go fast enough and you could be riding on tar; slow down and your wheels dig in, sink below the surface, the handlebars begin to twist from side to side like a horse trying to throw the bit; the rear wheel loses traction, flings sand, begins to dig itself into a pit of its own making. Keep the throttle pinned with little or no forward motion and, eventually, your bash plate will rest on the sand, your rear wheel dug down to the hub. Climb off, then, and walk away: your bike won't fall over. It won't move forward either, unless certain things are done.

Of course, the faster you go, too, the more damage you're going to do to yourself or your bike if you come off, hit a rock, fly through the air from the steep crest of a dune or somersault when your front wheel drops into an unseen hollow. It's a fine balance between speed and safety that not even the Dakar riders always get right.

I say to Mike, "You've *got* to get your speed up. You need to be at least in second gear - just *hit* it. Rev the guts out of it. Get the wheels on top of the sand."

He nods, uncertain. We press on, blinded by the rising sun, blundering across a wild landscape of small dunes and hummocks of sand, looking for the track. We've left the village behind now. Mike is making better progress but still very slow, lagging behind. At this stage I'm pretty certain we'll have to give up. 350ks to Choum across sand like this, and Mike struggling already, simply not possible.

And then, to my relief, random tyre tracks begin to coalesce out of the desert into what might almost be called a "road"; to our left, the rail line, laid on a raised sand causeway, disappears into the sun-haze; in front and to our right, a flat sand sea that extends to the horizon. I am filled with a sense of euphoria - we've found the track and it's firm and clear. My fears begin to drop away; we can do this thing and, if it's like this all the way, it'll be a breeze.

I stop and Mike pulls up next to me. I want to express my excitement but he is still unhappy. He admits that the first few hundred metres through the village had drained him physically and mentally. An experienced biker, he had suddenly been confronted with riding conditions he hadn't encountered before and which, as yet, he didn't believe he could master.

We press on, following the track as it makes its way across a firm desert surface. Gareth had downloaded his year-old track onto my

GPS and there it is, a thin red line across the screen, comforting and secure. All I have to do, I tell myself, is follow it. I can ignore the myriad tracks that fan out across the desert, diverge and reunite; tracks that might lead somewhere but all too often disappear into wind-blown sand. I must admit to being a little fearful. Mike doesn't have a GPS and mine is old and had stopped working twice on the way down the Moroccan coast. I no longer trust it. My deepest fear is that it will pack up half way across and the comforting red line that I cling to like a visual security blanket will disappear. Of course, there is always the rail line and, however far we go off track, by late afternoon the setting sun will show the direction of north and we'll find it again.

The track angles away from the rail line and it disappears. It would do this for two days, creeping towards the rails and running alongside them then angling away into the dunes until all sense of direction is lost. But I have the thin red line on my screen. If we follow it, it will lead us eventually to Choum.

Mike is getting the hang of it, as I knew he would. His many years of riding are coming to his aid. Occasionally the firm track disappears under long stretches of soft sand and, riding faster now, he is managing. We are making progress.

And then Mike, who at that moment is ahead of me, crests a small rise and his front wheel drops into a hole. If I'd been in front it probably would have been me. Pure chance. You can't see it until it's upon you - and then it's too late. He goes down hard. When I reach him, he is holding his wrist and side.

"You OK?" I ask him, concerned.

He nods. Nothing is broken. Although he's in pain, we lift his bike out of the sand and press on.

The sun lifts itself higher above the horizon; colour, what there is of it in the desert, leaches away and shadows all but disappear. The desert stretches to the horizon in every direction, pale and empty. During a water break, Mike looks out across the sand, and says, almost to himself, "The *endlessness* of it..."

And yet, as anyone who has travelled through the Sahara will know, the desert is ever changing: the sand varies in colour from a blinding white, deepening through every shade - pale brown, red, even, in places, a black so deep it seems to shine; soft, firm, yielding, deep-soft and, in places, the dreaded *fetch-fetch* that seems to suck your bike down, sap all the power from the engine, leave you fighting for forward momentum. Rocks of every colour and texture: small, sharp, rounded, large, isolated erratics and long sinuous ridges emerging from the sand. Sometimes you crest a dune and, before you, stretching into the smudged heat-haze of the horizon, is a flat plane, white, pale brown or dark grey like a bruise and you relax, knowing that, at least for a while, it will be easy riding. And you fly along, the wind cooling your face and you know that you can do this all day, loving it. Then you look up and, in front of you, as far as you can see, are lines of dunes, a heaving sea of sand, how deep, you cannot tell, but there are no gaps, no flat-bottomed valleys to ease your way through: you've got to ride *over* them and your stomach tightens.

The sun overhead destroys perspective and the first dune could be high and far away or low and right *here*; your eyes play tricks on you; everything is the same and there's nothing for your brain to latch onto, nothing to compare, just a continuous, uniform surface of pale sand where all visual cues are lost. Then the dune is upon you and you accelerate, wondering whether your front wheel will sink away and fling you over the handlebars, but you can't slow down, you must hit it with speed and take your chances, hope you've judged it just right so when you reach the crest you'll slide gently down the other side, not tap off too early and dig in on the crest or hit it too fast and tumble down a steep slip-off slope. The dune is firm and you sail up its side and you are happy; you take the next and the next and life is good.

At some time during the day I hit a patch of very soft sand, the bike slews this way and that and, despite allowing her to make her own way, as you do when riding sand, down I come, my left leg trapped under my soft pannier and twisted rather painfully. I know Mike is somewhere close and hope he's seen me go down, won't discover my absence too late and lose me amongst the confusing sameness of the dunes. I try to pull my leg out but it won't move; I try again, feeling claustrophobic, my face pressed into the sand but it's trapped.

This is why I wouldn't solo this track, I think to myself.

In retrospect, if I'd been alone I probably would have got free, given time and a little patience. I could have dug my leg out - the sand is soft and yielding. Even though I am face down in the sand, I believe I could have unstrapped my soft pannier or cut it free with the Gerber multi-tool I always keep in my riding jacket. But it's good to hear Mike's engine slow and then pause as he turns and comes to my aid. The KLE is heavy and, laden with my extra fuel, water, spares and camping gear, it takes Mike three attempts before he can lift it off my leg.

Sweating, we strip off our kit and drink water. When not moving, the heat rises from the sand like an oven.

"How you doing?" I ask him, thankful for his company in this fearful ocean of nothingness.

"Good," he says, telling me that he's now passed "beyond enjoyment and into endurance". He shares again how traumatic the morning had been: "We were looking for a track but there was no track. We were leaving civilization behind. You were supposed to be leading but you seemed to be lost. Then you disappeared into the distance and I couldn't follow. I thought, *'He can do this but I can't.'* But you told me to gun it so I did and suddenly I realised I could. I just needed to get over my fear of crashing and *gun* it, get my speed up and suddenly it was OK."

I know the feeling, remember my first experience of sand, the fear of it until Gareth and I learned what to do, how to read the surface, begin to understand the contours of the desert.

"I feel good now," he admits. "I've overcome my limitations, but I know I can do better."

By late afternoon we are both flagging. We've covered about 200ks and are hoping to make it to the Ben Amera monolith before we camp. This strange massif rises 633 metres from the flat desert plain, the largest monolith in Africa and smaller only than Ayers Rock in Australia, second largest in the world. But both Mike and I are tiring when we hit a bad section of soft sand. Battling to keep my bike moving forward, revving my engine in an abusive manner to break it free, I can smell that my engine is overheating. I glance down and see that my temp light is on but I can't stop, need to get clear of the deep sand first. I keep the throttle wide open until I can feel the sand begin to firm then switch off. It is then that we discover that my fan has packed up. My radiator is boiling, spewing precious water into the sand.

Once again fear grips me. There's nothing we can do. Mike checks the motor and, although he can get it running, it hesitates and limps and won't start without a helping flick. We wait a while, staring out into the endless void of sand all about us. With the engines off, the silence is very loud and strangely disconcerting, frightening in a way. In our normal world, we are not used to this absence of sound.

When my engine has cooled sufficiently we press on. We have to stop twice more to allow my engine to cool before we cross the rails onto the northern side and make our way over a flat plain sculpted with dunes towards a smaller massif that rises from the sand and, on its far side, casts a lengthening shadow. We stop the bikes close to a small, stunted thorn tree, instinctively looking for anything *living*, anything that isn't *sand*. We've been riding for ten hours.

Taking bottles of water, we labour up a long slope of soft sand that has gathered against the leeward side of the massif where there is shade and sit looking out across the desert, pleased with what we've accomplished.

Other than my broken fan, the bikes are coping well; Mike's confidence has grown throughout the day; he's beginning to "read" the sand, learning to allow the bike to find its way instead of fighting it, discovering its sweet spot. There is, at this moment, a deep sense of closeness between us, something that is felt, I am sure, by all who share adversity together and overcome.

The shadows lengthen; we return to the bikes and erect our tents. Later, as the sun sets golden over the horizon, I walk out into the desert and sit quietly by myself, watching the stars begin to appear in the surreal half-light of reflected sand and listen to the deep silence all about me. And I understand why holy men throughout the ages have sought communion with God in lonely desert places like this.

The second day dawns clear and still. We pack up in the cold half light and make our way through a small dune field to the rail line, cross it and find the track. The early morning is crisp and cool, favouring our bodies and my engine, the low yellow light seeming to set the small grass tufts that grow between the dunes ablaze. Occasionally we come upon small habitations, a building or two and a few camels. There are no wells here: water is kept in large bladders that lie on the sand; these, we are told, are kept filled from water carriages pulled by the train. Most of the structures are made from abandoned metal railway sleepers which litter the desert surface close to the tracks. These are particularly dangerous as occasionally we come across them unexpectedly, half buried in the sand. Once I hit the sharp edges of one that lay on the slip side of a small dune. I was sure I must have punctured my tyres but we are running at normal pressures because of this very reason and all is well.

This is always a dilemma when riding across the desert: soft tyres travel easier over loose sand, the softer the better, but with so many rocks on the desert surface and half-buried under the sand, you are bound to puncture a tyre. And repairing a puncture in the heat of the desert doesn't bear contemplating; rather ride with hard tyres and struggle a little more in the sand than hassle with punctures.

At one lonely shack made from sleepers and mud and flattened oil drums, we are invited in by a solitary man tending his camels. We sit in the shade on carpets laid soft on the sand and he heats water for tea, serving us the bitter liquid in clear glass tumblers sweetened with lumps of rock sugar the size of a baby's fist. We drink together in companionable silence, expecting nothing more from each other than the blessing of human proximity in this empty and lonely part of the world.

Meeting men who, with the generosity one always finds in the loneliest places of the world and who offer you all that they have, is a humbling experience and compels one to look again at the selfish and affluent lives we ourselves lead.

Thankful for this brief meeting and with the bitter-sweet taste of tea still in our mouths, we fire up our engines and press on. The endless variety of the desert landscape continues to inspire and challenge, each surface requiring a different level of skill, a different approach.

Two surfaces stand out in terms of enjoyment, though: first, the horizon-wide flat plain of firm sand where you open wide the throttle and, in top gear, your tyres sing across the sand at sixty miles an hour; and you know you're riding too fast but you can't slow down, thinking: *Can I push it to seventy? Seventy five?*

And then there are the dunes. Crossing high virgin dunes takes one back to the childhood joy of the roller coaster, the surge and lift as one rises from the plain, the dune surface smooth and firm like an unmarked snow *piste*; above, the skyline is blotted out by the crest-line hiding a sharp dip of unknown steepness. Judge your speed to breast it just right, a slight tightening of the stomach muscles because behind is a hidden land that will only be revealed once you're committed, yes, all clear, just a steep, smooth sand-slide to the firm plain on the other side or, perhaps, a short flat section to pick up speed before the front wheel rises up the whale-back of the next dune.

Sometimes we would come across old tracks, deep and filled with blown sand, the ridged edges just protruding above the surface. Tracks like these, some say, will remain etched into the desert surface for years. One learns to be wary of them, however, because the sand that fills them is very soft and getting a front wheel caught in one wants to have you over. In fact, on this second day both Mike and I dropped our bikes a second time. Nothing serious, just a more pronounced wobble than usual progressing to violent oscillations in the sand; it's too easy, then, for the weight on the pannier rack to drag you down.

We cross the rails again to eat a brief meal at the foot of the Ben Amera monolith, this strange, smooth dome of rock rising incongruously from the flat plain, then we press on, just 64 miles to Choum and the end of the track.

Once I stray too far south and we have to turn sharply across the desert to find it again. We are a few kilometres away from the rail line and all around me are small dunes, humps and hillocks of sand, the sun almost directly overhead. The responsibility of leading falls heavy on me at this time and it is a relief when we find the track again and, later, see the dark outline of the rails in the distance heading like a dark, ruled line across the sand.

By now, deep-sand riding has become unconscious for both Mike and me, muscle memory taking over: an automatic feeding the engine more fuel when a sudden de-acceleration signals soft sand, quickly shifting down as the engine begins to lug, finding that sweet spot where you're travelling on *top* of the sand, not wading through it; your engine is unstressed and happy and you've got a handful of throttle and a few gears to spare.

Mike tells me that he's moved now from "concentrating on riding to just riding", and he's right. Now we can relax and enjoy the image of a vast, flat plain emerging from a band of confused dunes, knowing that, for a time, the going will be easy, then seeing, in the distance, the pale yellow crests of a dune field kilometres wide and, in place of fear, the knowledge that, although difficult, we have the ability to cross it.

It is later that I come again to realise the importance of not travelling alone in the desert. Carelessly, I ride into a wide, deep bowl of very soft sand; *fetch-fetch* is the term I have heard used for this horrible stuff, sand that reacts in many ways like water. I feel my wheels sink deep, the engine note drops quicker than it has before and I know I'm in trouble. Quick change down, and again, and again, the engine note falling instead of rising with each downshift, my forward motion dropping to a slow walk. First gear now, the engine screaming, back wheel already settling into the sand. I struggle across the base of the bowl and start clawing my way up the other side, paddling with my feet. But I know I'm not going to make it. As a last resort, I swing the bike to one side, attempting to turn down the slope again and get a run back at the other side... then I give up. My bash plate rests on the sand, rear wheel buried to the hub.

Mike, riding behind me, has seen me struggling and powers across, parks his bike on firm sand. My body rapidly overheating, I strip off my gear. What to do? Together we lift the front wheel and drag it free (thank goodness it's not a GS1200) then dig the sand away from the rear wheel and engine. There is a small hump of firm sand in the base of the bowl and, together, we push and drag my bike onto it. Resting, we plan our next move, select what looks like the best line; then, with Mike pushing, the small momentum given by running down the firm side of the hump and me paddling and revving the guts out of my overheating engine, we make it out.

Could I have got out alone? Probably, but it was good to have Mike with me. Alone, I would have stripped off all my luggage, lain the bike on its side to free the wheels, dragged it to face the base of the bowl, let the tyres down to .5 bar and, yes, I think I could have got it out.

But I'm glad I didn't have to.

At last the desert begins to ease; there are small signs of humanity amongst the endlessness of sand. The track becomes more clear, wider and firmer, more like a dirt road. A 4X4 passes us, the fine dust hanging still in the air. We come across the iron ore train, stationary, men throwing stuff from a wagon onto the sand while other men, wearing the traditional *boubou* and turban, drag it away and load it onto battered Series 2 Land Rovers.

The low, squat buildings of Choum appear. We have made it. We fill our tanks with fuel decanted from plastic drums kept in a dark, dusty shed then sit on plastic chairs and, amongst the flies, drink strong, sweet coffee which has never tasted better.

First published in Overland Magazine, Issue 31.

I always welcome contact from my readers so, whether you have a comment or a question, you can get in touch with me here: lgbransby@hotmail.com

Other books by Lawrence Bransby:

Travelogues

Venture into Russia: Three Motorcycle Journeys

A Pass too Far: Travels in Central Asia

There are no Fat People in Morocco

The Wakhan Corridor : A Motorcycle Journey into Central Asia

The Plymouth/Dakar Old Bangers Challenge

Trans-Africa by Motorcycle : A Father's Diary

By Motorcycle through Vietnam : Reflections on a Gracious People

Two Fingers on the Jugular- A Motorcycle Journey Across Russia

Novels

A Matter of Conscience

Second Sailor, Other Son

Life-Blood - Earth-Blood

Novels for YoungAdults

Down Street
Winner of the MER Prize for Youth Literature

Homeward Bound
Book Chat Southern African Children's Book of the Year 1991
Short listed for the MNET Prize

Remember the Whales
Winner of the J.P. van Der Walt Prize

A Mountaintop Experience
Book Chat South African Book of the Year 1993

The Geek in Shining Armour

Of Roosters, Dogs and Cardboard Boxes

The Boy who Counted to a Million
Winner of the Sir Percy Fitzpatrick Prize

Outside the Walls

Printed in Great Britain
by Amazon